Emmanuel Levinas

'To read *Emmanuel Levinas: The Genealogy of Ethics* is an education from which anyone could benefit. John Llewelyn not only provides his readers with a profound study of Levinas's ethical philosophy, he also teaches them how to read philosophy with care. This is the most important full-length study of Levinas in any language, because one completes the book both better informed and a better philosopher.'

Robert Bernasconi, Memphis State University

'Emmanuel Levinas must now be judged to be one of the most influential figures in contemporary Continental philosophy. I can think of no better guide than John Llewelyn to lead us through the thickets of Levinas's prose. For those of us working in the embattled enclave of Continental philosophy in Britain and North America, Llewelyn's work has had a singular and special place, marked as it is by a quasi-Austinian analytic attention to linguistic and semantic detail, a dazzling breadth and depth of textual knowledge in the Continental tradition, and an absolute integrity and seriousness of intellectual and moral commitment. Bursting with questions, multiple references, cascading citations and multi-lingual puns and nuances, this book is the compelling record of an intellectual obsession. Taking as its guiding thread the theme of genealogy, the book gives a broadly chronological and impressively manageable presentation of the whole sweep of Levinas's work. I have read nothing more finely grained, more balanced and less dogmatic than Llewelyn's book on a whole range of Levinasian themes.'

Simon Critchley, University of Essex

John Llewelyn has been reader in Philosophy at the University of Edinburgh and visiting professor at Memphis State University and Loyola University of Chicago. His other publications include *Beyond Metaphysics?*, *Derrida on the Threshold of Sense*, and *The Middle Voice of Ecological Conscience*.

Warwick Studies in European Philosophy
Edited by Andrew Benjamin
Senior Lecturer in Philosophy, University of Warwick

This series presents the best and most original work being done within the European philosophical tradition. The books included in the series seek not merely to reflect what is taking place within European philosophy, rather they will contribute to the growth and development of that plural tradition. Work written in the English language as well as translations into English are to be included, engaging the tradition at all levels – whether by introductions that show the contemporary philosophical force of certain work, or in collections that explore an important thinker or topic, as well as in significant contributions that call for their own critical evaluation.

Walter Benjamin's Philosophy: Destruction and Experience
Edited by Andrew Benjamin and Peter Osborne

Bataille: Writing the Sacred
Edited by Carolyn Bailey Gill

Emmanuel Levinas
The genealogy of ethics

John Llewelyn

London and New York

In memory of little Granville,
brother from time immemorial,
and of Tony Palma and Ruth

First published 1995
by Routledge
11 New Fetter Lane, London EC4P 4EE

Simultaneously published in the USA and Canada
by Routledge
29 West 35th Street, New York, NY 10001

© 1995 John Llewelyn

Typeset in Times by LaserScript, Mitcham, Surrey
Printed and bound in Great Britain by
Biddles Ltd, Guildford and King's Lynn

British Library Cataloguing in Publication Data
A catalogue record for this book is available from the British Library

Library of Congress Cataloguing in Publication Data
Llewelyn, John.
    Emmanuel Levinas: the genealogy of ethics/John Llewelyn.
    p. cm. – (Warwick studies in European philosophy)
Includes bibliographical references and index.
ISBN 0–415–10729–6 (hard). – ISBN 0–415–10730–X (pbk.)
    1. Levinas, Emmanuel. 2. Ethics. I. Title. II. Series.
B2430 .L484L54   1994
194 – dc20   94-33895
                                        CIP

ISBN 0–415–10729–6
ISBN 0–415–10730–X (pbk)

Contents

Part III

la mia solitudine
l'altrui dolore
ghermiva
fino alla morte

est-ce qu'en étant, on n'a pas opprimé quelqu'un?

Nietzsche n'est-il pas le souffle exceptionel pour faire
résonner cet 'au-delà'?

Il faut passer par l'interprétation pour dépasser
l'interprétation

Levinas est donc très près et très loin de Nietzsche

Abbreviations

The following abbreviations accompanied by page numbers are used in the text in referring to writings by Levinas.

ADV   *L'au-delà du verset*, Paris, Minuit, 1982.

AE   *Autrement qu'être ou au-delà de l'essence* (1st edn, 1974), The Hague, Nijhoff, 1978.

AHN   *A l'heure des nations*, Paris, Minuit, 1988.

BTV   *Beyond the Verse*, trans. G. Mole, London, Athlone, Bloomington, Ind., Indiana University Press, 1994.

CPP   *Collected Philosophical Papers*, trans. A. Lingis, The Hague, Nijhoff, 1987.

CWC   'Philosophy and Awakening', trans. M. Quaintance, in E. Cardava, P. Connor and J.-L. Nancy (eds), *Who Comes After the Subject?*, New York, Routledge, 1991.

DC   'The Trace of the Other', trans. A. Lingis, in M. Taylor (ed.), *Deconstruction in Context*, Chicago, University of Chicago Press, 1986, pp. 345–59.

DE   *De l'évasion* (1st edn, 1935), Montpellier, Fata Morgana, 1982.

DEE   *De l'existence à l'existant* (1st edn, 1947), Paris, Vrin, 1981.

DF   *Difficult Freedom: Essays on Judaism*, trans. S. Hand, London, Athlone Press, 1990.

DL   *Difficile liberté: essais sur le judaïsme* (1st edn, 1963), Paris, Albin Michel, 1976.

DMT   *Dieu, la mort et le temps*, Paris, Grasset, 1993.

DVI   *De Dieu qui vient à l'idée*, Paris, Vrin, 1982.

EDE   *En découvrant l'existence avec Husserl et Heidegger* (1st edn, 1967), Paris, Vrin, 1982.

EE   *Existence and Existents*, trans. A. Lingis, The Hague, Nijhoff, 1978.

EEI   *Ethique et infini*, Paris, Fayard, 1982.

EI	*Ethics and Infinity*, trans. R. A. Cohen, Pittsburgh, Duquesne University Press, 1985.
EN	*Entre nous, essais sur le penser-à-l'autre*, Paris, Grasset, 1991.
HAH	*Humanisme de l'autre homme*, Montpellier, Fata Morgana, 1972.
HLR	*The Levinas Reader*, ed. S. Hand, Oxford, Blackwell, 1989.
HS	*Hors sujet*, Montpellier, Fata Morgana, 1987.
ITN	*In the Time of the Nations*, trans. M. Smith, London, Athlone, Bloomington, Ind., Indiana University Press, 1994.
MT	*La mort et le temps*, Paris, L'Herne, 1991.
NP	*Noms propres*, Montpellier, Fata Morgana, 1976.
NTR	*Nine Talmudic Readings*, trans. A. Aronowicz, Bloomington, Indiana University Press, 1990.
OB	*Otherwise than Being or Beyond Essence*, trans. A. Lingis, The Hague, Nijhoff, 1981.
OS	*Outside the Subject*, trans. M. B. Smith, London, Athlone, 1993.
QLT	*Quatre lectures talmudiques*, Paris, Minuit, 1968.
SMB	*Sur Maurice Blanchot*, Montpellier, Fata Morgana, 1975.
SS	*Du sacré au saint*, Paris, Minuit, 1977.
TA	*Le temps et l'autre* (1st edn, 1933), Montpellier, Paris, Fata Morgana, Quadrige – Presses universitaires de France, 1983.
TEI	*Totalité et infini: essai sur l'extériorité* (1st edn, 1961), The Hague, Nijhoff, 1980.
TI	*Totality and Infinity: An Essay on Exteriority*, trans. A. Lingis, The Hague, Nijhoff, 1969.
TIHP	*The Theory of Intuition in Husserl's Phenomenology*, trans. A. Orianne, Evanston, Ill., Northwestern University Press, 1973.
TIPH	*La théorie de l'intuition dans la phénoménologie de Husserl*, Paris, Alcan, 1930.
TO	*Time and the Other*, trans. R. A. Cohen, Pittsburgh, Duquesne University Press, 1987.
TRI	*Transcendance et intelligibilité*, Geneva, Labor et Fides, 1984.

Preface

This book is a response to an invitation from the general editor of the series in which it appears to bear witness to those who do not already know the work of Emmanuel Levinas that his writings demand not to be left unread. I welcome the opportunity this invitation gives me to reread those writings and to treat them more amply than I was allowed to do by my topic in *The Middle Voice of Ecological Conscience*. As its subtitle states, this earlier volume undertakes a chiasmic reading of responsibility in the neighbourhood of Levinas, Heidegger and others. It uses and, as I expect Levinas himself would say, abuses certain of his ideas to make out a case for not limiting to human beings the range of beings to whom or to which underivative responsibility is due. I hope that, despite the critical stance I adopted in that book and despite the difficulties I still have with some of his ideas, I can make it plain to readers of the following pages that not to read those published by the author with whose philosophy this study is primarily concerned would be to neglect one of the most important thinkers of our time. In this time after 'the death of God' some prospective readers, including those who have read Nietzsche, may be put off Levinas's philosophical work by the increasing use or mention made in it of what he refers to as the extraordinary word 'God'. My chapters therefore give increasing attention to the question whether that stumbling block can be circumvented without scandalizing those other prospective readers of his work who might consider its recourse to that word one of its strengths. That question first comes into focus in chapter 12. A shorter version of that chapter will appear in the proceedings of the conference held in 1993 at Loyola University of Chicago and the University of Chicago to be published under the title *Ethics as First Philosophy*.

For giving permission to use that material again here I thank the publishers, Routledge, and the editor, Adriaan Peperzak. To the responses he, Robert Bernasconi and others have already made to Levinas, my own is far more indebted than can be indicated by the mere occurrence of their names in my bibliography. Although their names do not occur in it, David Krell's scepticism was provocative, the interest shown in my project by Charles Bigger, George Davie, Basil O'Neill, Jill Robbins and the late Donald MacKinnon was reassuring, and the partnership of my wife was a *sine qua non*. For help with translation from Hebrew I thank Peter Hayman and Rabbi Shapira. I thank Adrian Driscoll, Nicholas Gillard and Emma Davis at Routledge for their guidance, and, for her indefatigable attention to ways of improving the layout of my manuscript and removing un-clarities, I am very grateful to Marguerite Nesling.

In my own translation from French I usually employ the capitalized 'Other' for Levinas's *Autrui* or *autrui* and for his capitalized *Autre*, where this last means the Other in contrast to the Same, *Même*. The latter contrast covers, for example, that drawn in Plato's *Sophist*. But Levinas's *Même* sometimes refers specifically to the first-person self or *Selbst*. By far the most frequently my 'Other' will translate *Autrui* or *autrui*, but it will sometimes translate *Autre*, which, unlike *Autrui*, admits a grammatical plural. I write 'other' for Levinas's *autre*, meaning the other or alterity in general, but since it is sometimes the personal Other Levinas intends when he uses this more general pronoun in the lower case, I sometimes use the lower case with the same intention and sometimes the upper case. I give the French where the risk of confusion is high.

I have often modified and sometimes departed altogether from the published translations of works cited in my bibliography or notes.

Introduction

As used in the title of this book the word 'genealogy' is intended in more than one sense. At least one of these senses will be operative in each chapter. It is employed most determinately of the stage of Levinas's teaching for the exposition of which he invokes the nomenclature of the family tree. More generally, it refers to what with reservation may be called the logical order in which that and the other phases of his teaching are generated. Still more generally, it refers to the order in which his thinking develops historically from one publication to another. Most generally, it refers to the way his philosophy, including his philosophy of philosophy, is related to the history of philosophical thinking – not least Nietzsche's thinking of the genealogy of morals – and to the very idea of generality that has dominated that history.

A cursory outlining of a genealogy in this fourth sense will provide a rough and preliminary indication of the space occupied by the notions to be described positively in later chapters. In this Introduction I shall list more or less chronologically and comment on more or less briefly some of the philosophers Levinas mentions and some of the doctrines he associates with them. This summary of points at which his own thinking starts and from which it departs will begin to show how radical and deracinative that thinking is. It should give weight to the argument for reading on to discover what he writes in the space thus marked out and how what he writes there may require another reading of the philosophical classics. Another and otherwise reading of, for example:

Plato. The positing of a good beyond being in the *Republic* opens a path for what is said about speech assisting at its word by Plato in the *Phaedrus* to be interpreted by Levinas in a way that goes beyond the Platonic doctrine of teaching as recollection (*anamnêsis*) and denies priority to the collective State. What, we may ask, following Plato and Levinas, is the place, *chôra*, of this good that is *epekeina tês ousias*?[1]

Aristotle. Notwithstanding Aristotle's exclusion of singularity from science, in which the particular is always a case falling under a genus, Levinas defends a non-particular singularity of the ethical which interprets otherwise the sense of accusativity carried by Aristotle's word 'category' and the sense of Aristotle's remark in *De generatione animalium* about the active intellect, *nous*, coming in, godlike, from outside.[2] How might we understand passing beyond being otherwise than as passing away, dying, and otherwise than as a transition from temporality to supratemporality (*AE* 3, *OB* 3)?

Plotinus. How might the trace of the Plotinian One be retraced in a manner that allows it to be non-ontologically and non-mimetically generative of existents without these latter and the One from which they proceed being resumed in a Parmenidean monism (*EDE* 201, *HAH* 62, *CPP* 105–6)?

Hobbes. Does the just State proceed from the war of all against all or from the responsibility of the one for all, responsibility that is the rationality of peace (*AE* 203, *OB* 159–60)?

Descartes. What is the significance and of what kind is the significance of the positive infinity of the idea of God that overflows every idea? Is a clue to the significance of this positivity given when at the end of the third of the *Meditations Concerning First Philosophy*, having discovered that this positive idea of infinity is anterior to the truth of 'I think', Descartes pauses 'to contemplate this all-perfect God, to ponder at leisure His marvelous attributes, to intuit, to admire, to adore, the incomparable beauty of his inexhaustible light, so far at least as the powers of my mind may permit, dazzled as they are by what they are endeavouring to see'? Is this 'not a stylistic ornament or a prudent homage to religion, but the expression of this transformation of the idea of infinity conveyed by knowledge into Majesty approached as face' (*TEI* 187, *TI* 212)? Is metaphysics as first philosophy on the way here to being discovered as ethics?

Spinoza. Can ethics stem uniquely from Proposition VI of Part III of Spinoza's system called *Ethics* which asserts that 'Every thing, in so far as it is in itself, endeavours to persevere in its being'? What if the thing, the person, bound by ethics is not in itself, or for itself, or in-itself-for-itself? Might this not mean that either a system of ethics cannot be complete or that ethics *sub specie aeternitatis*, viewed through the lens of eternity, is ethical and optical violence?

Kant. Is it not also violence to equate ethical regard for a person with regard for the universality of the moral law? Although, claiming to follow Plato, Kant posits ideas of reason, the idea of infinity is an ideal with respect to an always uncompleted approach. It presupposes the finitude of extensible sensible experience. But if, more Cartesian than Kantian, we say that the infinite exceeds my powers and free will not by being too great for them but by calling into question power and freedom of will themselves, perhaps we can say that it is affect or experience *par excellence* (*TEI* 170, *TI* 196).

Hegel. 'Hegel returns to Descartes in maintaining the positivity of the infinite, but excluding all multiplicity from it' (*TEI* 170, *TI* 196). For Hegelianism the other is never other than the allergic negation of the same which returns to it like Ulysses on his way home. Perhaps a more instructive figure of alterity is provided by Abraham who remains for ever in exile (*EDE* 191, *DC* 348, *HAH* 40, *CPP* 91). Like Hegel, Levinas writes a drama of the education of the psyche. Its *dénouement*, however, is not thinking anonymously thinking itself, but a recurrence in responsibility that traumatizes thinking without forfeiting rationality and without cancelling the singularity of named human beings or preserving them only as moments of a conceptually universal whole.

Kierkegaard. Kierkegaard resists the neutrality of the Hegelian concept in the name of inwardness and the salvation of subjectivity. Although that subjectivity has passed to a religious stage via the sensible particularity of the aesthetic and the universality of ethical institutions, in so doing it substitutes the violence of neutral totality for the violence of the secret. However sublime Kierkegaard's thirst for salvation may be, does it not repeat the perseverence affirmed by Proposition VI of Part III of the *Ethics* of Spinoza? Does not the ethical as defined by Kierkegaard call to be redefined in a way that forestalls the turn to inwardness by eliciting an outwardness that exceeds public generality and permits a singularity whose centre of gravity is located neither in religious fear and trembling nor in the privacy of the ego but in an absolute outside (*NP* 100–4)?

Nietzsche. If the Dionysian artist becomes a work of art and the philosopher becomes an artist, is not philosophy being returned to the aesthetic? Would it not therefore be outrageous to suggest, as does the subtitle of this study, that the name of the author of *On the Genealogy of Morals* is rarely mentioned in Levinas's texts, by comparison with the frequency of mention of names of certain other philosophers who might be supposed to be most in question within them, for the same reason as the one he gives for not citing Franz Rosenzweig's *The Star of Redemption*: that that writer's work is too often present in his own? But Nietzsche's mockery of a certain Platonist, Christian and Kantian idea of a being behind the scenes, as too his sortie beyond the good that is opposed to evil, are akin to Levinas's questioning beyond essence in that they are moments in the history of philosophy that go beyond the strictly ontological and theological beyond. Indeed, already at the beginning of philosophy, according to Levinas, Plato's One itself is another such moment. It is Levinas himself who writes that to get beyond this onto-theological beyond 'One should have to go all the way to the nihilism of Nietzsche's poetic writing, reversing irreversible time in vortices, to the laughter which refuses language' (*AE* 10, *OB* 8). Unless, refusing to refuse language, one can go beyond nihilism by going beyond the distinction between the distinctions of good and evil and good and bad that *On the Genealogy of Morals* makes, beyond the passivity that the tenth section of the first essay of that book associates with resentment, beyond the warlike activity it associates with the upright hero of noble descent (*gennaios*), to the passivity beyond passivity, activity and reactivity, and to the call to peace before war announced by Levinas's genealogy of ethics for those who have ears fine enough to hear. Although one of the aims of this examination of Levinas's philosophical work is to indicate how his genealogy crosses Nietzsche's, references to the latter are restricted to the bare minimum necessary for the achievement of that aim.

Bergson.   Although Bergson's critique of Aristotelian and Kantian chron- ometric theories of time points toward a notion of the creation of the absolutely new, the absolutely new requires the absolutely old. If, in the terms of Bergson's title, *la pensée* falls short of *le mouvant*, and if the temporality of movement is continuous and lived, *durée vécue*, absolute alterity requires that this continuity be interrupted by dead time, *temps mort* (*TO* 122 *TEI* 260, *TI* 284).

Husserl.   Although Husserl's proto-impression is another claimant to absolute novelty, the proto-impression and the noetic-noematic intentionality of his phenomenology call for supplementation by a super-impression and an intentionality that is reversed. Husserl's practical, axiological and ethical variations on intentionality are still noetic-noematic in structure. Therefore what Husserl calls the ethical is according to Levinas ethical only in name.

Heidegger.   The name 'ethics' is employed by Levinas for what in comparison with its classical employment, for instance by Aristotle, Spinoza and Kant, it might be less misleading to name 'proto-ethics'. But Levinas maintains that what he calls ethics in his 'emphasized' sense is precisely what makes ethics what it is, disruptive of the 'what it is'. Whether or not Heidegger gives thought to the proto-ethical in *Being and Time* or elsewhere, that book states that it is not concerned with ethics in the classical sense. It is a treatise in fundamental ontology. Why fundamental ontology is either not fundamental enough or too foundational to be proto-ethics or ethics in Levinas's sense is a question that is most fruitfully approached through the approximately chronological reading of some of his earliest works. They are treated below in Part I.

Part II treats chiefly of *Totality and Infinity*. Part III treats chiefly of *Otherwise than Being or Beyond Essence*. All three parts invoke other philosophical essays by Levinas and some of the many interviews he has given. From time to time appeal is made to his Talmudic exegeses, but not without keeping in mind his statement, to be reproduced in due course (in chapter 10), about how he sees the relation between them and the more philosophical texts.

What I have called three 'parts' could have been called three 'acts'. It is as though a plot unfolds from the earliest of Levinas's writings to the most recent. One cannot but be struck by the degree to which he seems to have a foresight of what he intends to say in detail later on. There are changes of order, style and stress. A later work may make more or less radical adjustments to what is said in a predecessor. Reading the writings in the order of their composition one is again and again taken by surprise. Yet hindsight frequently reveals that the ground for the unexpected turn of events has been prepared in one of the short early essays. It is as though those early essays are produced with the later masterpieces in view and remain in the author's mind during his production of the latter. Because they keep so much in reserve and because they are so comparatively brief, the kind of challenge they present to comprehension is different from that experienced in reading *Totality and Infinity* and *Otherwise than Being*, where it is the multiplicity and fineness of detail that puts demands upon one's attention. I have found that despite the above-mentioned differences of order and so on, a grasp of what Levinas is arguing in the *magna opera* is facilitated by a grasp of the framework outlined in the early *opuscula*. That is one reason why the latter are the topic of the first part. Another is that they merit examination in their own right. A third is that without examining them the subtitle of this study fails to apply in one of the senses of genealogy defined at the beginning of this introduction.

Part I

1 Ontological claustrophobia

A NEW WAY OF POSING AN OLD PROBLEM

With hindsight it can be seen that the essay *On Evasion* published in 1935 announces the issue with which all Levinas's philosophical writings will be preoccupied: the issue of the issue from ontology. Why does he state already in this essay that 'the ancient problem of ontology' has to be posed in a new way? Why does he consider the new way of posing it attempted by Heidegger in *Being and Time* (1927) still not new enough?[1]

Why is Levinas so concerned with the new? A historical answer to this question is that he inherits the topic from Bergson who, when Levinas was a student in the 1920s at Strasburg, was being hailed there as the leading thinker in France. Indeed, in the year preceding that in which *De l'évasion* (*Of Evasion*) was published the Alcan edition of the works of Bergson had appeared. It was the wide interest in Bergson's philosophy of time, Levinas notes, that prepared the ground for the reception of Heidegger in France.[2] Bergson's interpretation of psychological time as duration and his notion of creative evolution as *élan vital* purport to show how there can be an intuition of radical newness despite the conception of physical time which, he argues, is reducible to space, and which permits to intelligence only the uncreative fake novelty of geometrical reconfiguration. It is to the bustle of such mere re-arrangement, *remue-ménage*, that Maurice Blanchot refers to illustrate what he means by 'the neuter' and later, with Levinas, the there-is, the *il y a*.

In lectures published under the titles *La mort et le temps* and *Dieu, la mort et le temps* Levinas cites the following sentences of Bergson's *Creative Evolution* (1928):

> All living beings are linked one with another, and all yield to the same tremendous drive. The animal takes its stand on the plant, man bestrides animality, and the whole of humanity, in space and time, is a gigantic army galloping alongside, in front of and behind each one of us in an

all-embracing charge capable of overcoming every resistance and of clearing [*franchir*] many obstacles, perchance even death.[3]

Death according to Bergson is the translation of duration and its inter-penetrating phases into space divided into spaces according to more or less arbitrary convention. It is the reduction of quality into quantity and of differential energy into entropic equilibrium. It is not nothing or non-being. The idea of nothing is an idea of being:

> the idea of an absolute nothing, in the sense of the annihilation of everything, is a self-destructive idea, a pseudo-idea, a mere word. If suppressing a thing consists in replacing it by another, if thinking the absence of one thing is only possible by the more or less explicit representation of the presence of some other thing, if, in short, annihil-ation signifies before anything else substitution, the idea of an 'annihilation of everything' is as absurd as that of a square circle.[4]

It is this absurdity, the impossibility of nothingness, that is being ack-nowledged, Levinas suggests, when Macbeth laments that it cannot be truly said of death 'And there an end', and when Hamlet realizes that the 'not to be' is, perchance, not to be. What these characters in the so-called tragedies of Shakespeare are expressing – and Levinas remarks that it sometimes seems to him that the whole of philosophy may be regarded as a meditation on Shakespeare (*TA* 60, *TO* 72) – is that they are beyond the tragedy of tragedy. If there is still tragedy in a conflict between fate and freedom where the hero or heroine is able, like Juliet, to say 'I keep the power of death', Hamlet is beyond tragedy. For he understands that if death is nothingness perhaps he does not have the power to die, even by his own hand. 'Suicide is a contradictory concept.' I can take life, but I cannot take death. Death comes without my being able to assume it. Beyond my capacity, out of reach of the 'I can', death, as Heidegger says, is impos-sibility. But it is not, as he also says, the possibility of impossibility. It is the impossibility of possibility.

Coming toward me rather than that which I am toward, death is not non-being before which I am anxious, but being before which I am afraid. It comes toward me across a gap over which, as over my shadow, I am forever unable to jump. This interval will suddenly be closed by the arrival of my death. It is this interval rather than the arrival that is what occasions my dread. For if 'Prior to death there is always a last chance', the chance that the hero, the heroine or the saint grasps in ultimately tragic hope, there is also always a last risk, the risk of my committing murder. This, rather than my death, is what rouses dread.

In this sense, I do not die alone. And it is this that gives sense to death, as for Bergson it is this, and no longer the *élan vital* which according to *Creative Evolution* may perchance even leap over death, that comes to give sense to time when in his *The Two Sources of Morality and Religion* (1932) duration comes to be the fact that one human being calls out to another.[5] We shall see that this is the fact that will allow Levinas to put a new interpretation upon a word that occurs in one of the passages from Bergson cited by him and reproduced above: the word 'substitution'. To consider at this stage what Levinas will mean by this word would be to move too quickly ahead. Not to stay longer with Levinas's very early publication *Of Evasion* to ask what is anticipated there would be to miss an opportunity to understand the nature of the anticipation that his genealogy of ethics involves and so the genealogicality of this genealogy itself, its logic, or its 'logic'. To understand this must be an aim of any reading of his works. It is a principal aim of the reading we are engaged in here. It should be kept in mind as we proceed; as we proceed to ask, to begin with, of what kind of escape this early essay treats.

ESCAPE

Levinas tells his readers that although the word used in his title is borrowed from literary criticism the escape in question is not that of so-called escapist literature or of literature as such regarded as escape. In these latter contexts the need to escape is the need to escape 'harsh reality', 'bourgeois conventions', 'boredom' and suchlike. It is a need to escape a certain style of existence. What the title of Levinas's essay refers to is the need to escape existence as such, to escape the elementary and, as he also describes it, brutal truth that there is being, *il y a de l'être*. That the momentum of the *élan vital* will offer no chance of exit from sheer existence is already plain. That urge, however allegedly creative, however deconstructive of inherited frames, leaves one state of being only to enter another. It does not achieve the issue from being as such that would be the only remedy for what we might call ontological, as distinct from ontic, claustrophobia. Although it may, to employ Bergson's word, clear (*franchir*) death, depriving it of its sense, as in his paraphrase Levinas says (*MT* 62, *DMT* 67), this is *transcendence* to a new estate of existence. It is not the *excendence* that would be the exit from existence, turning the senselessness of death into sense.

We have still not read further than the first of the eight parts of *Of Evasion*. Yet it has already raised questions that will be of primary importance in the interpretation of Levinas's entire future work. For example, his recourse to this word excendence may be compared with his use of the word 'need', words that occur together in his phrase *besoin d'excendance'*. Levinas introduces this neologism apologetically, as though he might have preferred to stay with words in common currency. This will not be his last coinage, but we shall find that he generally prefers not to invent or to change words, but to bring out in old words an overlooked, overheard sense. The word *besoin* ('need'), is a case in point. *Of Evasion* employs this word in a dual capacity. On the one hand it is used, as it is usually used, in the sense of that which implies an expectation that would be met by something that is missing. But such ontic need is not the need for excendence. No satisfaction of a lack can meet that. Although in later writings Levinas will tend to restrict his use of the word 'need' to the ontic dimension and the difference between the ontic and the excendent will be marked by the difference between lower-case and upper-case initials for the word 'desire', a certain dramatic force is carried by the dual role given to the word 'need' in this early work. Its duality answers to the duality Levinas attributes here already to the self-identity of the human being, a certain duality that will turn out to be other than that of self-reference traditionally attributed to the identity of the self since Descartes at least, though in Descartes himself that duality of self-reference is no more than the beginning of the story he tells about the duality of human identity. The full story, as Levinas continues to tell it, will reveal that this duality takes on a *forme dramatique*.

> Existence is an absolute that affirms itself without referring itself to anything other. It is identity. But in this reference to himself man distinguishes a kind of duality. His identity with himself loses the character of a logical or tautological form; it takes on, as we shall go on to show, a dramatic form. In the identity of the ego [*moi*], the identity of being reveals its nature as enchainment because it appears in the form of suffering and it is an invitation to evasion. So evasion is the need of going out of itself [or the need to go out from itself (*le besoin de sortir de soi-même*)], that is to say, *to break the most radical, most irremissible enchainment, the fact that the ego is itself.*
>
> (*DE* 73)

Will Levinas go on to tell us that the tautologicality of self-identity gives way to heterologicality? All we have been told up to this point about heterologicality is that it is – otherwise than being. Why should this be a reason for saying that identity with oneself takes on a dramatic form? Are we to expect, in the words with which one dictionary defines 'drama', a 'set of events having the unity and progress of a play and leading to catastrophe or consummation'? Does his 'dramatic' have the force it has when used of utterances that are, as the same dictionary says, 'not to be taken as one's own', when instead of being attributed to an authorial 'I' the words are put in the mouth of a *dramatis persona,* whether a she or a he, an *il* – or an *Il*? We can perhaps expect at the very least that the word 'dramatic' here is being used with its root meaning, from *draô* ('to do, be doing, accomplish or fulfil'). If this is so, however, the doing in question cannot be the activity (*activité*) of creation that Bergson ascribes to the *élan vital*. It cannot be that of Bergsonian creative becoming because Levinas has just been arguing that however successfully that becoming escapes the prison of the present by immediately making it past, the creative activity itself is still in the service of being.

Yet, if this dramatic deed or accomplishment is not activity or creation in Bergson's sense, in what sense can it be suffering? How can the dramatic ✔⋅ form be a form of suffering? How is this duality to be understood? One clue to be followed is the statement that the identity of the self's being reveals itself as imprisonment because it appears as suffering. Being is suffered as imprisonment, as being riveted, enchained. Experienced as suffering, being is already an invitation to escape. The 'and' of 'and it is an invitation to escape' seems to be an implication of rather than an addition to the suffering, just as the first word of the sentence immediately following this clause seems to introduce not simply independently but as a consequence the idea that the escape to which the suffering of being invites the self *is* the need of going out of itself. This is an idea that calls for a closer scrutiny of the 'is', of being itself. Could it be that being is not itself? Could we say that where there is being, where *il y a de l'être*, there is evasion, *il y a de* ✔ *l'évasion*, so that just as books entitled *De la grammatologie* and *De l'esprit* might help their readers understand what they are about by giving them a helping of grammatology and spirit or wit, the *De* of *De l'évasion* might be not simply a preposition, but also a partitive pronoun, so that while the title announces an essay about or concerning evasion, it could at the same time announce an essay that is in some way a performance, a dramatic performance of evasion?

But of what sort is that other interesting 'of' in the assertion that evasion ✔ is the need of going out of oneself? The logic of this would be odd if evasion or escape here meant the same as going out of oneself (and how could the Latin root *evadere* not mean 'to go out'?), for in that case the assertion would be that going out of oneself is the need of going out of oneself. In the light of our analysis of the sentence immediately preceding it it looks as though we are being given to understand that the very identity of the oneself incorporates the need of being quit of oneself, and that the second *de* of the phrase *le besoin de sortir de soi-même* admits translation both as 'from' and as 'of'. One's self is from the start the need to leave oneself. The unity of the self labours in the pain of a need to be outside itself. Its unity is a disunity. Oneself is a twoself.

Is its labour labour lost? Is its pain pain in vain? If the tie I need to break is strictly irremissible, the need to break it can never be met. Levinas says however that the need in question is to break 'the most irremissible' enchainment. His admission of degrees means that whether the need can be met or not remains to be shown. The paragraph is avowedly proleptic.

NEED

When, however, in the second section of the essay Levinas reminds us that the need in question is not a privation, his explanation is that privative needs are needs of *what* is: they have to do with the *ti esti*. Whereas the need here in question has to do with the self's *that* it is: its *hoti esti*, the very fact that it is. Now that has no degrees. So does this mean that the need to go outside myself can never be satisfied? If so, this would not mean that I cannot not exist. This is no ontological argument by which my immortality is guaranteed. Levinas is not here treating of third-personal or impersonal logical truths of the kind that an imaginary independent onlooker might constate and process in a logic machine. The fact of existing that refers only to itself, as he first says, is the fact of existing as lived or existed by a self that poses itself or, *sich setzt*, as the German Idealists would say. Though it is less the idiom of German Idealism than that of Austrian, Husserlian phenomenology as modified by Heideggerian ontology that in this essay Levinas is beginning to adapt. It is from some of the implications of this phenomeno-ontological idiom that he feels the need to escape. But he does not feel the need to escape from the concreteness of the point at which thinking in this idiom begins. That is evident from the beginning of the thinking that goes on in *Of Evasion*, thinking that is a thinking of the beginning. However, this thinking of the beginning is not a thinking of the origin. That thinking and the thinking of death can be properly undertaken only when the analysis of evasion has reached a more advanced stage. And here we get no further than an introduction. This essay is provisional, Levinas says, thereby repeating another gesture Heidegger makes with reference to the analysis of *Dasein* in *Being and Time*.

There may be a third parallel with Heidegger if Levinas abandons the intention he here declares to return in a later study to a demonstration of the ontological character of nothingness and eternity. It may be granted that the first part of this programme is carried out in the brief discussion of some of Bergson's ideas reported above. As for the second part, that it may still not

have been carried out by the time *Totalité et infini* (1961) has been com-
pleted is suggested by what is written just before the section of that book
which announces Conclusions:

> Messianic triumph is pure triumph; it is secured against the revenge of
> evil whose return infinite time does not prohibit. Is this eternity a new
> structure of time, or an extreme vigilance of the messianic consciousness?
> The problem exceeds the bounds of this book.
>
> (*TEI* 261, *TI* 285)

Let us leave open the question whether that problem falls within the bounds
of another style of book. Let us say for the moment only that the escape of
which the need is being studied in the essay published more than a quarter
of a century before *Totality and Infinity* is not escape from time or flight
from death. One of the conclusions of the essay is repeated as one of the
Conclusions of *Totality and Infinity*. The very last words of that book return
to the figure of heroism to which we have already referred. They repeat that
the idea of a solo soul being saved through eternal life is incoherent if it
takes its monadic identity with it. If the salvation I need is salvation *from*
identity, salvation *of* identity gives victory to, in the words Levinas cites
from Baudelaire, 'ennui, fruit of the mournful incuriosity that takes on the
proportions of immortality'.[6] If salvation is my preservation it is unequal to
the need for evasion.

   In his essay on evasion Levinas tells us more about the nature of this
need, enough to confirm that the need being analysed is not that of saving
one's soul or one's life. Nor, for the same reason, is it a finite being's need
to overcome its finitude. An infinite being is still encumbered by being. The
need to be rid of that is not a need that can be satisfied. It is more like a need
from which one can only be delivered. One is not delivered from it by
applying empirical or technical knowledge. If teaching – Levinas's word
here is *enseignement* – is relevant to deliverance, it is not the teaching of
theoretical or technical information: not Kantian rules of skill or counsels
of prudence; not technology. Only in later writings will Levinas explain in
what sense *enseignement* may be relevant to deliverance. Only then will it
be possible to judge what his response would be to Heidegger's pro-
nouncement 'Only a god can save us.'[7] We do not have to wait until then,
however, in order to be able to discern another point of proximity with
Heidegger, the fourth to which the evasion essay has drawn our attention so
far. Heidegger contrasts anguish and fear. Fear has an object. Anguish
before nothingness does not. Nor, according to Levinas, does the need
before being. It has no term. It has a positive indeterminacy. The need to get
out is not a need to go to a particular destination. This is why no theoretical

or practical knowledge is relevant to it. Dare one say that this need has a teleologicality without *telos*? The malaise which is the mode in which the suffering of the need manifests itself is at least dynamic, we are told (*DE* 78). But it is less a movement toward than a movement away, an e-motion. It is an inner restlessness that will not be put to rest, unlike needs for which satisfaction brings an at least temporary peace. If even satisfaction is accompanied by disappointment ('Is that all?'), perhaps the need that can be satisfied is in some sense inferior to the restlessness that does not seek rest, the inquietude in which there is another exigency. Note that a certain need, and it must be the 'higher' need that is meant, has applied to it the adjective *déchirant*, piercing or tearing. We shall meet this and cognate words again when Levinas later develops the thoughts set out in the essay of 1935, entitled *De l'évasion*. To be precise, it is of the exigency or urgency of the uneasiness or, as Kierkegaard might say, sickness intrinsic to what we have just called the higher need that Levinas says that it is *peut-être supérieure*. If this reference to superiority has any evaluative implications it is because it is primarily to logical status that it refers. That what we may provisionally call ontological disquiet is the condition of specific ontic disquiets explains why the satisfaction of ontic needs – and it is only ontic needs that admit of satisfaction – is yet tinged by an unsatisfiable insufficiency. It is a disappointed satisfaction. For the disquiet of ontological need is not stilled. This also explains why Levinas goes on to talk of needs without always distinguishing the higher from the lower. If the nature of ontic need is informed by ontological need, then an analysis of the one will be informative about the other, and it will be of need quite generally that Levinas will affirm the thesis that satisfaction is never enough. This thesis is supported by an analysis of pleasure.

PLEASURE

If malaise is not a passive state, no more is the pleasure in which is manifested the satisfaction of a need. If satisfaction leaves something to be desired, so too does pleasure. Completeness is a state. Pleasure is always underway, outward bound, though not to any specified place. Rather than being a filling, pleasure is an emptying. If pleasures are – as Plato allows at least of physical pleasures – concomitant with or consequent upon a process of filling, their pleasurability must be seen in the context of a pleasure that is or accompanies a process of emptying. This is not however an endorsement of the 'leaky bucket' theory attributed to Callicles according to which the continuance of the pleasure of satisfaction would require that satisfaction to be incomplete.[8] It is not simply that with the filling there has to be a concomitant leakage of the substance with which the vessel is being filled. What is called for by the pleasure in which is made manifest the satisfaction of a need is not a leakage of substance but a leakage of substantiality. Properly understood, pleasure is a movement of dispersal that desubstantializes being and splits the moment of time. It is as though the filling of the vessel has to be interpreted not only as an analogy for drinking, but also as an analogy for being drunk. Pleasure is an insobriety, a relaxation of the density and weight of the pain of ontological malaise: a ∨ glimpse of escape from being through liberation from being one's first-personal self.

If, as Levinas says, pleasure is dynamic, it is not what the Scholastics, following Aristotle on *energeia* ('actuality' or 'activity'), call *actus purus*. Pure activity is free of all potentiality. Levinas also says however that pleasure is a movement. So it is *kinêsis* ('movement' or 'motion') with latent power. While agreeing with Aristotle that pleasure is not pure and simple activity, Levinas does not agree that it is what supervenes on activity like the bloom of youth. The latter conception fails to do justice to the kinetic nature of pleasure and to the promise of emancipation from being that pleasure brings with it. If pleasure is to augur escape from being then the categories of being cannot apply to it. It cannot be a state of being. This is why pleasure is an affect. It is affective rather than effective because affectivity is recalcitrant to the categories of activity or will and of being and of thought. If affectivity were amenable to the categories of activity or what in traditional terminology goes under the title of 'conation', it would have to be amenable to the categories of being. For activity presupposes a being that acts. If it were amenable to the categories of thinking, to the cognitive faculty as traditionally understood, the categories of being would be in its scope. For cognition is of beings and what is predicable of them. In the traditional trichotomy affection is distinguished from cognition and conation. So it is not surprising to find Levinas denying that it is reducible to the categories applicable in the other two spheres. This does not mean that affects cannot become objects of knowledge. It means only that an objectivating psychology of affects must be derivative from a non-objectivating access to them. As Bergson would say, the movement of e-motion is misconstrued when quantitatively described. As Levinas says, the affectivity of pleasure attempts to break the forms of being.

It fails in this attempt. It succeeds only in breaking itself. Its promise of evasion is not kept. This is to some extent recognized both in the experience of shame and in the idea advanced in the *Philebus* (36a–b) of pleasures mixed with pain, for instance the pleasure and pain which a thirsty person experiences when his thoughts combine the idea of what would quench his thirst with the idea that no beverage is near. This pain is not to be confused with the pain of the thirst. Nor is it to be confused with, for example, the pain resulting from setting one's expectations of pleasure too high or with the pain caused by the unhappy consequences of a life too devoted to pleasure. The pain of a mixed pleasure would be intrinsic to the pleasure. Likewise, Levinas argues, in its very nature as affect pleasure is always a deceit. And at the moment of breaking the promise that it appeared about to keep pleasure is swallowed up in shame.

SHAME

Appearances notwithstanding, one is ashamed not simply of an immoral or other misdeed. The sharpness of shame – and the adjective *déchirant* is used again here – derives from a conjunction of not being able to understand how one could have done such a thing and not being able to deny one's identity with the being of the person who did it. One is ashamed of oneself because one is ashamed of one's self. One has no power to break away from oneself – and the word 'break' (*rompre*), used here will take on further significance in Levinas's later work. The origin of original shame, and therefore of shame over what one regards as a lapse, is the impossibility of concealing from oneself one's nakedness. Either original shame does not depend on original sin, or the origin of original sin is one's being riveted to oneself, incapable of evasion. Of Evasion. Adam was naked, and he hid himself. But even if he could hide himself from Eve or from God, he could not hide his nakedness from himself. He could not hide his self from himself. And original shameful self-consciousness does not have to wait for shame in the sight of others. Furthermore, seeing oneself from outside as the unembarrassed striptease artist does is a way of clothing oneself, like Hans Andersen's Emperor, with one's unclothedness. Nakedness is not being unclothed. It is the need of an apologia for one's existence. It is not motivated by a sense of having done something wrong. It is not conditioned by one's being finite. It is the condition of one's being.

If it is not already obvious that Heidegger is one of the philosophers uppermost in the author's mind throughout *Of Evasion* (one of the others is one sometimes uppermost in the mind of the author of *Being and Time*, Hegel, on whose vocabulary both authors draw), it must become so when toward the end of the section of the essay in which he has been analysing shame he writes epigrammatically 'Ce que la honte découvre c'est l'être qui se *découvre*' ('What shame reveals is being's self-*revelation*') (*DE* 87). Where being is unconcealed or concealed, there lies the root of all shame.

NAUSEA

In connection with Levinas's response to Heidegger it will have to be asked in due course what is implied for being as such, *Sein*, by these analyses of human being, by Levinas's *Daseinsanalytik*, his analysis of being there, *d'être là* (*DE* 91). Meanwhile, under that analysis the nakedness of the presence of one's being there reveals itself as the experience of being about to be sick. Not sickness unto death. Being unto death assumes reflection on one's being. In the sickness of nausea there is not knowledge, reflective or pre-reflective, of one's state. One is not in a state. Not yet. As yet there is nothing to constate. There is only the pure there is, the pure being of being oneself. This 'of' of one's belonging to one's being is the 'of' of the irremissibility of being by which we are asphyxiated. One is stuck with oneself – stuck to oneself as Levinas says (*DE* 90) and as Sartre will say.[9]

Nausea reveals more patently than shame that this ontological claus- ∨ trophobia, this experience of being 'enclosed within a suffocatingly tight circle' (ibid.), does not depend on the fact that one is a member of a society. It does not depend on the thought that one has infringed some social norm. Poverty is not in itself a crime, yet one can be ashamed of the nakedness left uncovered by one's rags. One's being ashamed of one's nakedness does not depend on what one imagines others would say. And, as already noted, it does not depend on what others would see. It does not depend on others at all. The monadic ego of which Husserl writes in the earlier parts of the *Cartesian Meditations*[10] is not immune to this ontological nausea. 'Without a window on anything else' (*DE* 92): being-there without being-with, a *Dasein* without *Mitsein* would experience it too. It has nothing to do with intersubjectivity. On the contrary, the presence of others might seem to offer a temporary escape. For this sense of being *mal dans sa peau*, the malaise of feeling oneself shut into the subcutaneous substantiality of one's subjectivity, could expect at least intermission through being given the guise of a malady which one might hope a therapist would be able to diagnose and treat.

Levinas is pointing to a powerlessness beyond the power of the self, a *Nichtkönnen* that adheres to *Seinkönnen*. But his impower is not a corollary of human finitude. Human being is being at a limit, at the point at which, wretchedly retching ineffectually, one would like to but cannot be sick. At the limit at which inclination (*Mögen*) and inability (*Unmöglichkeit*) meet. So the impower is not that of being unable to accomplish a deed exceeding one's power. Nor, as we have more than once observed, is this impower the impossibility at the horizon of possibility that Heidegger equates with death. Nor again is it the impower over our coming into existence, the already-having-been-thrownness (*Geworfenheit*) of our birth. It is the im-power of the very accomplishment of our existence, of its *plêrôsis*, that is to say, its total lack of lack. An accomplishment. Not a negation or privation, but the positivity of the self's self-posing, the affirmation of its being. A *sui generis* accomplishment, Levinas writes, using a word (in which resounds among others *Vollziehung*, Husserl's word for 'accomplishment', 'per-formance' or 'fulfilment') that will recur in later works, a word that may be a key to an understanding of the genealogicality of his ethics and of how a non-generality can emerge from generation or what he will call 'creation', adopting the word from Bergson – though one should not forget the role this word also plays in Nietzsche's genealogy of morals.

2   Ontic accomplishment

CONCRETENESS

More than once *Of Evasion* couples together the nouns that appear in the title *De l'existence à l'existant* of the book published in 1947 incorporating a discussion of the there-is, the *il y a*, published as a separate article in 1946. Just as this book, published in English under the title *Existence and Existents*, is announced by *Of Evasion*, so it in turn postpones but explicitly promises the more detailed analyses of time and the Other begun in *Le temps et l'autre* (*Time and the Other*) which will also be published in 1947. In *Existence and Existents* 'Le temps et l'Autre' is the subheading of a brief section only, following one that claims to be only on the way to time, 'Vers le temps'. Levinas is touching there on topics which, as he says of eternity in *Totality and Infinity*, exceed the limits of the present study (*DEE* 147, *EE* 85). The approach is again provisional. It is as though Levinas is writing within the framework of *Being and Time* in order the better to engage with it and explode it at its seams. Heidegger advises his prospective reader that his study is prospective: 'Our aim in the following treatise is to work out the question of the meaning of "*Being*" and to do so concretely. Our provisional aim is the Interpretation of *time* as the possible horizon for any understanding whatsoever of Being.'[1] It could be said that any aim is pro-visional, *vorläufig*, and that Heidegger's adjective is redundant. The redundancy would be avoided if the provisionality of the aim meant that the aim is not the ultimate one, but one adopted for the time being. That is how one might describe the aim of an analysis of *Dasein* that will give way to an analysis of being as such, as the third division of the first part was going to do under the title 'Time and Being'. That too is how one might describe the aim of the first division of the first part of *Being and Time*, which is concerned with the existential analysis of the being of *Dasein* and qualified as preparatory (*vorbereitend*) in the index of the book in relation to the second division of the same part which proceeds to express the preceding analysis in terms of temporality. That progression at least is mirrored in the agenda drawn up for himself by Levinas.

It is not beyond credibility that when in the passage cited Heidegger uses the adjective *vorläufig* he is anticipating, running ahead to, the second division's analysis of being-towards-death as anticipation or running ahead toward a certain possibility: the possibility of impossibility by which all *Dasein*'s possibilities are embraced. This and these possibilities are concrete. There is no reason why the philosophical working out of the question of the meaning of being should not be possessed of the concreteness of this ultimate possibility. And if Levinas is ultimately to propose that death is not the possibility of possibility and impossibility but the impossibility of possibility, there is every reason why his philosophical working out of the response that precedes questioning should be no less concrete.

In this quest for concreteness Heidegger and Levinas are following the example of Bergson and of Husserl, the dedicatee of *Being and Time*. Up to a point. For Heidegger rejects what he takes to be Bergson's doctrine that the abstract quantitative time of objects in the world results from an externalization of inner qualitative duration. Bergson's account of objective time belongs on Heidegger's reading of it to the Kantian tradition whose shortcomings Bergson's account of duration was meant to make good. Through Kant it belongs to the ontological tradition going back to Aristotle. Heidegger holds that 'The question of Being does not achieve its true concreteness until we have carried through the process of destroying the ontological tradition' (*SZ* 26). Levinas holds that this question does not achieve its true concreteness until both the Greek tradition and the Heideggerian alternative have been 'destroyed', that is to say, de- and reconstrued.

However, both the Heideggerian and the Levinasian destructions follow Husserl in stressing the importance of concreteness, even where they disagree with the philosopher whose lectures they both attended. Husserl contrasts the *concretum* with the *abstractum*. This contrast is equivalent to that between the independent and the dependent (or non-independent) as exemplified by the distinctions between whole (e.g. a coloured surface) and part (e.g. a part of a coloured surface) examined in the third of the *Logical Investigations*.[2] This logical and ontological notion of concreteness is carried over into *Ideas*, volume 1 (e.g. §15), but in that book a methodological and phenomenological notion of concreteness is derived from the so-called principle of all principles which applies to every 'object', concrete, abstract or whatever. This principle of 'bodily selfhood' states that '*immediate "seeing"* (Sehen) . . . *in general as primordial dator consciousness of any*

*kind whatsoever, is the ultimate source of justification for all rational state-
ments'.*[3] This is a principle of concreteness, but in the sense of concreteness
of eidetic essence, not in the sense of empirical 'individual concrete being'
(*Ideas*, vol. 1, §3) or in the sense of mystical insight (ibid.). As Husserl
insists in the book for the French version of which Levinas was one of the
translators, 'Phenomenology's purely intuitive, concrete, and also apo-
dictic mode of demonstration excludes all "metaphysical adventure", all
speculative excesses' (*Cartesian Meditations* §60).[4] While being a positive
principle of concreteness this 'first methodological principle' (ibid. §5) is a
principle of caution and criticism. It affirms not only that '*whatever
presents itself in "intuition" in primordial form (as it were in bodily
reality), is simply to be accepted as it gives itself out to be*', but goes on at
once to warn 'though *only within the limits in which it then presents itself*'
(*Ideas*, vol. 1, §24). It is therefore a principle of gradualism:

> It is plain that I, as someone beginning philosophically, since I am
> striving toward the presumptive end, genuine science, must neither
> make nor go on accepting any judgment as scientific *that I have not
> derived from evidence*, from 'experiences' [*Erfahrungen*] in which the
> affairs and affair-complexes in question are present to me as '*they
> themselves*'. Indeed, even then I must examine its 'range' and make
> evident to myself *how far* that evidence, how far its 'perfection'
> [*Vollkommenheit*], *the actual giving of the affairs themselves*, extends.
> Where this is still wanting, I must not claim any final validity, but must
> account my judgment as, at best, a possible intermediate stage on the
> way to final validity.
>
> (*Cartesian Meditations* §5)

Whether or not phenomenology is always 'on the way', and whether or not
this principle of gradualism is already evidence that there must be a phenomenology that is a genealogy, a phenomenology subject to the law of
'oriented' constitution (ibid. §58), it merits repetition that this principle
remains a principle of rigorous rationality when adopted and adapted by
Heidegger and Levinas. This rigour and rationality require methodological
concreteness that has ontological concreteness as its aim. Analysis into
abstracted pieces, parts, components and levels must keep the synthesis of
the manifold in view. Thus the first division of the *Daseinsanalytik* of
Being and Time ends by asking 'Has our investigation up to this point ever
brought *Dasein* into view *as a whole*?' Given the biological 'root' of the
word's meaning, one cannot read without a sense of irony Heidegger's
repeated demands for con-creteness (from *crescere*, 'to grow'), despite the
fact that he is analysing what he allows himself to call *Dasein*'s everyday

life. Do these last three words not verge on incoherence in the context of the strictures he puts upon philosophical biologism? Do not these strictures make it very difficult for him to agree that all human *life* is *there*, *da*? Or are we meant to imagine that the last of those three words is flanked by inverted commas? Husserl and Levinas have no such compunction. Concrescence is an entirely apt description of the incremental way in which their analytico-synthetic genealogies of the *life*world proceed.

However, just as Heidegger warns against 'verbal mysticism' (*SZ* 220), so Levinas will take pains to argue for the extreme rationality of what in his redefinition of metaphysics may seem from a traditional point of view to be extreme irrationality. Heidegger will redefine phenomenology ontologically to allow its subject-matter, the 'phenomenon', to include not only 'experiences', what discloses itself, but also what conceals itself, being. So Heidegger's fundamental phenomenological ontology is not limited to an analysis of the noetic-noematic structures to which Husserl's analyses are confined, despite the fact that the hyphen here marks Husserl's insistence on the concreteness of these structures and despite the fact that their noematic objects are not just representations in the empiricist or Kantian transcendental sense. That limitation is one of the chief targets of the criticism of those analyses made by Levinas in *The Theory of Intuition in Husserl's Phenomenology* (1930). But notwithstanding the precedence Heidegger gives to readiness to hand over presence at hand in his analysis of everyday life, and despite Heidegger's turn and return to the question of being as other than a being, Heideggerian ontology is still in the strict sense a phenomenology, that is to say, it is still concerned with the giving and given in light. The 'seeing' may be less narrowly conceived than it is in Husserl's already broad reconception of sight, but, as is suggested by Heidegger's attribution of forms of spection (*Sicht*) to *Dasein*'s *Da* in §§15, 31 and 36 of *Being and Time*, seeing remains for his phenomenology 'the prince of senses' that it was for St Augustine.[5] This is one misplacement that Levinas sets out to correct in *Existence and Existents*. He also continues there the meditation on 'the tragedy of being' begun in *Of Evasion*. Third, rather as Fichte, Schelling and Hegel undertake the task of repairing what they regard as Kant's failure to deduce the categories, so Levinas undertakes to make good what he sees either as Heidegger's failed attempt to deduce the ontic from the ontological or as his failure even to make that attempt.

CONSTITUTION

In *Existence and Existents* this undertaking and that correction are accomplished together through the meditation starting from a phenomenological description of the concrete conditions of effort, lassitude and fatigue. The relevant meaning of accomplishment is not explicitly defined here but can only be gathered from the many contexts of its use. We found it employed in the last paragraph of *Of Evasion* which speaks of 'an event that in the very accomplishment [*accomplissement*] of existence breaks that existence' (*DE* 99). The phrase raises a question that will haunt the reading of *Totality and Infinity*. How can being exceed itself? How can ontology *par excellence* find itself to have been what Levinas calls the *fait accompli* of non-speculative 'metaphysics', 'ethics', even 'religion', long before speculative metaphysics approaches what Heidegger calls its *Vollendung*, that is to say, its closure?

At one of the many places where the notion of accomplishment returns in *Totality and Infinity* the 'accomplished' is offered as an alternative to the 'constituted'. The phrase 'is constituted or is accomplished' (*se constitue ou s'accomplit*) occurs in a section entitled 'Subjectivity', following a section entitled 'Against the Philosophy of the Neuter' in which Levinas declares himself convinced 'of having broken with . . . the Heideggerian Being of the existent whose impersonal neutrality the critical work of Blanchot has contributed so much to bringing out, with Hegel's impersonal reason, which shows to the personal consciousness only its ruses' (*TEI* 274–5, *TI* 298–9). The break with that neutrality, and what Levinas is bold enough to call as early as the 1930s and 1940s a resolution of the tragedy of being, are begun precisely with the accomplishment or constitution of subjectivity. So prima facie, this resolution is sought in a return to the human subjectivity that Heidegger's analysis of *Dasein* would leave when he locates what he refers to as a resolution of the tragedy of being in the √ coming to presence of the present as in the overcoming of the dis- of dis-order denoted by Anaximander's word *a-dikia*.[6] The word 'constitution' has a root in the Latin terms *sto*, *stare*, *stans*, and so on, meaning 'to stand and hold oneself up', *se dresser* or, as Levinas writes in the section entitled 'Subjectivity', *se tenir*. But the same terms are at the root of the words 'existent' and 'existence' as is more apparent in the *existant* of Levinas's French title than in the *Existents* of the title of the translation. This etymological clue is not enough to point to an exit from Heideggerian being, of course, because Heidegger's analysis of *Dasein* too trades on the link that the word 'existence' has with the same Latin terms and their Greek predecessors. However, whereas in Heidegger's analysis of *Dasein* the *sta* of the verbs *stare* and *sistere* are prefixed by *ex-* or *ec-* to express the ways in which *Dasein* is ec-statically extended through time, in Levinas's analysis of subjectivity the *sta*, and so on, are prefixed by *in-*, as in 'instant'. If Heidegger were to see this as a regress to a German Idealism, he would be wrong. For Levinas's account of the 'I' makes as many reservations as does his about the voluntarism that the German Idealist account of the 'I' inherits from Leibniz. It would not be entirely wrong to see here, however, a return to something like the Cartesian notion of the 'I' as the *chose qui pense* whose shortcomings are spelled out in *Being and Time*. For Levinas does employ the word 'substance' in characterizing its status. In doing so he has Bergsonist and other process interpretations of the self in view. But his recourse to this term is made as a challenge to the continuism of these interpretations, not in order to argue that the stance of the substance of the subject is static. On the contrary, he maintains that movement is involved. Not the movement of a present inheriting the burden of a past, like the snowball of Bergson's analogy, or weighted down by the having-been that according to Hegel is the essence of presence. Nor the movement of a present protending or projecting a future as in Heidegger's analysis of *Dasein* in which futurity is the temporal ecstasis that is stressed. Rather, the movement of an instant understood not as a mere limit, but as a present interruptive event.

This accentuation of presence returns to being at hand (*prae-esse*) an importance that is ascribed to it in certain realist and idealist theories but which is diminished when it is derived from readiness to hand in the analysis of everyday life conducted in *Being and Time*. If the subject's way of being in the world is primarily with things in their readiness to hand and is therefore a being-able (*Seinkönnen*), the being of subjectivity is inevitably ecstatic existential reaching, imperial *reichen* and thorough reaching-through: *durchreichen*. But if being in a *Reich* is the primary and ultimate order of subjectivity, if being in the world is the fullest concretion of being-there, there can be no hope of evading the there-is.

Now, as has already been said, Levinas insists that there is no hope of evading the there-is. This does not mean that the there-is is all there is, that there is nothing for which one may hope, or only nothing, non-being, to fear. Being is the first and last motivation of fear, and this is fear-of, rather than, as for Heidegger, fear-for. More specifically, it is of the unspecific neutral impersonality of the *il y a* of being that I am afraid, as of the impersonality marked by the pronoun in *il fait nuit* (strictly, 'It nights'), rather than of the night itself and what might go bump in it, which, in being an in principle locatable what, is no different in principle from what goes bump in the light. Yet it is in the close atmosphere of the sickroom of allegedly fundamental ontology, no less oppressive than the closure of speculative metaphysics, that, like the oxygen bottle in the grandmother's bedroom in Proust's *Le côté de Guermantes*, is provided at least provisional relief. How does Levinas begin to show that where this most fearful danger lies there does rescue grow?[7] By showing that from existence grow up existents with their feet planted on the earth.

HYPOSTASIS

But, as has also already been said, the standing of hypostatic existents is not static. Even their standing still is the accomplishment of a movement, the accomplishment of commencement, a fresh start that interrupts the droning ground-base of impersonal being. Personality is born. It is to the assumption of existence in this birth that one must first look, not to the assumption / of our being toward our death, if there is to be any hope of resolving the tragedy of being, a tragedy deeper than the tragedy that can be resolved by the heroic assumption of death. It is not in human finitude, the endingness of humankind, each person's being toward the end of its being or the end of metaphysics, that the tragedy of being is resolved. That tragedy outlives the end of the world. For the end of the world is not the end of the *il y a*. In thinking this Levinas is giving a twist to a thought that is expressed in *Being and Time* itself, where it is already a repetition of an idea expressed in *Ideas*, volume 1. In §49 of the latter book, the section entitled 'Absolute Consciousness as Residuum after the Nullifying of the World', Husserl asks: supposing a subject capable of unifying the contents of consciousness, 'is it still *conceivable*, is it not on the contrary absurd, that the corresponding transcendental world should *not be*?' It is a version of this question that Heidegger is answering when he says 'Being – not beings – is something which "there is" ['*gibt es*'] only in so far as truth is. And truth *is* only in so far and as long as *Dasein* is' (*SZ* 230).

These statements mimic statements (emphasized in the original text) where Husserl distinguishes a certain contingency from a certain necessity:

> Immanent being is therefore without doubt absolute in this sense, that in principle *nulla 're' indiget ad existendum*. On the other hand, the world of transcendent '*res*' is related unreservedly to consciousness, not indeed to logical conceptions, but to what is actual [*aktuelles*].

However, Heidegger sets aside Husserl's terminology of consciousness, *Bewusstsein*, restricting himself to that of *Sein*, on the grounds that

> The ideas of a 'pure "I"' and of a 'consciousness in general' are so far from including the a priori character of 'actual' [*wirklichen*] subjectivity that the ontological characters of *Dasein*'s facticity and its state of being are either passed over or not seen at all.

(*SZ* 229)

This reflects and reflects on statements (in which the emphases are Husserl's except for the last) that Levinas must surely have had in his mind when choosing his title *De l'évasion*: 'Consciousness, considered in its *"purity"*, must be reckoned as *a self-contained system of being*, as a system of *absolute being*, into which nothing can penetrate, and from which *nothing can escape*'. Whereas into Husserl's text Heidegger reads his *es gibt*, Levinas reads into it the *il y a* which, he writes in the preface to the second edition of *Existence and Existents* (1973), was never meant to convey the implications of generosity and abundance associated with Heidegger's use of his phrase. Not grace but gravity characterizes the *il y a,* like the weight of the chains that bind one to existence, as Levinas was held in the *Stalag* when describing the *il y a* in *Existence and Existents*, 'written for the most part in captivity' (*DEE* 10, *EE* 15).

DEDUCTION

In the years immediately following the Liberation from the captivity in which he described captivity by the *il y a*, before the publication of *De l'existence à l'existant* in 1947, could Levinas have read or at least heard of Simone Weil's *La pesanteur et la grâce* which was published in the same year?[8] At any rate he writes in that book the following disillusioning words: 'La liberté du présent n'est pas légère comme la grâce, mais une pesanteur et une responsabilité' (*DEE* 150): 'The freedom of the present is not light like grace, but a weight and a responsibility' (*EE* 87). The movement of the initiative instant is a movement from '*consumation*' *inextinguible* in the fire of the neutrality and indeterminacy of the there of there-is (*DEE* 93–4, *EE* 57), the anywhere of its *y* and the impersonality of its *il*, into the frying-pan of a determinate, posited, *gesetzt* here, the *ici* where the ego finds itself tied irremissibly to itself. Adapting Levinas's figure of speech, one could say that it is as though the prisoner's chain has been lengthened but not untied. Although my instantaneous present is freed from the past and the future, underived from the reach of time of the world, I am not freed from myself. I keep my own company. Levinas is alert to the possibility that this may look like nothing more than the dramatization of a tautology. Given his recourse to the language of German Idealism it would be interesting to compare his alleged 'deduction' of posited beings from being with the deductions of the categories from 'I am I' that Fichte and Schelling purport to carry out. As well as because of the important place Schelling occupies in the thinking of Franz Rosenzweig's *The Star of Redemption* and the importance for his own thinking that Levinas ascribes to that book (*TEI* XVI, *TI* 28),[9] comparison with Schelling would be especially relevant because of Levinas's interest in Bergson, Bergson's interest in Schelling and Schelling's interest in the Neo-Platonist tradition mediated by Böhme and Tauler. That tradition, mediated by the Gaon of Vilnyus and Rabbi Hayyim of Volozhyn's *Nefesh Hahayyim*, makes an impact on Levinas's thinking, as is apparent from the preface he contributes to a translation of that book.[10] Suffice it to note Levinas's reference in that preface to Genesis 2:7, which, he points out, does not say that when God formed man of the dust of the ground by breathing into his nostrils man became a living *being*; it says that he became a living *soul*; it says that he became *Nefesh Hahayyim*. As such he becomes with his Creator a co-creator responsible for the world and needed by God. A Trinitological version of this doctrine is expressed in *The Ages of the World* and elsewhere where Schelling draws on the idea that the Father achieves actuality only by becoming past in relation to the presence of the son as Reconciler, the *Sohn* as *Versöhner*.[11] Heidegger draws on and away from the same idea when he expresses the thought that being needs the human being. This is the thought from which Levinas withdraws when he deduces and hopes to rescue the presently existent being from the neutrality of being. The being that is deduced is the soul of life of which Genesis and Volozhyn write. No wonder that, in connection with Heidegger's history of the epochs of being's dissimulation of being as a being, Levinas objects that his response to Heidegger is being oversimplified when it is interpreted as a reversal of the hierarchical ordering held to obtain in the latter's conception of the ontological difference between being and beings (*DEE* 12).

The history of Heidegger's own thinking of the ontological difference rules out a simple answer to the question whether, as against Levinas's so-called deduction of a being from being, he deduces being from a being. When in the fourth edition of the Postscript to 'What is Metaphysics?' he takes back his earlier assertion that being holds sway without beings, he opens the door for a passage in both directions.[12] Indeed Levinas appears to do likewise when on one page of *Existence and Existents* he refers to the adherence of beings or existents to being or existence (*DEE* 16, 28, *EE* 17, 23) and on another to the adherence of existence to existents (*DEE* 27, *EE* 22). What is going on here? Not, as we have seen, a dramatization of an abstract tautology. Not overmuch ado about being and its vacuous repetition by a being: what is is. But a drama and a *répétition* in the theatrical sense, a rehearsal enacting the concrete phenomenology of the experience that the adherence of neutral existence to the existent can appear as a coming unstuck. A deneutralization takes place. We shall return to this appearing in the next chapter.

Notwithstanding the complications to which allusion has just been made, it can at least be said, and we have earlier done so, that the original programme of *Being and Time* is to proceed to the question of being as such from the concreteness of the being of a certain being. *De l'existence à l'existant*, on the other hand, proceeds, as the title of the book indicates, to the existent from, in the words of the subtitle of one of its sections, existence without existent, the neutral there-is, from, therefore, in the words of the title of the chapter in which that section falls, existence without world. Heidegger's deduction from *Dasein* cannot possibly be a deduction from existence without world, for the concreteness of *Dasein*'s being cannot be that deduction's point of departure unless that point is its being in the world with its pastward and forward ecstases. Levinas's contention is that Heidegger is wrong to suppose that subjectivity entails worldhood in that sense, as he does as soon as the unity of *Dasein* is attributed to care, specifically care for being, specifically its being, even though this may embrace concern and solicitude for other beings. Levinas argues, as David Hume and Joseph Butler did in different terms before him, that care does not have to have an ulterior motive. I do not always eat to live. Although I may use instruments, knives and forks, as means to eat, eating is not in its turn another means. It can be directly and, as Levinas says, sincerely motivated by hunger or the enjoyment of what is on my plate. I can care for cabbage without this care being subsumed within a care for being.

The intentionality of my desire to eat is the duality of the relation of a substantive subject and a substantive thing in the world, but the horizon of this worldhood is not the multiply tensed verbality of ontological care (*Sorge*). Its focus is narrower than that. Not that it is outside time. Nor that it is outside being. It is outside the temporality of the care of being toward my death. It is bio-ontological, not thanato-ontological. Nor is time negated when the focus is narrowed still further to the present of position that relates only to itself. In this focus something like the occasionalist doctrine of causality and duration advanced by Malebranche in his *Search after Truth*, *Dialogues on Metaphysics*, and elsewhere is confirmed, though so far only the accomplishment of a creator with a small 'c' is invoked by Levinas to preserve the seriature across the caesura of the vanishing present (*DEE* 128–9, *EE* 74–5). His claim is that this instance of hypostasis is an interruption and recommencement that makes possible time and with time being which would turn into non-being if there were no more to the present than the evanescence it undergoes when it appears to be absorbed into the past or what is 'presently' to come. Because this rescue of being is a rescue from being's anonymity by the hypostasis of a substantive subject, a being that can bear an identifying name, and because being or existence is unnegatable even by nothing and death, Levinas has indeed deduced the existent from existence.

3 Before time

METHOD

What, more precisely, does Levinas mean by deduction? Deduction is production. Not production in the sense of an explicative leading out of something implicit according to rules of logical inference. Production rather in the sense of a *mise en scène*. What is productively deduced is given its place in the drama or general economy of being (*TA* 18, 83, *TO* 39–40, 90). In *Totality and Infinity* the word 'production' is introduced as a technical term, a term of art, to perform some of the work done in *Existence and Existents* by the word 'accomplishment'. This latter word, we have noted, is nowhere formerly defined in this latter book, but, as we have also noted, it is probably an adaptation, perhaps accomplishment, of what Husserl calls *Vollziehung*. It continues to be used frequently in *Totality and Infinity*. No formal definition of it is forthcoming there either. But the preface of the book does contain a formal definition of 'production', a term corresponding to Husserl's term *Leistung*. In this preface Levinas announces that the book will affirm the philosophical primacy of the idea of infinity over the idea of totality. He goes on:

> It will recount how the infinite is produced [*se produit*] in the relationship of the same with the other, and how, not to be *aufgehoben* [*indépassable*], the particular and the personal somehow magnetize the very field in which this production of the infinite is acted out [*se joue*]. The term production indicates both the accomplishment [*effectuation*] of being (the event 'is produced', an automobile 'is produced') and its being brought to light or its exposition (an argument 'is produced', an actor 'is produced'). The ambiguity of this verb translates the essential ambiguity of the operation by which the being of an entity at one and the same time realizes itself [*s'évertue*] and reveals itself.[1]

Between the Husserlian stem and Levinas's notions of production and accomplishment an intermediate branch is grafted when at the beginning of the 'Letter on Humanism' Heidegger translates the Greek *poiêsis* and the Latin *producere* by *Vollbringen*, understanding by this the unfolding and leading forth of something into its essence, *etwas in die Fülle seines Wesens entfalten, in diese hervor geleiten*. *Vollbringen* is translated by *accomplir* in Roger Munier's translation published in *Questions III* (1966) and in works by Alphonse de Waelhens to which Levinas refers.[2] The idea of production will enable Levinas to distinguish the idea of the infinite from the idea of totality. Although totality is not the same as neutrality and distinction is not the same as separation, the thin end of the wedge that will accomplish this distinction between totality and the infinite is inserted when the analysis of concrete manifestations of the concretion of existence and the existent begins to separate these.

A wedge can both hold two pieces tightly together and split them apart. It so happens that Levinas uses the word 'unwedging' (*décalage*) for the division and delay that an analysis of position or hypostasis or *setzen* discovers. His word *position* must be understood as the act of positing that takes place even when one is in a state of repose. The maintaining of oneself in a location is a *main-tenir*, a taking of oneself in hand that is prior to both readiness to hand (*Zuhandenheit*), and presence at hand (*Vorhandenheit*). Before the presence before something of *Vorhandenheit* is the presence before oneself of the present moment, the *maintenant* or the instant. The subject's standing *here* stands under the understanding (*Verstehen*) that according to *Being and Time* is primarily a mode of *Dasein*'s projectivity in the *Da*, the there of the world. And the subject's finding itself posed before itself in this particular location now is already older than the disposition (*Befindlichkeit*) that according to Heidegger is primarily a mode of *Dasein*'s finding itself having been projected. Presupposed by position as *Ortschaft*, site and sighting in a world, is position as an act. But the act has to be correctly deduced. It is not to be construed in terms of effort exerted against the resistance of matter, which is the paradigm most favoured by philosophers. The correct method of deduction will be to investigate not simply the subject's engagement with objects in physical space. It will be to exhibit the espacement of the internal dialectic of its engagement with its own existence. It will be to spell out the concrete logic of accomplishment.

This is the nearest Levinas comes in *Existence and Existents* to a formal presentation of his method. And just as what he means by accomplishment is to be collected from the contexts in which the word is used, so for further clarification of this brief statement of his methodological principle he refers the reader to the applications of it throughout the book as a whole (*DEE* 42, *EE* 30). Three decades later he will express regret over the unwrittenness of the more interesting books that could have been written by authors who devoted their time instead to propounding methodologies. He explains his own reticence by admitting that he does not believe that there can be transparency in philosophical method or indeed in philosophy as a whole. If we press him to give us his formula, the most he will say is that his method is the method of emphasis. In French, he reminds us, this word can mean provocative and exasperating exaggeration. 'Exasperation as philosophical method!' he exclaims (*DVI* 142). In what sense his philosophy can go in for rhetorical heightening, perhaps force, is something else we shall learn only when we have more experience of his philosophy in effect. We shall therefore postpone further comment on this notion of *emphase*. For the time being let us simply note, as he also reminds us, that the word has the same Greek root as the word 'phenomenology', which need not imply showmanship but quite simply show, bringing to light (*phaô*). And we were about to say that in *Existence and Existents* he shows us the dialectic of the accomplishment of the instant through an analysis – or quasi-analysis, for there are no ultimate simples to be reached – of the primary lassitude, laziness, effort and fatigue, and so on, that are modes in which the instant accomplishes itself before they can seem to be no more than mental states resulting from one's active and passive involvements with other existents.

LASSITUDE

Lassitude appears as such a state when reflected upon by ontic psychology.

What Levinas calls 'phenomenological excavation', phenomenological *fouille*, uncovers below weariness with regard to particular things or events in the world, below even world-weariness, that is to say, below weariness of the world as a whole, weariness of being as such and of the existent subject's own existence. This lassitude prior to letting-be (*Seinlassen*) is internal to and constitutive of the subject's self-position. It is an event, not a state: the very event of the constitution or accomplishment of the self. Lassitude is the mode of appearing of what in his earlier essay Levinas calls the need to escape, the *besoin* that is sooner than the ontic or ontological *soin* or *souci* that in *Being and Time* Heidegger calls care, the *Sorge* that diversifies itself into concern with things, *Besorgen*, and solicitude toward other human beings, *Fürsorge*.

Heidegger misrepresents care, Levinas maintains. Care is not toward being via being toward nothing. It is not existential-ontological through being existential-meontological. Care is immediately ontological. Without detour by way of the void, care goes direct to the fullness of being, burdened by the *embarras de richesse* that belongs to the existent that also belongs to it. In this respect more Parmenidean than Heidegger is in his account of the belonging together of *Sein* and *Dasein*, Levinas's ontology is also in this respect more Bergsonian. However, whereas according to both Heidegger and Bergson the burden is an inheritance from or of the past, according to Levinas what is irksome is the very accomplishment, event or act of beginning the instant of presence in which the existent subject takes on existence in refusing it. Lassitude before negation and nihilation is the existent's pre-predicative gesture of renegation of existence that cannot be refused. It is therefore an impossible refusal – 'almost a contradiction', Levinas might say, as he says of fatigue (*DEE* 51, *EE* 35). Almost, perhaps because there is full contradiction only where there is diction as *dictum*, and there is no such diction prior to predication. But there is confliction, and this allows Levinas to say that the instant of hypostasis, the moment of the positing and presenting of oneself, is accomplished or produced dialectically (*DEE* 31, *EE* 42).

This dia-lectic is not a dialectic through tri-dimensional time. It is a dialectic of the instant, of hypostasis *en ce moment même*.

Does this mean that the dialectic cannot be diachronous? Does not the instant have at least a beginning, a middle and an end? For reflection it does. For *connaissance* it appears as an enduring process or state. But the instant is the sheer beginning of an act of existence or existance: institution, constitution, creation, birth, *naissance*. It has an existantial status that Levinas compares with that of those statues by Rodin where what matters is the relation between the formed thing and the unformed matter out of which it grows (*DEE* 88, *EE* 55). In the sculpture entitled 'The Creation of Man' the hand that shapes the clay into human limbs itself merges with and emerges in co-creative concrescence from the mass out of which the handful of clay has been scooped, *geschöpft*.[3] This status is prior to statement and to thoughts, feelings or acts of will as reflected-upon states of mind.

DILATORINESS

So when Levinas speaks of the accomplishment of the beginning it is to the beginning as itself accomplishment that he refers, not to something that succeeds the beginning, of which the beginning falls short. In his phrase 'the accomplishment of the beginning' the genitive is subjective. The words denote beginning as accomplishment, and accomplishment as at once realization and revelation. The ambiguity that the preface to *Totality and Infinity* will discern in production is discerned in accomplishment when *Existence and Existents* suggests that the reluctance to begin of dilatoriness is 'the revelation of the beginning that every instant accomplishes through its virtue as instant [*par sa vertu d'instant*]' (*DEE* 34, *EE* 26). Is it fanciful to see this noun *vertu* as an anticipation of the verb *s'évertue* in the definition of production provided in *Totality and Infinity*? In both places what is being proposed is a notion of effort prior to the notion of effort that figures in accounts of action based on the mechanistic idea of a subject's resistance to external forces, an idea that remains operative in Maine de Biran's anti-mechanism, though in Levinas's mind here too are Scheler and Dilthey's defense of this idea in an article referred to in *Being and Time* (*SZ* 205, 209).[4] As already suggested, Levinas's notion of a primary effort exerted in the subject's being with itself has a precursor, despite major divergencies, in Fichte's doctrine of primary *Anstoss*, a check unposited by the positing self yet a condition of the I-am-I. And it may not be premature to recall the primacy that Fichte ascribes to the ethical.[5] It is probably premature to recall on the other hand that *vertu* shares a virile genealogy with the word *virtù* that plays so significant a role in Nietzsche's *On the Genealogy of Morals*.

S'évertuer is to strive, *streben*, another Fichtean word. It is to exert power. But power is rarely *pouvoir* as possibility in the exposition of the positive side of Levinas's existantial analysis. When these words or their cognates occur in Levinas's text they can very easily mislead. For example, what are we to make of the sentence 'Dilatoriness is an impossibility of beginning or, if you prefer, it is the accomplishment of beginning' (*DEE* 34, *EE* 26)? If the beginning is accomplished how can it also be, if one likes, an impossibility of being? The most plausible explanation is that when Levinas writes of this impossibility of beginning he means that it is not a possibility in the sense of the *Seinkönnen* or *Möglichkeit* of *Being and Time* which are *Dasein*'s temporally prejective–projective ecstasis. Dilatoriness is, to employ a phrase Levinas will employ frequently in his later writings, a *manière d'être* (mode or modality of being). This phrase parodies Heidegger's word *Seinsweise* in order to suggest that more primordial than his temporal existentials are the modes of being of beginning, adverbial modes of the action by which the subject accomplishes the substantivity of a stance in the sun. Note that when thus understood in the context of a rejection of the claim to primordiality Heidegger makes on behalf of his modes of being, Levinas's reference to impossible beginning and impossible refusal cannot be made consistent with his reference to the accomplishment of beginning by a softening to 'almost impossible' on analogy with the phrase 'almost contradictory' used in connection with fatigue.

Before attention is turned to some of the other details of what Levinas writes in connection with fatigue rigour requires that attention be returned to a difficult detail in what he writes about dilatoriness in a paragraph of which a part has been previously reproduced. The difficulty becomes visible when other parts of that paragraph are also reproduced:

> Dilatoriness is related to the beginning as if existence did not accede to it straight off [*n'y accédait pas d'emblée*], but had a life previous to it [*la prévivait*] in inhibition. There is more here than a space of duration flowing insensibly between two instants; unless [*à moins que*] the inhibition in [*de la*] dilatoriness is also the revelation of the beginning that every instant accomplishes through its virtue as instant.
>
> (*DEE* 34, *EE* 26)

The only feminine nouns earlier in the sentence where the text says *la prévivait* are *existence* and *paresse*. If what Levinas intended to say was either that existence or that dilatoriness precedes itself, he would have used the reflexive *se prévivait*. Therefore, either he means that it is as if existence precedes the dilatoriness or the *la* is a slip for *le* and by this is meant the beginning. The Lingis translation takes the second of these options. If this is judged to be rash, while taking *y* to refer to the beginning and *la* to refer to dilatoriness, *prévivait* could be taken as a transitive verb to yield the idea that it is as if existence with its insistent *il y a* holds up (perhaps both in the sense of sustains and in the sense of detains), does not accede to (perhaps both in the sense of assent to and in the sense of attain) the instance of the existant and the existance (*sic*) of the instant by transitively living or existing dilatoriness and its inhibition.

Lingis's translation also renders *à moins que* as 'or perhaps'. This 'or' must be non-exclusive if the 'also' (*aussi*) is meant to indicate a junction with the preceding clause. In view of the positioning of 'also' late in its clause it is more natural to suppose that it is meant to indicate the junction within its own clause of 'the inhibition in dilatoriness' with 'the revelation of beginning'. Translating *à moins que* as 'unless' sets up a disjunction and introduces second thoughts that qualify the idea of a space of duration flowing smoothly between two instants and specify, contrary to the first thoughts, that there need be no more than this durational stretch if the instants between which time flows are understood as initiative positings that are paradoxically revealed – and realized, that is, ambiguously 'produced' – as inhibitory postpositing or deferral inherent to the very performance of an act. It is dilatoriness essential and intrinsic to action that Levinas is describing, not deliberative dithering. In the terms of William James's often-cited paradigm, this existantial shrinking is posterior to the resolution to rise from one's bed and interior to the action of placing one's feet on the floor.

The paradoxicality of this analysis would be alleviated if Levinas's phrase *l'inhibition de la paresse* were translated 'the inhibition of dilatoriness'. For it is not difficult to equate the inhibition and ending of dilatoriness with the beginning of the act. But the subjective rather than objective genitive is what seems to be implied by Levinas's statement that it is dilatoriness, not the inhibition of it, that is the accomplishment of the beginning. Furthermore, 'dilatoriness', the first word of the first sentence of the passage, is equated with the last word in that sentence, 'inhibition'.

Despite these difficulties of interpretation, it is fairly clear that the aim of the sentences in question is to challenge the adequacy of Bergsonian continuist and Heideggerian ecstasist accounts of temporality. By implication Aristotelian and other theories of chronology are impugned. The main point being made in these sentences is that without excluding flow from instant to instant the beginning of each instant suffers a delay. Perhaps 'suffers' is a dangerous word to use here in the light of Levinas's denial that the generic term *douleur* conveys the specific nature of the trouble, *peine*, of the effort to begin. This is why Lingis's 'indolence' (from *dolere*, like *douleur*) is also a risky word to translate *paresse*. Yet this word could come to be seen as the most appropriate one when 'emphasized' and when we have come to understand better what for Levinas a word's being emphasized means. 'Laziness' would be the first English equivalent of which one would think, but that does little to bring out the force of which the French word is capable thanks to its derivation from *parare*, to prepare. The essential laziness and lethargy with which Levinas is here concerned is a precedence essential to the accedence to a start. Just as lassitude is refusal, so *paresse* is a prevaricatory preparation that constitutes or accomplishes the effortfulness of the beginning of the instant. As through heaviness and labour the human existant is born. And as though in Rodin's 'The Creation of Man' the hand presses and is oppressed by the very clay out of which it is made.

FATIGUE

Like essential dilatoriness and lassitude, essential fatigue is the self's resistance to existence, a refusal that as such presupposes existence. So the moment of polemic between the existant and its existence can be at most only *almost* contradictory. It can be only that also because in this very same momentary *Augenblick* (see the first section of chapter 5 below) there is, although not a lapse into two moments of time by which contradiction might be forestalled, a certain lateness that Levinas denominates essential fatigue. This 'almost' is not enough to distinguish from negative dialectic the dialecticality Levinas admits into the moment of self-positing and, as we shall discover, elsewhere. For by the standard of the principle of contradiction of purely formal logic all dialectic, including that of Kant's dialectical antinomies, Hegel's logic and Hegel's phenomenology, is a dialectic of the almost contradictory. In this respect the dialectic articulated in Levinas's emphasiology is no different.

How does fatigue, as another modality of the moment of beginning, differ from dilatoriness and lassitude? It will be found that many dictionaries enter each of these terms under each of the other two. Etymological dictionaries point in the direction of greater precision. We have observed how etymology suggests that in Levinas's use of the word *paresse* is preparatory to the beginning of the act. It is in some way directed upon a future (*DEE* 39, *EE* 29). Levinas says 'in some way' because it is not projected toward the future in the manner of *Dasein*'s being ahead of itself in the world. What could be called Levinas's existantials (*sic*) are more fundamental than the *Seinsweisen* of the self-styled fundamental ontology of *Being and Time*. 'The only task this entire work sets itself', he writes, 'is to make explicit the implications of this fundamental situation' (*DEE* 52, *EE* 36). The situation here referred to is not a site in the world but the act of positing by which the self, before it finds itself as found (*befunden*), as described in the analysis of the state of *Befindlichkeit* conducted in §29 of *Being and Time*, founds itself as existant. The future of the act upon which dilatoriness is somehow directed is the future of the act of hypostasis. The manner in which it is directed upon the future is abstention, holding back. So there is some sort of oppositing in the act of positing. There is a tension between abstention and what is in some way a protension. There is what could be called an existantial protension. So if tragedy implies some sort of contradiction, there is some basis for speaking, as Levinas does, of the tragedy of being.

Levinas speaks also of dilatoriness as fatigue of the future. This reinforces the impression dictionaries give that the three terms are casually interchangeable. But by Levinas's own analysis of these terms his description of *paresse* as 'fatigue with regard to the future' must be understood as a figure of speech. Strictly speaking, the direction of fatigue is not the pre- of preparation but the re- of retardation. *Décalage* can be an opening up of distance by unwedging. It can also be the putting back of a clock. Fatigue, like dilatoriness, has to do with the act. Whereas dilatoriness is a sort of fear of beginning, fatigue is that in spite of which an effort already begun may continue to exert itself. Fatigue troubles the forward flight of effort. It is that from which, *ex*, e-ffort forces itself forth. To speak in Bergson's terms, there is no pure *élan* or pure *durée* in the travel of the travail of existence. That *Erfahrung* is conditioned by arrest, stayed, *étayée*, by stay. For what is under consideration here is an activity that may be inactivity. Levinas is purporting to describe the remainence or maintenance of the existant's being *here*, whether or not the existant is covering any distance in the space of its being in the world, as according to Heidegger *Dasein*, the being of distances, is doing all of the time. Hence, when Levinas contrasts dilatoriness with repose he means repose as contrasted with movement in the world, not the existantial repose that is the restlessness of worldly rest and the re-positing of self-positing.

Hence also, to speak the language of Newton, rest and so-called uniform motion in a straight line always have internal forces acting upon them where existantial effort is concerned. Inertial forces are not extrinsic to e-ffort's *ex*. The so-called dynamism of the *élan* is not just anticipation of the future. It is the resultant of anticipation and fatigue in the instant of an existant's self-presenting. Fatigue is what accomplishes the di-stance in which the stance of presenting eventuates as existantiation. This distance is essential if the present is constituted by the taking on, the *prise en charge*, of the present (*DEE* 49, *EE* 34), and if the being of the existant being that accomplishes this present and presentative *prae-esse* is the dialectical assuming of being not heroically, but as the affirming of being in refusing it (*DEE* 51, *EE* 35).

Whereas Heidegger (followed by Sartre) says that each *Dasein* has to be its being, *je sein Sein als seiniges zu sein hat* (*SZ* 12), Levinas says of the existant that it exists itself, *on s'est* (*DEE* 38, *EE* 28). In *Existence and Existents* fatigue, dilatoriness and lassitude are shown to be concrete ways in which this reflexivity of assuming one's existence, which is not yet an assuming of the world or its time, maintains with regard to its own personal existence what with regard to impersonal existence in the essay *De l'évasion* considered above in chapter 1 was called a need for evasion.

SOLITUDE

Before bringing this chapter to a close a few more remarks on lassitude require to be made.

If as well as being a response to Heidegger Levinas's account of fatigue is a response to Husserl's account of retension in the upsurge of the present, and if dilatoriness is his revision of Husserlian protension, with respect to what tension – or *distentio* – is lassitude a gloss or an alternative?[6] This is not easy to say. Although fatigue and dilatoriness are explicitly related to the act whereas lassitude is related to the self's existence or being, Levinas also describes fatigue as fatigue of being (*DEE* 50, *EE* 35). Furthermore, the discussion of fatigue and dilatoriness is introduced by the comment that they are both concrete forms of the adherence of the existent to existence (*DEE* 28, *EE* 23). Since we know that for Levinas existence is an act, namely the reflexive but not reflective act of assuming existence, and since fatigue and dilatoriness have been associated with the tensions or tenses of the effort of enduring which he argues are presupposed by durational or ecstatic anticipation and recollection, it is tempting to associate lassitude with a present tension or tense. Because the present is constituted in part by fatigue and dilatoriness, lassitude would be perhaps the mood or modality that straddles or embraces these. It would not be then a concrete way of being of presence as opposed to the concrete ways of preparation and retardation. It would be rather a concrete form of the present's essence as evanescence which the other two concrete forms help to explain, but not through a dialectic of negation as in the corresponding argument in the *Encyclopaedia* where Hegel writes:

> The *finite* present is the *Now* fixed as *being* [*seiend*] and distinguished as the concrete unity, and hence as the affirmative, from what is *negative*, from the abstract moments of past and future; but this being is itself only abstract, vanishing into nothing'.[7]

Moreover, would not fatigue with regard to a given or, better, taken instant of effort be deferment with regard to the instant to come? And would not deferment with regard to the instant to come be fatigue with regard to the instant already initiated? We can only speculate here. Words are lacking at least in Levinas's text. But, since the text tells us explicitly, we do not need to speculate whether the three tensions taken together are forms of the gravity of labour rather than forms of the grace of innocent play. They accomplish the laboriousness to which one is condemned when one is freed from impersonal being to being oneself. It is to this laboriousness, to the very burden of being, Levinas remarks, and not only to the specific labours of fetching and carrying in order to survive in the world that Genesis 3:19 refers when Adam is told 'In the sweat of thy face shalt thou eat bread'. Work is an affliction, an evil. God's curse is a malediction. What is mistakenly said to be the joy of work is always the joy of something extraneous to it, for example its results. Lassitude is a proneness to faint and fall asleep under the burden of being. It is the *évanouissement* in the evanescence of the present. Lassitude is the *Last*, as German has it, the load. It is the weight that makes one late. It is what has to be lasted out, *hat*, as Heidegger's German has it. It is the *Leistung*, the endurance in duration.

It is a response to a charge. *Nulla lassitudo inpedire officium debet.* No lassitude should hinder the carrying out of one's responsibility. Existantial responsibility is the one-must-be, before the one-must-do. Older than the falling, *Verfallen*, that according to *Being and Time* is older than original sin and yet is connected in that book most closely not with the past but with the present ecstasis of time, lassitude is perhaps the *il faut* of a failing that is not a lack but a *falloir* that is both a fault and a binding that not even the radical sceptic can dodge: a must that he or she affirms in denying it. One must be *one*. *Un* Levinas writes here (*DEE* 51, *EE* 35), though not yet *unique*. For he also writes here, by way of a final comment on *par-esse*: 'it announces perhaps that the future, a virgin instant, is impossible for a solitary subject' (*DEE* 40, *EE* 29).

4 Announcing time

ASSUMPTIONS

The *avoir* of the impersonal *il y a*, the having (compare Heidegger's *hat*) of the anonymous there-is, becomes contracted to a point of focus (*foyer*) the instant there exists a solitary monad that, although still possessing no door and no windows, possesses itself and a name. It possesses itself because it possesses no doors and no windows. For its self-possession is a turning in on itself. And this possession of itself is a being possessed by itself. At the birth of the instant the existant is preoccupied by the existence (with) which it has contracted. Preoccupied, obsessed, con-cerned. If one is to remain in touch with what Levinas will be going on to say, it is important to grasp from the beginning the preposterousness of his analysis of the beginning.

For instance, why does he say that before being a source of pleasure (*jouissance*) one's self-prepossession is a source of concern? This state-ment appears to imply that the neutrality of the care (*Sorge*) that Heidegger does not limit to care or concern as worry, *Besorgnis* (*SZ* 192,197), is undercut by what Heidegger would call its deficient mode. The very rich-ness of self-ownership through one's belonging to being, the generosity of the Heideggerian *es gibt*, is cause for disquieting concern. Not only does the underlying menace of dispossession by the *il y a* persist, but the will to persist in one's own being is, so to speak, unwillingly bad. Prior to will, so prior to the freedom of will, the existant freed from the anonymity of the there-is remains inscribed in being. It has entered into a contract with existence. Indeed its very existence is this contracting or assumption. Levinas tells us even that this assumption is an assumption of responsibility. Responsibility, contract, inscription, charge, even possession as property and the having- of having-to-be are all ethico-legal terms. From the first instant, in the court of first instance, there is a dialectic of the ego with its inalienable self. This is a dialectic of departure from itself and return

(*TA* 36, *TO* 55). When Levinas writes that through no fault of its own, or because of the fault that yawns open between the ego and the intimate self that pursues it like a shadow, it is not, like Narcissus, innocently alone, is this non-innocence equivalent to non-in-nocence? Does it mean that the ego is noxious, responsible for harm? Is the tie of the ego to its dilatory, fatigued and lassitudinous self an obligation it has inevitably contravened, not because of anything it has or has not done, but simply because it exists? These are the questions that must be answered if one is to answer the question where for Levinas philosophy must begin.

It is beginning to look as though the answer to these questions is answerability. Ontological answerability, responsibility for being. Ontological responsibility is a pervasive theme in the lectures Heidegger delivered in Freiburg from 1929 to 1930.[1] It is difficult to believe that this theme did not surface in discussions in which Levinas participated during his presence in Freiburg from 1928 to 1929. In any case, it had already surfaced a year still earlier in *Being and Time*, for example in the sections on ontological conscience. What is said there is under criticism when Levinas claims that Heidegger admits no third beyond the alternatives of *Dasein*'s self as authentic and *Dasein*'s self as the impersonal *das Man* (*TA*18, *TO* 40). Even in authentic being towards my own death I am only *with* others as alter egos assumed within a world that remains monistic when my monad has been provided with windows and doors.

The sense 'assumption' has here must be distinguished from the sense it has elsewhere. The two senses are distinguished in *Time and the Other* more clearly than they are in *Existence and Existents*. Despite Heidegger's distinction between categories, for example readiness to hand and presence at hand, to which un*Dasein*ish beings belong, and existentials, for example care and its modes, which belong essentially to and are ways of *Dasein*'s being, existentials still resemble the categories of Aristotle, Kant and Hegel in that they reign over and, as the Greek *katêgoreô* says, arraign the concepts, objects and subjects of which they are predicated. They 'go out and get them', as the *hinnehmen* even of the a priori forms of time and space says in Heidegger's interpretation of the schematism of Kant that was so decisive in the former's reinterpretation of being and time. Kant's so-called forms of receptivity acquire a degree of spontaneity as schemata mediating the application of the categories of the understanding to the pure forms of sensibility. Hence the phrases 'act of receptivity', 'spontaneous receptivity' and 'take in their stride' that are used for Heidegger's *hinnehmen* and its cognates.[2] This is one of the senses in which Levinas speaks of assumption, the sense that the Latin-German word *Subsumtion* has in the chapter on schematism in Kant's first *Critique*.

A clue to the second sense in which Levinas speaks of assumption is offered by the Greek *kategguaô*, meaning 'to make responsible, to oblige to give security or bail'. Assumption in Levinas's second sense would be the acceptance of this responsibility imposed on me by another. It would be the acknowledgement of that charge, endorsement of the justice of an accusation to which the subject is subjected. In *Totality and Infinity* he will speak also of welcome, though that word too will have two senses equivalent to those that *Time and the Other* distinguishes for 'assume'. In the latter book he speaks also of the assumption of death. But death is precisely what cannot be assumed in the sense of taking in one's stride.

So here is another duple: assume–assume. It remains to be seen whether the second sense of 'assume' is an assumption of the first. Whether it is its production–production or *emphase*. And whether assumption might be a dialectical but not negative *Aufhebung* of *Aufhebung*. An *Aufhebung* not via 'not', but via 'is', provided one could produce a non-Hegelian, non-totalizing sense of 'to be' which is not exclusive of 'not to be'. That is the question. And because Levinas's answer to this question is 'Yes' it is more than a rhetorical flourish to say that the whole of philosophy might be regarded as a commentary on Shakespeare. This is what *Time and the Other* begins to explain. It explains also the genealogy of ontological and ethical responsibility. It explains the genealogy of genealogy itself. Assumption–assumption, responsibility–responsibility, genealogy–genealogy. *Time and the Other* explains how these repetitions remark time.

FROM TIME TO TIME

Time and the Other remarks the time of the solitary existant as time of the Other. Does it say that there is time before the time of the existent? Does it allow that this question makes sense? Levinas recalls Heidegger's reliance in *Being and Time* on the distinction between 'beings', *Seindes*, as a substantive or verbal noun and 'to be', *Sein*, as a verb. If, as German says, a verb is a *Zeitwort*, a time-word, the question 'Is there time?' would already seem to have given itself an affirmative answer, provided the being of time is understood as *es gibt* rather than as *ist* or 'exist'. Only beings exist. But, as underlined in the quasi-Berkeleian sentences reproduced above (in the third section of chapter 2) from page 230 of *Being and Time*, the existing of *Dasein* is presupposed by the 'giving' of being, and, in the terms Levinas says he prefers for reasons of euphony, the existence of the existant is presupposed by existence or, rather, by *exister* to exist, as he prefers to say in *Time and the Other*, suggesting that he thinks the verbality to which Heidegger draws attention is insufficiently marked in the title

De l'existence à l'existant. It is intriguing to note that in the table of contents even of the 1981 edition of the latter book *existance*, with an *a*, is given as the last word of the subtitle that in the text itself is printed as *La relation avec l'existence*, with an *e*. Assuming that the meaning of *Sein* and *exister* is time, as following the clue of their grammatical category as time-words Heidegger maintains in *Being and Time*, this typographical slip provides a word that would at least seem to keep open the question whether the temporality of existence is different from the temporality of what can be referred to as the existance rather than the existence of the I. What is Levinas's answer to this question?

Taking Heidegger again as his point of departure, he agrees that there is little sense in the notion of an existing without something that exists. But he adds that the notion of an existing as though prior to each existant is introduced along with the existential that Heidegger calls *Geworfenheit*, the phenomenon of finding oneself as though uncontrollably thrown into existence. And it is this notion that Levinas redescribes under the pseudonym *il y a*, there-is. The question just raised must therefore be posed as follows: Is there, *y a-t-il*, time before or, in case that preposition is too provocative, independent of the positing of the existant? It will be recalled that from the analysis of positing conducted in chapter 3 it seemed that Levinas was at pains to show that although this positing is a beginning which has modes of endurance, these are not modes of the duration of an I. The *il y a* admits no I. It is impersonal. It is without subjectivity, so it is without the beginning that subjectivity implies. It can therefore be likened to eternity, Levinas proleptically suggests. His reference to it also as the place (*endroit*) where positing is produced, suggests a comparison with the incomparable placeable place (*chôra*) of the *Timaeus*. The *il y a* is the first incomparable in the order of exposition of Levinas's ethics, though not necessarily the first in the order of being or of being's eminent *emphase*. And the *il* of the *il y a* is a repetition of the *es* of Heidegger's *es gibt*, a repetition however that deprives the latter of the gift by which it enables a passage to authentic selfness from the inauthenticity of *das Man*, the impersonal they or people or one which is not to be confused with Levinas's personal one who is some determinate one, *un*, who stands out from the anonymity of the *il y a*.

It is to this anonymous *il y a* from which the existant stands out that Levinas is referring when he writes that the event of hypostasis, that is to say, the present, has a past and a history without being that past or that history. This does not conflict with the argument just recalled from chapter 3 that the instant of positing or hypostasis is an instant of enduring without duration. The present has the past as memory, but it is itself a tearing in two and rejoining not of an already constituted duration, but of the thread of an eternity that has neither beginning nor end, an infinity, Levinas says, a bad infinity, one might say, the pedagogically first infinity. Without mention of the name of Kant, since that is rendered otiose by the frequent mentions of the author of *Kant and the Problem of Metaphysics*, published in the second year of Levinas's presence at Freiburg, Levinas suddenly starts talking about an ontological schematism. The present is so described because it performs a function analogous to that accomplished by the schemata of the first *Critique*. Levinas says that the schema is a function, and this is the word Kant uses of the procedure of the understanding in producing schemata. For Kant this is a procedure in the legal sense of the term in that it is a procedure of judgement for determining what is on the right and the wrong side of the law constitutive of experience. Kant's pages on schematism are tantalizingly few. Levinas's are fewer, but they occur at as crucial a moment in his critique of fundamental ontology as Kant's do in his critique of dogmatic metaphysics. Although no more than outlines are traced in the pages of *Time and the Other* where the word 'schematism' is used and although no table of schemata is hinted at there, is it not Levinasian schemata that are being described in *Existence and Existents* under the names of 'lassitude', 'dilatoriness' and 'fatigue'? Like Kant's schemata, these are limitrophic forms. They are, Levinas says in that book, concrete forms of the adherence of existence to the existents. In *Time and the Other* the schema of the present is said to be the eventing, the *événement* – one might say after Heidegger the *Ereignen* – of hypostasis which occurs at the limit between existence or being and the existent or the being. Its situation is that of the ambiguous threshold between the verbality of the *exister* of being and the substantivity of the id-entity and idem-tity of beings. It is the tension between the timeless eternity of unnamable being and constituted existents persisting in given, datable time (*TA* 38, *TO* 57). This time is *given* time, the homogeneous continuum which in the first *Critique* is a given form of sensibility. Hence the ambiguity of the Kantian schemata which the Levinasian schemata reflect. The Kantian transcendental schemata have to be sensible concepts if they are to be able to accomplish the application of the formal concepts of the understanding, for example substance and the inherence of properties, to particulars existing in time. Application is instantiation. But the instantiation of properties in substantial objects, inherence, is itself a function and production of subjects. So that the instantiation of properties in present at hand objects and the logical and epistemological schematism that it presupposes, presuppose in turn the production and self-positing of subjects accomplished in the act of presenting that Levinas calls the 'instant'. And the inherence of properties in objects presupposes what he calls the adherence of the existent in existence and ontological schematism.

The word 'schema' is cognate with the Greek verb *echô* meaning 'to have, hold or possess', as in the possession or holding of property, properties or oneself. It is not far-fetched to use it therefore to expound the idea of status, standing and stance. The root verb, like the Latin *habeo* from which (along with habit, clothing) the French *avoir* derives, can also mean to have power or mastery. And schematism as described by Levinas is precisely the empowering of an existent with mastery over the impersonality of existence. A schema in Greek can be a person, a figure or shape. Its meaning as outline, diagram, sketch, project and indeed scheme, is spelled out by Kant. Its German translation as *Entwurf* is implicit in Heidegger's jectile words *Geworfenheit*, *Entwerfen*, and so on.

Levinas himself uses the verb *s'esquisser*, meaning 'to sketch or make a first draft', at the beginning of his analyses of the three concrete forms of stantiation that might be regarded, we have noted, as schemata. What is singular about these schemata is that they accomplish mastery, the first but not the last mastery in Levinas's exposition, through separation. There is adherence, but at the same time or rather before time, separation. The separation is separation from the there-is. Separation, be it observed, not just distinction. In Levinas's judgement it is only as far as distinction that Heidegger goes in what the latter calls the ontological difference, the difference between being and beings, which Levinas considers to be the point where the thinking of *Being and Time* is at its most profound. This separation, the first separation in the order of Levinas's exposition, can be described from two points of view. On the one hand it is the separateness of neutral existence without beginning or end from the existent with whom beginning begins. On the other hand it is the active separating that this beginning accomplishes. As well as describing this as a tear (*déchirure*), Levinas at one point calls it a *mue*. A *mue* can be a moulting, a sloughing off of skin or the breaking of the voice. It is evidently a more dramatic alteration than the unceasing pseudo-alteration of the *il y a* that he and Blanchot call its *remue-ménage* and which Levinas likens to Heraclitus's river in which according to Cratylus one cannot bathe even only once.

Schematism then is crucial in Levinas's deconstrual of Heidegger's construal of it because it is that which makes the difference between the way they each think of the ontological difference. Heidegger claims, as Levinas reads his teaching on *Jemeinigkeit*, that existence always belongs to an existent. Repeating Husserl's experiment of imagining the destruction of the world, Levinas casts doubt on what he takes to be Heidegger's claim. He proposes that the connection between existence and the existent is that which is effected by a schematism which is also a disconnection. Schematism spells schism.

He confirms his finding by appealing to the fact of insomnia. Insomnia is sleeplessness but not consciousness. A person who is conscious is a person who is capable of sleep. In insomnia I am not asleep, yet I can be awakened from it. I cannot awake myself from it, not least because in this waking state, the first waking state before I am awakened, I am not present as an I. There is presence, *il y en a*, but it is a pseudo-presence because it is without beginning. It is without beginning because it is indistinguishable and inseparable from a past to which it is, in Levinas's metaphors, soldered, riveted, enchained. The enchainment to this eternally present past would be broken if only it were a past that could be remembered. But this is an immemorial past. This is the first immemorial past we encounter in Levinas's exposition. There is another on the way.

ON THE WAY FROM THE FUTURE

The first immemorial past is so closely present that there is no distance from which to stand and look back. With the in-stance of the existant is produced dis-tance, the *Entfernung* that makes possible the estimation of closeness, the removal of farness, *Ent-fernung*, as one might say with the Heideggerian hyphenation that brings together and sets apart. But if the immemorial past is to be repeated it must be repeated as an immemorial future.

There is no future in the instant of the existant's hypostasis. Even its present is evanescent. As the present of beginning coming sheerly from itself it cannot have a past, for if it did it would not come sheerly from itself. So it cannot have a future, since that would be a future with respect to its past. That is why the present is effacement. If the present of hypostasis can be said to have any time, it is not hypostatized time, the time of durational spread. It is not time that is, time that is given, *le temps donné*. It is the time of the giving of that time, that time's generation. It is the tense time of the procedure of schematism, of a *Verfahrung* of which, as Kant says, there can hardly be any *Erfahrung*; it is beyond experience because it is a root hidden in the depths of the soul. So, as Levinas says, although phenomenology may be a method of radical experience, this may be a root that its experience fails to reach. This is not Levinas's last word on the scope of descriptive phenomenology. For two reasons. It is not his last word on experience. In later writings he will say that experience in the Kantian and Heideggerian senses just adverted to is not what experience *par excellence* is. Anyway, one does not need to go that far to recognize that since disappearing is related to appearing as darkness is to light, and since each term of each of these pairs derives its meaning from the other, a phenomenology of hiddenness is not a contradiction in terms. It is phenomenology in this slightly extended sense that is performed in *Being and Time*. And in that sense phenomenology is not even slightly extended beyond the sense it has in the lectures by Husserl edited by Heidegger in 1928 under the title *The Phenomenology of Internal Time Consciousness*. Witness the following often-quoted sentences from §36 which Levinas has in mind in his reference to Heraclitus and in the paragraphs from this that have been and are about to come under our review:

> It is evident, then, that temporally constitutive phenomena are, in principle, objectivities other than those constituted in time. [. . .] To be sure, one can and must say that a certain continuity of appearance, namely, one which is a phase of the temporally constitutive flux, belongs to a now, namely, to that which it constitutes, and belongs to a before, namely, as that which is (one cannot say was) constitutive of the before. But is not the flux a succession? Does it not, therefore, have a now, an actual phase, and a continuity of pasts of which we are conscious in retentions? We can say only that this flux is something which we name in conformity with [*nach*] what is constituted, but it is nothing temporally 'Objective'. It is absolute subjectivity and has the absolute properties of something to be denoted metaphorically as 'flux', as a point of actuality, primal source-point, that from which springs the 'now', and so on. In the lived experience of actuality, we have the primal source-point and a continuity of moments of reverberation. For all this, names are lacking.[3]

The present of the self's hypostasis depresents itself. But by what in a Kantian context would be called 'double affection' and in a Husserlian context 'double intentionality' the act of hypostasis can become the object of a hypostasis that locates the original non-durational hypostasis at a point in the course of hypostatized time.[4] This very presentation of the presencing of the actuality of the living present is its depresencing. It is the living presence's petrification and death: its entombment. Precisely this takes place when one fails to distinguish in Levinas's text the extant substantial subject that can bear a name from the movement of *parousia* to it which can no more be named than can the impersonal existence from which the existent is torn. The chances of this confusion are increased because Levinas's texts do not always distinguish the subject from the ego and the I, the *je*. This is a difficulty they inherit from the texts of Husserl. It is very likely however that what in the passage before us Husserl refers to as absolute subjectivity and point of actuality is what Levinas has in mind when in *Time and the Other* he writes that the I, the *je*, is not initially an existant, but a mode of existence itself: initiation (*TA* 33, *TO* 53). It is natural to ask whether this initial initiation occurs only once, at an absolute beginning, or whether it can be repeatable at different times. Levinas himself compares an act performed dilatorily with driving along a road which is so bumpy that every instant is like a new beginning. This is however a comparison, the comparison of constitution with the constituted of which Husserl speaks, where, as his translator puts it, the one is conformed to the other. The uncommon sense of the instant as an active stance and presencing which Levinas describes as the *perpetual* birth of the I cannot but find itself gravitating toward the common sense of the instant as a chronological point (*DEE* 143, *EE* 84). *Absconditus*, the nameless *parousia–apousia* of the presencing that is the initial enabling of names can be described only by analogy and metaphor. Strictly speaking this presencing has no given name because it is not itself given. So it can be given no date. Hence it makes no sense to say that it takes place only once or again and again. What Levinas calls beginning (*commencement*) is the way of being of the I; and what he calls *événement* is less misleadingly described as an eventing rather than an event, as indicated above by the suggestion that his word may be put in apposition with Heidegger's *Ereignen* and *Ereignis*.

It can now be added that Levinas's *commencement* is closer in its grammar to Heidegger's *Anfangen* and *anfänglich*, which denote originarity rather than a beginning in historiographical time. So that when Levinas writes that the present has a past, but in the form of memory, and that it has a history but is not history, he is perhaps saying that the history it has is a borrowed one, one borrowed from narrative as the history of events in the more usual sense of the term (*TA* 32, *TO* 52). I say only that perhaps he is saying this because I am taking his *histoire* in the sense of dated history or the chronicle of such a history. If one interprets his word in the sense of the existential historicality, *Geschichte*, that Heidegger attributes to *Dasein*, then, without this second interpretation being incompatible with what is being claimed according to the first, Levinas must be taken to be disagreeing with that attribution. This disagreement is in any case implied by the fact that his analysis of the event of presencing is, as was shown in chapter 3, an analysis of presencing that is not a presencing in the world. It claims to be independent of worldhood. Whereas existential historicality is a mode of being in the world.

5 Announcing the Other

THE MOMENT OF WAITING

Presencing, it has just been noted, is described by Levinas as a perpetual birth. The perpetual, from *peteo*, to seek, is some kind of quest. Petition, quest, questioning mean waiting. So too does *Gegenwart*, the usual German word for the present which means literally a waiting against or toward. This German word is omnipresent in *Being and Time*. It is widely employed by Husserl in the phrases *lebendige Gegenwart* and *lebendige Selbstgegenwart* to be found on pages that are seminal for Levinas and often referred to by him, for instance – an instance particularly relevant to our topic here – in his 'La philosophie et l'éveil' and 'De la conscience à la veille' (*EN* 101–2, *CWC* 212–13, *DVI* 34–61). This sense of at-tensionality, the manifest sense of the French *attendre*, is hinted at in the English adverb 'presently'. It is not obviously present in Levinas's *le présent*. Perhaps it could be argued that it is pre-sent in the original *prae-*. Whether or not this is argued, it should be recalled that Levinas's articulation of the modes of this presencing *parousia*, suspended gerundially between verb and substantive, include dilatory and preparatory *par-esse*, 'deferment and delay'. In the moment of presencing momentum is fused with an inclination to stay. It is the moment of waiting to see. And of waiting to hear. The one after the other or the other after the one. Or simultaneously. We must wait and see or hear. It is too early to tell what priority, posteriority and posterity can possibly – or impossibly – be in Levinas's genealogy of ethics.

In the language of Heidegger's translation of Kierkegaard's word which Levinas translates into French, this momentous moment is an *Augenblick*. A *Blick* is a look, glimpse, glance or regarding. But maybe already in some of its appearances in German philosophy and almost certainly in some of its philosophical appearances in French the *Blick* of the *Augenblick* has become also a blink. This is so if it is the meaning of what Kierkegaard calls the beautiful word *Øieblikket* that some recent French philosophers are intending to convey by the expression *clin d'oeil*.[1] This expression at least does bring with it the idea of a wink or a twinkling of the eye, and along with this the glance acquires the chance of irony. The history of this idea remains to be told. As well as taking into account the Danish and German philosophers just mentioned, that history would reach back from Derrida to Husserl, Nietzsche, Schelling and to Hölderlin's meditations on the wake and the work of mourning, of *deuil*, via Rosenzweig on the – in French in the text of *The Star of Redemption* – *coup d'oeil*. Perhaps for the interpretation of Levinas this dubious lexicography can yield no more than a hint, what in Heidegger's German is called a *Wink*. The darkness when in the wink of an eye the lid is momentarily lowered would announce the way that in waking life in the world the light of consciousness, as Levinas maintains, is suffused with the darkness of unconsciousness. Not an unconsciousness or 'the unconscious' imagined as an underworld stratum of nocturnal consciousness lying below the consciousness of everyday life. Rather an extinguishing of itself that distinguishes the very brightness of the light of consciousness, like the twinkling of a star (*DEE* 172, *EE* 100).

As was reported earlier, Levinas considers that consciousness is constituted by one's ability to sleep. He proposes that consciousness might be better defined by this ability to escape vigilance than by vigilance itself. This would at least prevent our supposing that consciousness is implicit in the *il y a* of existence. If Levinas supposed that consciousness was implicit in the there-is he would have taken a step back from Heidegger and rejoined idealist and other philosophers of consciousness. Despite the objections he makes against Heidegger's so-called fundamental ontology, at least in the publications we have been examining so far and in *Totality and Infinity*, what he writes about consciousness is embraced by what he writes about being, rather than the other way round. A possible inconsistency between what he writes about consciousness and the at least provisional primacy he accords ontology is avoided when he suggests that although the *il y a* of existence implies vigilance, it is the vigilance of insomnia rather than of consciousness.

BETWEEN SLEEPING AND WAKING

Sleep, hence consciousness, but not insomnia, is the promise of an exit from the oppression of the *il y a* of existence. Levinas sometimes compares sleep to the interspace occupied by the gods according to the Epicureans. It is significant that a polytheism is in question here and that the gods are meta-cosmic, nowhere in the world.[2] In an essay no less significantly entitled 'God and Philosophy' to which we shall return in later chapters, the very idea of the meta- is said to come from what Levinas calls the meta-category of insomnia. It is a category beyond categories understood as forms of mind that constitute the world thereby making it mine and thereby forestalling an escape from ontological solitude despite my being ontically with others in that world. It is a category of what is beyond the space of the known world. It is a category that is closer to the passive of *kateggua ô* than to *katêgoreô* in that it is a category where the centrifugal intentionality of virile dominative assumption gives way to centripetal attentionality (see above, the first section of chapter 4).

Indicative too is the fact that although Levinas is commenting here on the prefix 'meta-', and so on the preposition of the title of his *Otherwise than Being or Beyond Essence*, and although in the *Epicurea* the word used is *metakosmiois*, it is Cicero's translation *intermundia* which is the closer ancestor of the *interstices de l'être* in which Levinas locates the Epicurean gods. This is an interesting phrase because *sisto*, 'to stand or present oneself', is a root that 'interstice' shares with 'exist'. It is arguable therefore that an interstice of being is an interstice that is in some way in being. This could be an interstice, an excluded middle, which the dichotomy of being and non-being fails to cover. Another space that will call to be watched as we proceed with our reading of Levinas is the exteriority of which the subtitle declares *Totality and Infinity* will be a study. This will turn out to be an exteriority exterior to that of the perceptually and conceptually known world without being an exteriority of an unknown world behind that known world. Levinas's study of exteriority reveals a more complex notion of exteriority than that which is simply contrasted with interiority, a notion of exteriority other than that of the beyond of the thing in itself and the hidden god ranked among the prejudices of the philosophers from the first pages of *Beyond Good and Evil*. This is why in studies published already a decade and a half before the publication of *Totality and Infinity* conciousness is not directly opposed to sleep or to 'the unconscious' supposed as a mysterious hinterland. But it is instructive to take together what is said on this subject in those earlier works with what is said in essays published a decade and a half after *Totality and Infinity*.

It can look as though a variation in Levinas's distribution of meanings among the terms *veille* and *réveil* takes place during these three decades. In the earlier texts the first of these terms means the sleeplessness of the insomniac which however cannot be properly described as his or hers because the there-is of insomnia is impersonal. It is more like *cogitatur* than *cogito*. *Ça veille*. In certain essays of the 1970s however it is as though Levinas gives *veille* the sense of *réveil*, apparently the opposite of the sense it had for him in the 1940s.[3] However, this apparent inversion is more accurately called an emphasis in the style of what it amuses Levinas to describe as his method of exasperation, as noted in the discussion of method above in the first section of chapter 3. As also noted, in so far as he is ready to talk about his method, Levinas is sometimes prepared to describe it as a dialectic, though not a dialectic of negation. It cannot be this at the moment of dialectic we have now reached, not if the dialectic of negation is a dialectic of conciliation. The wakefulness, *veille*, of insomnia as an ontological category, is ended by the awakening, *réveil*, to the light of day in which personal subjectivity comes back. But the subject is only half-awake in that this personal subjectivity is an assumption of a world in which it is absorbed, because it and the objects and other persons in it reflect back to the subject the cognitive categories it has imposed. It becomes fully awake only if that subjectivity intending its world, awakened *to* it, is interrupted by the Other, *Autrui*. Borrowing a word from Heidegger, who borrows it from Kierkegaard, Levinas says of this interruption that it is a sobering, not simply a sobriety. The word implies that the contentment of living monadically is a kind of drunkenness, a word of which Nietzsche makes much use, as we shall have occasion to remind ourselves before we reach the last page of this book. A kind of drunkenness too would be the sleep in which one's dreams might be peopled by the gods of polytheism or the mythical families on which psychoanalysis relies. To rise and begin the agenda of another day is one way of escaping the disquiet of insomnia. To sleep, perchance to dream, is another. But in no case is this something that the insomniac self can do. It is not there to be able to do anything. It is not possessed of self, not self-possessed. Not self-possessed, insomnia is in one respect more ready to become possessed by the Other, possessed in the sense of the title of Dostoevsky's novel. The insomniac becomes a maniac. Deranged and psychotic, as Levinas says. Perhaps it could be said that that possession is figured in the presence to one's thought of ancestors when in the earliest hours of the morning one is lying half-awake and half-asleep. Perhaps this thought lies behind Levinas's reference to insomnia as *la veillée de l'éveil*, where *veillée* could refer to a funeral wake or watch. It could refer, that is, to the death of the Other that disturbs the symmetry of being together and equal with others in being toward one's distinctively own (*jemeinig*) death, so giving determinacy to the unfocused disquiet of insomnia and disestablishing the complacent identity of the man of substance, the man of property.

So the *veille* of insomnia is in one respect close to the heightened *veille* of possession by the Other. Despite its monotony, it is the chance of what with precaution could be called a monotheistic alternative to polytheism.

But in another respect the intermediate position of being an established burgher in the world of everyday life is closer to the stage of emphasized *veille*. For although this state of civil society is atheistic, it has been reached via the trauma of suddenly coming to life, to presence, through the first awakening or *(r)éveil* from neutrality. But no other trauma or *thauma* can be similar to that of the advent of the Other. Here analogy breaks down. Despite the passage from vigil to a first and to a second awakening by comparison with which the light of day is darkness at noon, the *logos* suffers a shock that is not comparable with Fichtean counter-shock (*Anstoss*) or Biranian *résistance*. Moreover, although the *Augenblick* in which one is blinded by light is the moment when opening one's eyes is called to make way for opening one's ears, what one hears is unassimilable in a Hegelian dialectic of the determinate negation of negation. That absolute idealistic dialectic – and the dialectic Kierkegaard would put in its place – is no doubt what leads Levinas to describe as dialectical the genealogical transitions his own thinking describes, describes in the sense both of marking and in the sense of moving through. It remains to be seen in more detail how this genealogy can be neither analogous to the Hegelian version nor an inversion of it. It remains to be seen in detail how the word of its Greek logocentrism is broken. And how when the story of Odyssean return gets interrupted by the story of Abrahamic exile, when the monad becomes the nomad, one must be careful if one supposes that words break for a reason analogous to that on account of which theology adapts the way of analogy or negation when it speaks the extraordinary non-names of God.

One must be no less careful if it is supposed that a simple extrapolation can be made to Levinasian genealogy from the sentence 'For all this, names are lacking' with which the limits of the genetic phenomenology of Husserl are inscribed. When it begins to seem that in certain of Levinas's analyses of Husserl's texts – for example the analyses of analogical pairing in the *Cartesian Meditations*, of the *waches Ich* in *Phenomenological Psychology* and of *Weckung* in *Analyses Concerning Passive Synthesis* – nothing is being said or left unsaid other than what is being said or left unsaid by Husserl, the reader is likely to be told all of a sudden that in Husserl none of all this can be found; it is beyond the letter and horizon of his texts.[4]

DOGMATIC SLUMBER

What is to be found in Husserl, what Levinas finds there, is a precursion that nevertheless helps to clarify the precursion within the levels of the genealogy Levinas produces from what he finds in Husserl. Already in 1930, in *The Theory of Intuition in Husserl's Phenomenology*, Husserl is being hailed as the philosopher who overcomes Bergson's opposition of intuition and intellect. But in the works available to him at that date Levinas judges Husserl's philosophy too intellectualist. Although, like Bergson, Husserl attends to the concreteness of life, it is life no longer lived but represented. This means that Husserl fails to do justice to the non-representational historicity and temporality that is of the essence of human being. So Levinas here underlines the importance of the contribution made by Heidegger. The neutralism which Levinas will find to be a shortcoming of Heidegger's ontology is here found to be a weakness of Husserl's phenomenology, indeed a corollary of phenomenological reduction itself. 'The reduction is an act by which the philosopher reflects on himself and so to speak "neutralizes" in himself the man living in a world, the man posing this world as existent, the man playing his part in this world' (*TIPH* 221, *TIHP* 157). The neutralization is a transition from a natural attitude to the world posed by man in a state of 'dogmatic slumber'. Kant's phrase is cited by Levinas in the 1974 essay 'De la conscience à la veille', and in the 1930 book he cites §61 of *Ideas*, volume I where Husserl characterizes man in the naïve natural attitude as a 'born dogmatist' (*DVI* 46, *TIPH* 222, *TIHP* 157). The natural and human sciences are dogmatic until the actuality they posit for their subject-matter has been suspended by the imagined 'destruction' of the world, phenomenologically reduced to a field of 'consciousness in general' (*DVI* 55). Note that the Husserlian transcendental consciousness in general not only shares a certain neutrality with the Levinasian there-is. Just as Levinas says of the latter that it is a kind of eternity, so Husserl says that the transcendental consciousness is eternal. In documents dating from 1922–3 published as section 10 of appendix VIII of the *Analyses Concerning Passive Synthesis* Husserl says of transcendental consciousness what Levinas says of the there-is, that it knows no birth or death. Whatever becomes of the body and soul of the natural human being, the transcendental I is neither created nor destroyed – there is, as German interestingly expresses it, no *auf-hören*. No wonder that the vigilance of insomnia, proposed in *Existence and Existents* as an empirical illustration of the there-is, can seem to become one in Levinas's thinking with the vigilance of reawakening, or that the latter is the emphasis of the former, the soul of the soul, the psyche psyched and sobered up.

The transition from the naïve to the phenomenological attitude, like the Kantian transition from dogmatism to criticism, is a transition from theory to theory. This common denominator may well ease the passage that some of Husserl's commentators have found so difficult to explain in his terms, but it remains difficult to understand how in those terms motivation to adopt the phenomenological attitude can be explained.[5] Almost all Husserl says on this difficulty in writings published by the time Levinas publishes his book on them is that we carry out the reduction because we can. Almost but not entirely all. In the final paragraph of his book Levinas reminds his reader that despite the primacy given to theory by Husserl, the latter's phenomenological method requires that the structures and dynamics of concrete life be examined with a view to placing them, as Levinas would say, within the economy of being. Aesthetic and practico-ethical structures are among those whose ontological meaning (*Seinsinn*) calls to be described. So, Levinas asks in his final sentence apropos of the aforementioned difficulty: 'But is not the possibility even of overcoming this difficulty or fluctuation in Husserl's thought given with the affirmation of the intentional character of practical and axiological life?' (*TIPH* 223, *TIHP* 158).

Thus does Husserl set Levinas's agenda. In the execution of that agenda the aesthetic, in the sense of the word traditionally associated with the beautiful, the sublime and the enjoyment of artistic creations, will occupy a place subordinate to that of the ethical. In his placing of the ethical in the economy of being and in his placing of the economy of being in the non-economy of the ethical, Levinas will call into question the primacy of theory, that is to say of *theôria*, seeing. How can this be so, we may ask, given that in the essays dating from the 1970s, when the *Cartesian Meditations*, the *Crisis* and many other volumes embodying Husserl's descriptions of concrete life have been published, not only Levinas's reflections on those descriptions but also his supplementation of them are cast in the language of waking and the opening of eyes: *veille, éveil, réveil* and so on? To this expression of puzzlement several responses are due. To start with, it should be said that one can be awakened by the sound of an alarm. An alarm clock is a *réveil, réveille-matin* or *Wecker*. The members of Levinas's family of French terms are translations of Husserl's *wecken* and its various cognates which have to do with rousing and calling up; calling up a memory, for instance, as in the last footnote to §41 of the *Phenomenological Psychology*, though it is what exceeds memory that Levinas is especially concerned to evoke. So his language of bringing to light goes over into the language of calling up, telephony. Witness: 'Vigilance – awakening rising in(to) awakening – awakening reawakening the state into which wakefulness itself falls and freezes – is vocation – and concretely responsibility for the Other'; 'La vigilance – éveil se levant dans l'éveil – l'éveil réveillant l'état où tombe et se fige la veille elle-même – est vocation – et concrètement la responsabilité pour Autrui' (*DVI* 55).

The awakening in question is an awakening either from sleep or from the fixation upon objects presented to the light of consciousness. This fixation, no less than sleep, is a kind of stupor. Both of these ontic anthropological states fall under the meta-category of vigilance or insomnia. This is a meta-category because it transcends the categories under which fall the objects of consciousness. It also transcends the existential ways of being that Heidegger holds consciousness to presuppose; and it transcends the *Wächterschaft* and *Wachsamkeit* understood by him as vigilance for the ways in which being comes to pass.[6]

But there are grounds for thinking that Levinas does not want the meta- of this transcendence to be understood as a simple layering, notwithstanding the frequency with which this archaeological image is encountered in the writings of Husserl, though he too sometimes warns against the dangers of being misled by the metaphor of stratification, for example in §124 of *Ideas*, volume I. The transcendence is an excession that is the already-being-outside-itself of an inside. This would be a reason for mixing the metaphors of seeing (*theôria*) and hearing, thereby complicating the meta- of metaphor itself, discovering it to have the structure and destructure of a chiasm, as though the chiasm of the optic nerve were discovered to be hybridized with a chiasm of the aural nerve, and as though ontology were discovered to be in some sense, a *sensus communis*, already crossed with ethics, *phusis* with *ethos*.[7] This double crossing is expressed in the thought that although ethical transcendence is not vision or super-vision, not *viser*, so not a purely visual optics (*TEI* 148, *TI* 174), it is a 'spiritual optics', that is to say, it is an optics without synoptics. It does not originate in nor does it aim at the representation of an eschatological ideal in which it would be consummated. Rather is it the consummation of the visionary in that eschatological sense, its accomplishment, though Levinas's *consomme* can also mean to consume or disintegrate (*TEI* XII, *TI* 23). It can be a holocaustic end over whose eschatologicality there hovers an inextinguishable 'maybe'. This double crossing is, in the terms of the title of one of Levinas's essays, the ruin of representation due to the face, the visage that offers itself, gives, gives its word (*DE* 125–35). Defying comprehension, the moment of vision, the *Augenblick*, is at the same time, but time otherwise construed, a moment of audition, *audire*, *obaudire*, obedience. The comprehension of sense is disturbed by the call of exigence (*DVI* 98, *CPP* 156, *HLR* 169). Consciousness, *conscience*, is discomforted by bad conscience, *mauvaise conscience*, even menaced by it, as though by an avatar or ancestor of Descartes's evil genius. The transcendence of the *meta-katêgoria* is the transcendence *of* evil, Satan, that is to say, taking the Greek word to its Hebrew root, the accuser.[8]

EV(E)IL

Sleep, Levinas writes, and, it must be added, a gaze fixated upon objects, are tactics of evasion, although, as must also be mixed-metaphorically added, they do not cease to hear the menacing call, for how else could they be tactics of evasion? The badness of bad conscience is the goodness of the good beyond being, as might be expected with an-economical, meta-physical ethics beyond the economy of systematic ethics in which latter good and bad are mutually opposited terms. The good beyond being 'is' the bad beyond being. Levinas does not state this so starkly. If it is objected that this is not even implicit in what he says, consider his endorsement of the thesis that in its malignancy evil is an excess.[9] In saying that good too is an excess Levinas is not suggesting that evil is a dialectical negation of the other, or that it is the basis of a theodicy by being the basis from which comes a good that makes up for it. Evil is excess because it is *éveil*. It voices both the menace already lurking in the *il y a* and the malediction that awakens me to the smugness of my persisting in the world. It puts the forward drive of its intentionality into reverse. This is not a simple reversal within a dynamical system of action and reaction, any more than the 'reversal of evil and of the horror of evil into an expectation of the Good' (*DVI* 203, *CPP* 183) is a mere change of conceptual gears. In such accounts of evil there is a balancing of accounts. The reversed, centripetal intention-ality of the evil that befalls me – 'What have I done to deserve this?' – is a *sui generis* intentionality that overflows the capacity of centrifugal in-tentionality. The excess of good and the excess of evil (excesses that exceed the bounds of this chapter and that will be returned to in this book's *dénouement*) are their transcendence of economies of give and take and morality as bargain. But their transcendence of these economies and moralities of exchange is not the satisfaction of a lack or need that the immanence of such economies and moralities fails to fulfil. Their trans-cendence is the transcendence of need. It is the transcendence even of the need to escape, of the *besoin d'évasion*, in so far as it is expected that that need could ever be fulfilled. It is the transcendence of expectation. If it is a waiting it is a waiting for an arriving where nobody arrives, where nobody, *personne*, will ever have come to per-sonate in the rumour of the im-personal there-is. What is announced is always to-come, *à-venir, avenir*, the ceaseless adjournment of time future already 'momentarily' present in the deferment that is a schema of presencing. But how 'already'? And how 'already' when we say that the obedience that is hearing a call of bad conscience before there is law by which badness and goodness are defined, is already announced in the 'first' obedience to those laws and to the principles and categories that constitute worldhood? The answers to be given to these questions and to the question of the proximity of good and evil – which is also a question of the Nietzschean genealogy of morals – will depend on the interpretation of certain statements made in *Totality and Infinity* about the status of ontology, the logic of 'is' and the syntax of inverted commas. These topics will be taken up in the next chapter. That chapter and the one following it will take up again in more detail the topics enunciated in the title *Time and the Other* but only announced in that book and in this one so far.

Part II

6 Being faced

DISPLACEMENT

Levinas writes in *Time and the Other* that he has there omitted stages in what we are calling the genealogy of his ethics. This implies that he already has at least an outline plan in mind if not on paper for the book that will be entitled *Totality and Infinity*. In the preface composed for the second edition of the earlier book published in 1979 he observes that some of the topics dealt with in that earlier book are treated differently in the later one. The same will have to be said about the relation of a still later book, *Otherwise than Being or Beyond Essence*, to *Totality and Infinity*.

In the commentary on parts of *Totality and Infinity* which the present chapter begins it will be convenient to take as point of departure a sentence from an essay to which several references were made in chapter 5 and which was published in the same year as was published *Otherwise than Being*. The sentence contains the word 'substitution' that provides the title for what Levinas deems to be that book's most important chapter.

> Vigilance – reawakening in awakening – signifies the de-fection of identity, that which is not its extinction but its substitution for the neighbour – order or disorder where reason is no longer either knowledge [*connaissance*] or action but where, dislodged from its station by the Other [*désarçonné par Autrui de son état*] – dislodged from the Same and from being – it is in an ethical relation with the other [*autrui*], in proximity to the neighbour.
>
> [*DVI* 60]

If what is meant here by 'substitution' is to become clear, what is meant by de-fection of identity must be investigated.

What is meant by saying that de-fection of identity is not extinction? On the page facing the one on which these words 'not extinction' occur, right opposite them, reference is made to *la brûlure sans consumation d'une flamme inextinguible* (*DVI* 61). Strange to relate, these words refer in turn to words written nearly thirty years earlier in *Existence and Existents* and cited above in the fourth section of chapter 2. In the earlier work the *il y a* is described as 'this impersonal, anonymous but inextinguishable "consumption" ["*consumation*"] of being . . . "being in general"'. The sound associated with this by Levinas and Blanchot is mentioned in the same breath – the murmur which could easily be heard here as the sputtering of the flames of an earthly or subterranean inferno; scarcely yet as words; at most as the muttering (*muttire*) from which the *mot* will eventually emerge as the more from the less (*DEE* 93–4, *EE* 57, *SMB* 17). In the later text the inextinguishable flame that never burns out and does not leave even a trace of ash is a metaphor of the more in the less. And if *brûlure* carries also its usual meaning of the painful sensation of heat applied to the skin there is a further metaphor at work here, a furthering of the idea of the reawakening in awakening in which the source of illumination, the candle beside the insomniac's bed, becomes a source of ill, evil, lesion. The burden of being is doubled by the burden of responsibility for the other. However 'glorious' the responsibility for the other in the recto-verso of the face to face may be – and according to Levinas it is the wonder of wonders – the wonder remains a wounding, the *thauma* a trauma. For although the Other dislodges me, I continue to be lodged in my place in the sun. And the rays of the sun grow more searing beneath the Other's gaze. The passive intentionality of that intense gaze, more passive than the passivity opposed to activity in a system of energy exchange, *is* the intensity of the sun, of the Good beyond being. And the Good beyond being *is* simultaneously, yet at the same time dia-chronously, an unassimilable Evil beyond the simple opposition of good and evil. In Philippe Nemo's terms, as paraphrased by Levinas, while striking me in its menacing horror, evil 'reveals – or is already – my association with the Good' (*DVI* 203, *CPP* 183). In Kantian terms, there is a hidden common root of all evil and good deeper than the common root that the schematism of the time-generative productive imagination is for the passive sensibility and active understanding or reason. This deeper common root is a twofold, ambiguous root. It springs from a level below that from which Kant's second *Critique* sustains the first, a level at which sustainment is shaken to its root by such evil as that spoken of in Schelling's *Essay on the Essence of Human Freedom* and Heidegger's reflections on that treatise, but a level deeper even than evil grounded in freedom of will.[1] Deeper than transcendental conditions of the possibility of synthesis, deeper even than the ontological difference between beings and being, radical Evil/Good is a quasi-transcendental condition of the possibility and impossibility of synthesis, as the ethical difference between Evil/Good and particular evils and goods is more original than original sin.

Deeper. The more I respond for the other the deeper the subcutaneous wound. The more I answer, the more the other gets under my skin. The passivity is a subjection to suffering before it becomes an object of cognitive consciousness. Such consciousness of the presence of pain is a way of softening its sting and an opportunity to alleviate it by calculating its efficacy in a teleology consummated in good. Without consuming itself, the inextinguishable flame consumes consummation, contemns totting up, because it is the incessant hotting up of my sensitivity to my occupation of a place in the sun that my neighbour might have occupied. My complacency is ever more disturbed by my never being able to unplace myself. My displacement is always my replacement of another. Any place I would save for myself is one for which I am answerable to the other. That is to say, the irremovable burden of ontological responsibility under which I find myself not through any act or contract I have performed but simply because of the unwilled accomplishment of my self-identity, *is* my ethical responsibility for the other. That identity can no more be extinguished than the flame, too close for comfort, can be blown out. Rather is it strengthened by the other's breath. How could it be extinguished if ethics is a spiritual optics, if the breath of its life is the breath that is breathed in a call not simply to open my eyes, to sympathize and to universalize in the enjoyment of the still self-sustaining pleasure of good will, but to feed and clothe the Croatian stranger, the Serbian widow, the Somali orphan and the Palestinian or Israelite exile whom no one is willing to shelter from the desert heat or cold? Ethics is an optics only in so far as optics is operation, praxis or, where Levinas's 'fundamental ethics' is concerned, proto-praxis, prior to the opposition between knowledge and action, optics without option. That is to say, and Levinas approves of Marx for saying it, ethics has a base in economics. But Levinas's endorsement of this aspect of Marx's materialism goes along with a more complex conception of materialism and of what constitutes a base.

The basis of materialism is not the economic base or the primacy of the physical as opposed to consciousness or spirit. Where the spiritual is the holy within the bounds of reason and rationality is contrasted with the sacred as irrationality, 'Attachment to the sacred is infinitely more materialist than proclamation of the – incontestable – value in human life of bread and beefsteak' (*DL* 20, *DF* 6). Materialism accords primacy to the neuter even in Hegelian idealism and the late Heidegger's thinking of the belonging of being (*phusis*) to a saying which lets being lie (*logos* in the sense of 'saying' is cognate with *legein*, which can mean 'lay before' or 'let lie'), but which, on Levinas's interpretation of that thinking, does not belong to a face 'as a source from which all meaning appears, the face in its absolute nudity, in its destitution as a head that does not find a place to lay itself' (*TEI* 275, *TI* 298–9). It does not find a place to lay itself because, in a manner of speaking, that place is always already occupied by me in my self-identity.

Neither my isolated self-identity nor my self-identity as a worker united with others constitutes a base for the ethical, for the ethical also deconstitutes that base. This is what Levinas means by a de-fection of identity, that is, a falling away from and unmaking of identity, which is nevertheless not identity's death. The base is not a firm bedrock at a level deeper than a layer it supports. What is depth and what is height? What is identity? Precisely what it is, the identity of personal identity and with it the identity of the 'is' is what is put on parade and cross-examined when Levinas shuffles syntactic structure in saying that 'the Other [*l'Autre*], instead of alienating the unicity of the Same whom he disquiets and detains, calls him only to the deeper in him deeper than him' (*DVI* 48). Here Levinas's use of *Autre* rather than *Autrui* is a sign that he is interpreting Husserl rather than 'producing' him, but the depth-grammar of depth exposed here is already what Levinas will need when later in the essay he speaks in the voice, if one may so put it, not of the father but of the son. This very relationship between Husserl and Levinas, like the relationship between the Same and the Other in question in the sentence cited, is deeper than the oppositions between assimilation and alienation, Same and Other, I and you or *tu*. Deeper, but not geologically. Logically, but according to a logic that queries and queers the pitch for the principiality assumed by the classical principles of inference that prescribe or describe what follows from what. So that the metaphor of depth should not be assumed to be more profound than the metaphors of surfaces. This means that all this talk of hidden roots must be taken with a pinch of salt; which does not mean that whatever is superficial or ficial or facial is something that is easily seen. Something can be so close that it is overlooked or, like the sound in one's ears of the pumping of blood, unheard. The face is no less self-effacing than is being.

EFFACEMENT

If the face is the source from which all meaning appears, as Levinas says that it is, then the face is the source of the meaning of being. Time is the meaning of being according to *Being and Time*. Time is the meaning of being according to *Totality and Infinity*. But in the latter book time is construed from and beyond the face, and otherwise than as continuous duration or ecstasis. So being as thought in Heidegger's thinking beyond the being of classical metaphysics, being as thought, is in its turn surpassed. It surpasses or overtakes itself, Levinas can be read as saying on one construction of the pronoun in his statement that *l'être se dépasse*. Being passes itself departing from itself (*TEI* 278, *TI* 302).

Does being return to itself? Only if it does not start from and go to being construed, in the manner of Spinoza and Hegel, as a systematic whole, only if it starts from me as a separated being and goes as a host to the Other, welcoming the Other as guest, only in this manner can an eternal return within the interiority of the circle of being be escaped. For when I turn to the Other interiority turns into exteriority. The interiority of being is produced as exteriority not when in a multiplicity of subjects each competes with every other for a place in the sun. In conflict and cooperation the multiplicity reduces itself to one, to a totality of interacting selves in which the other is my other and I am his and hers. In true plurality society is not the polemical negation where free wills are rendered compatible by the universality of political law or where a peaceful outcome of the war of each ~~Girard~~ against all is achieved by the imposition of force. The political renders the ethical invisible. The State effaces the face. The true and just plurality of society is concretely produced in hospitality extended to the Other from within the economic base of a home in which the subject that enjoys and maintains itself in separation says to the Other 'Peace'.

But how does Levinas describe this concrete production? How concretely is economics accomplished as ethics? Not without an attentive and retentive study of the fine detail of the earlier chapters of *Totality and Infinity* can these questions be answered. Only that will enable us to understand the status of the question we are asking when the Conclusions lead us to ask whether the book concerns *being otherwise* or rather, in the words of the title of one of that book's successors, something *otherwise than being*. But it is also heuristically productive when rereading those earlier chapters of *Totality and Infinity* to have in mind this last question and the remarks made in the Conclusions that provoke it. Among these remarks are ones that treat of productivity.

ECONOMY AND ETHICS

Consider, to start with, some of the phrases and sentences to be read in the very last subsection of *Totality and Infinity*. Under a subheading that includes the phrase 'Being as Goodness' we read: 'To posit metaphysics as Desire is to interpret the production of being – desire engendering Desire – as goodness and as beyond happiness; it is to interpret the production of being as being for the Other' (*TEI* 281, *TI* 304). What force does 'as' have here? When A is posited or produced as B, is B the same as A, different from A or the same and different? Is one of these alternatives more in keeping than the others with the definition which the preface gives of production as ambiguously effectuation of being and being exposed in the light (*TEI* XIV, *TI* 26)? To posit or expose metaphysics as Desire is to bring to light that the metaphysical is not, as it is typically conceived in the history of philosophy, the sphere of theoretical principles that ground the principles of the physical in the narrow sense of that which is in time or space, of nature including human nature, and so of human need and desire. But how does natural desire 'engender' ethical Desire? How does it produce it? What kind of genealogy is posited or supposed? Does the production of being as goodness with which this engendering is equated mark a marking of time? Does being produce *itself* as goodness, so that being *is* goodness? It has already been mentioned that being overtakes itself, *se dépasse* (*TEI* 278, *TI* 302).

We have also been told that where being is not defined in terms of a system or whole but as the fact or act of starting from oneself, 'the act of starting from oneself and separation itself can be produced [*se produire*] in being only by opening the dimension of interiority' (*TEI* 276, *TI* 300). The 'can . . . only' here does not signify a possibility that may or may not be realized. The (f)act of starting from oneself *is* the opening of the dimension of interiority. Earlier in the same subsection it has been asserted that 'Separation is accomplished [*s'accomplit*] positively as the interiority of a being referring to itself and maintaining itself of itself [*se tenant de soi*] – all the way to atheism!' That the 'as' here is equivalent to an 'is' seems to be implied by the statement in the next paragraph that the positive accomplishment of separation is precisely what enables me, the subject, to welcome the other. When it is said immediately after this precision (and more will be said about Levinas's 'precisely' below) that 'The subject is host', is the 'can welcome' being replaced by a 'does welcome', or is it being left open whether a host may be unwelcoming? The most that Levinas needs to establish is that it is open to the subject to welcome the other. To affirm that separation entails welcome would appear to be at variance with his statement that 'self-reference is concretely constituted or accomplished as enjoyment or happiness' and that the essence of subjective existence is 'exhausted in identity'. So that when Levinas writes 'To metaphysical thought, where a finite has the idea of infinity . . . radical separation and relationship with the other are produced [*se produit*] simultaneously' (*TEI* 275–6, *TI* 299), the relationship in question is one that allows space for the individual subject in inner identification with itself and its own happiness, bliss or indeed salvation to welcome the other into its home. If the other were only my other dialectically opposed to, so posed by myself, this relationship would be in an internal relation with myself and therefore logically already in my home, within the economy of the self, constitutive of myself according to a universal logical law and needed for the fulfilment of my identity, in order that its finitude be made good. The other would have revealed itself as a mediator of my being saved through the 'production' of my separateness as part of the economy of a systematic whole. But it is my separateness that must be saved, and with it, however paradoxical it may seem, my capacity to enjoy myself and the fruits of the earth behind closed doors, if space is to be left for me to relate concretely to the singular other who faces. He or she is effaced as soon as the invisible ethical dimension of the face is made visible by being represented as a case falling under a logical law. Thus represented, apparently non-apparent ethical exteriority shows itself as only a logical part of an economy of interiority.

We are now in a position therefore to comment on the declaration 'Being is exteriority' which gives so much trouble to Levinas's readers.[2] It can be read in either of two ways. If, guided by the subtitle of *Totality and Infinity*, 'An Essay on Exteriority', we take exteriority to be the space of infinity and of the ethical as opposed to the space of totality and political economy, we shall be inclined to identify ethics with being. On that reading we shall be inclined to read *Totality and Infinity* as at most a treatise concerning being otherwise, rather than the otherwise than being. This would seem to be out of keeping with the subtitle 'Beyond Being' that Levinas gives to one of the sections of his Conclusions.

So we may choose to interpret 'Being is exteriority' as a statement about the relation to the Other of the being of the separately existing individual subject, to the effect that its interiority is outside and independent of the Other; that, as *Existence and Existents* has previously argued, the presence or instance of its existance is not being with others in a world (*Miteinandersein*). Picking up the first word of its title, *Totality and Infinity* asserts, under the subheading 'Beyond Being' to which reference has just been made, 'To exist has a meaning in another dimension than that of the perduration of the totality; it can go beyond being' (*TEI* 278, *TI* 301). By now we may have no difficulty with this assertion. But there remains the question whether when existence goes beyond being understood as the perduration of the totality, when it goes beyond metaphysics in a traditional sense, it goes beyond being when it goes to infinity, to the Other. For although Levinas refers at the end of the subsection in question to 'the relation with the Other, where being is surpassed' (*TEI* 278, *TI* 302) or surpasses itself, as we have earlier translated *se dépasse*, in the immediately preceding subsection he has written that fecundity, which has been treated in a section headed 'Beyond the Face', 'opens the subterranean, where a life called inward or merely subjective seemed to take refuge, upon being' and that fecundity and the perspectives it opens to an infinite and discontinuous time 'evince the ontological character of separation' (*TEI* 277, *TI* 301). The infinite time of fecundity opens up the interiority of separation, yet separation is ontological. It is as though interiority is opened up by exteriority thanks to fecundity which enables the separated self 'to be an other': not to be *or* not to be, but to be *and* not to be, as the father both is and is not his son, and therefore, it would seem to follow, as the son, Hamlet for example, is and is not his father. Is the simultaneous affirmation of the 'is' and the 'is not' made possible by what in the light of a traditional Aristotelian formulation of the principle of non-contradiction could be referred to as a difference of time or of respect or regard? If so, would there be any reason for saying that a non-Aristotelian logic and an un-Parmenidean and unfundamental ontology were here being invoked? And would this strange logic and ontology apply before the face and not only beyond it?

These questions will be considered more closely in the next chapter. But the ambiguity of the phrase 'before the face' is too obvious to go unnoticed here.

BEFORE THE FACE

The expression 'before the face' can denote either the ethical moment of the face to face discussed in section III of *Totality and Infinity* under the title 'Exteriority and the Face' or the economic moment of separation, enjoyment, representation and dwelling discussed in section II under the title 'Interiority and Economy'. How is this order of exposition related to what at least in the context of a discussion of classical, for example Cartesian, metaphysics would be described as the order of being? How are we to understand the claim 'Metaphysics Precedes Ontology' announced in section I of *Totality and Infinity* under that section's main title 'The Same and the Other'? How is the 'and' of that title to be read? As the 'and' of 'is and is not'?

When Levinas says that metaphysics in his sense, that is to say the ethical, precedes ontology, metaphysics in his sense is being distinguished from metaphysics as the study of being as such or the study of the being of beings, a sense in which it is one and the same with ontology. But at least three senses of ontology must also be distinguished: the traditional one just mentioned, ontology as fundamental ontology, and 'ontology' as used by

Levinas, though less and less frequently by Heidegger himself, for the latter's later thinking of being. Levinas identifies ontology in the second and third senses, along with the ontologies of Spinoza and Hegel, as ontologies of neutrality and totality. So there arise questions about the relation between being as totality and ethical infinity. Are these the same or other or both? How is the interiority of the economy of a systematic whole related to the exteriority of metaphysico-ethical infinity? These questions have to be distinguished from the one posed earlier in this chapter concerning the relation of the infinity of the metaphysico-ethical face to face to the being and economy not of the neutral totality but of the separated subject. Let us stay with this question, noting only that it would become absorbed into the question of the relation of infinity to totality if the being of the putative separated subject could be covered without remainder by the classical logic defined by the principle of non-contradiction or by the logic of dialectical negation. For under these logics everything that can be said about one being can be said truly or falsely about any other being of the same category. Not only is each being thus logically considered either a member of a class or a concept included under a genus, hence a term related to other terms of a system: already as a being it falls with other beings within the system for which being is defined by, for classical logic, the principle of identity and the principle of non-contradiction.

According to the Aristotelian formulation of the principle of non-contradiction the same attribute cannot belong and not belong to the same thing at the same time and in the same respect.[3] It is arguable that the identity of a thing is defined by its attributes. It is also arguable that if that is to be arguable definitive or essential attributes have to be distinguished from accidental ones, and that if position in a spatial, temporal or other series is an attribute it must be included among the non-defining ones. Otherwise the Evening Star could not be identical with the Morning Star. And if Chomolungma and Sagarmatha are the same mountain, then the points of view from the Tibetan or Nepalese geographic and cultural-linguistic sides respectively upon the mountain Westerners call Everest must count as different respects or regards of the kind anticipated in the tag 'in the same respect' by which Aristotle attempts to forestall a challenge to his principle of non-contradiction.

OF DRAMATOLOGY

But what if we take respect or regard in the sense intended in Levinas's doctrine of the face? As will be explained more fully in the next chapter, in that ethical or, more strictly speaking, proto-ethical sense – for the ethical as expressed by the face is the ethical as first philosophy, *prôtê philosophia* (*TEI* 291, *TI* 304) – the attribute or property (*Eigenschaft*) is significant because it can be alienated (*enteignet*) from my own domain (*Eigentum*): possession becomes dispossession because the I becomes emphatically 'possessed' by the other. Furthermore, the synchrony that Aristotle attempts to ensure by including the phrase 'at the same time' in his formulation of the principle of non-contradiction, thereby provoking Kant's comment that no reference to time and place need be made in such a purely formal principle of logic,[4] gives way to diachrony. And the visibility of the point of view is interrupted by invisibility. The third-personality of talk of points of view, their being seen laterally as points of view from a point of view which compares them, must be 'deduced'. But deduction, declared as an aim in earlier writings by Levinas, is distinguished quite explicitly in *Totality and Infinity* from deduction according to rules of inference and so-called laws of thought such as the principle of non-contradiction. Deduction as sought by Levinas destructures the structure of thought, fragmenting it 'into events which this structure dissimulates, but which sustain it and restore its concrete significance' (*TEI* XVII, *TI* 28). If these events sustain the very structure they explode, the deduction of them in Levinas's emphatic sense can lay claim to necessity, but that necessity cannot be the necessity of logical implication or transcendental presupposition of deduction as classically understood. It is not analytic necessity or the necessity of synthetic a priori propositions. For it is not the necessity of propositions. It is the necessity by which propositions and the formal necessities by which they may be connected are connected concretely to non-propositional events. To say that the propositional is concretely connected to the non-propositional is to state a proposition which as such conceals what it purports to reveal. The event, e-venting, occurring or *Ereignen*, as in a different context Heidegger would say, cannot be said or phenomenally shown. Neither the formally or transcendentally logical nor the phenomenological can constitute this; any more than a verb, for example the verb of all verbs, 'to be', can be a noun; any more than an act of speaking, an (o)uttering, even if what it purports to say is self-referential, can be simply the propositional entity that is what is said.

Yet Levinas calls this *événement* 'the ultimate event of being itself' (*TEI* XVI, *TI* 28). It is ultimate in the sense in which being-in-itself, the *kath auto*, which according to him is being for the other, is contrasted with the phenomenon. Here being is other than the purely nominal being of the separated subject. It is also other than the neutral being of classical metaphysics, of fundamental ontology and of the thinking of being. Neither the nominal being of an entity nor being parsed as a verbal noun, the being of the event of being is the being expressed by the verb. It is the being of the word as expression or act of speech.

But the word 'act' here is liable to mislead. *Being and Time* argues that acts of speech performed in everyday life are projective. Everyday life is primordially projective. The structure of projection is that of a referential though not necessarily significatory whole. Heidegger stresses the priority of this *Verweisungsganzheit* because one of his own projects in writing *Being and Time* is to bring out that the everyday world is not the totality of present at hand entities as which it has been commonly seen by philosophers. Levinas welcomes Heidegger's analysis to the extent that it is a corrective to what he also considers to be the overextension by Husserl and other philosophers of the noetic-noematic conception of being in the world. But this corrective and its holistic conception of being call in their turn for correction by the acknowledgement that 'the ultimate event of being itself' is not reducible to 'active interventions realizing projects' (*TEI* XVI, *TI* 28). These last words are taken from a footnote in the preface anticipating what will be said toward the end of *Totality and Infinity* under the heading 'Beyond the Face'. Whether or not we find reason to read back that beyond into the face to face, it does not seem unreasonable to apply what he goes on to say in this footnote to the face to face. For the face to face, no less than the beyond the face, is interpretable neither as noetic-noematic nor as projective interpretation 'nor, of course, as physical forces being discharged into masses' (*TEI* XVI, *TI* 28). What does he go on to say in this footnote? He goes on to admit that he would have liked to use the word 'drama' in the way that Nietzsche says he would have liked to use it in *The Case of Wagner*. Nietzsche's remark therefore deserves to be cited at some length:

> It has been a veritable misfortune for aesthetics that the word *drama* has been translated as 'action' [*Handlung*]. Wagner is not the one who errs here; all the world is still in error about the matter; even the philologists, who ought to have known better. The ancient drama had grand pathetic scenes [*Pathosszenen*] in view – it just excluded action (relegated it previous to the commencement, or behind the scene). The word 'drama' is of Doric origin, and according to Dorian usage signifies 'event' [*Ereignis*], 'history', both words in a hieratic sense. The oldest drama represented local legend, the 'sacred history or story' [*heilige Geschichte*] on which the establishment of a cult rested (consequently no doing, but a happening [*Geschehen*]; *dran* in Dorian does not at all signify 'to do' [*thun*]).[5]

Levinas comments that it is because of this risk of confusing drama with doing or active intervention that he does not use the word 'drama' of the 'conjunctures in being' he locates beyond the face. There seems to be no other reason why he should not be ready to use the word also of the 'conjunctures of being' of the face to face. This readiness is suggested by his statement that fecundity, which is the relation situated beyond the face, is only 'part of the very drama of the I' (*TEI* 251, *TI* 273). Only part. And 'The I is . . . drama in several acts' (*TEI* 258, *TI* 282). So its earlier acts are drama too, as a closer consideration of Levinasian earliness may eventually confirm.

The word 'drama' lends itself to a still wider application, application at the methodological level to deduction in Levinas's emphatic sense. For the deductions performed in *Totality and Infinity* turn on the effectiveness and accomplishment of the mode of address (*Ansprechen?*) in which the author faces his reader. Somewhat as it has to be said that the so-called deconstructions performed in the writings of Derrida are not simply deeds done by him, but that he intervenes rather as the occasional cause of a middle-voiced (neither simply active nor simply passive) *se déconstruire* of the texts worked through in those writings, so with the deductions performed in the writings of Levinas. The reader of those writings is witness to a *se déduire* or, as Levinas's definition of production in the preface to *Totality and Infinity* underlines, a *se produire*, a *ceci se produit comme cela* which is neither simply active nor simply passive in a sense opposed to active, but more passive than passivity in that simple sense. Absolutely passive, and absolutely past, as too could be in its own way Heidegger's *Gelassenheit*, for that is not only outside the opposition of activity and passivity, as is said in the dialogue which endeavours to 'place' that word, but is formed from the past participle of *lassen*, as in *Seinlassen* ('to let be'). Not an activity or doing in the common sense of these words, *Gelassenheit* is a 'higher doing', *ein höheres Tun*.[6]

Liddell and Scott say that the Attic equivalent of the Doric *dran* is *prattein*, for which they give as translations 'to effect' and 'to accomplish', observing that the primary sense seems to be 'to pass over' or 'to go through', *dia-*, as in 'diachrony' (to which in the next chapter we shall return). Although what Levinas calls deduction in an emphatic sense is not translation or logical inference, but a passover from identity defined by relations of formal or dia-lectical opposition to the concrete significance by which the foundations of these structures are both borne and shaken, he advises his readers that these deductions are marked throughout *Totality and Infinity* by expressions like 'this accomplishes that', 'precisely', 'that is to say' and 'this is produced as that'. It is precisely as though he does not always forget the 'as such' of metaphor, as Derrida says Levinas sometimes does. In *Totality and Infinity* at least he does not slip into 'etymological empiricism, the hidden root of all empiricism', which forgets that it is using the verb 'to be'.[7] There, in expressing the deduction of 'the ultimate event of being' through the expressions just reproduced, it is as though he is productively parodying Heidegger's statement in *Being and Time* that 'In our fundamental analysis of being, and of course in connection with the interpretation of the "is" (which, as a copula, gives "expression" to the addressing [*Ansprechen*] of something *as* something), we must again make the phenomenon of the "as" a theme and delimit the conception of this "schema" existentially' (*SZ* 360). In making the phenomenon of the 'as' a theme, and in dephenomenologizing it, Levinas delimits Heidegger's existential delimitation of this schema of the 'is' as 'as' in a manner that lets the manners of being (*Seinsweise*) of propositional truth and primordial proto-propositional *alêtheia* be as manners of being of the veracity of exposition to another in the face to face. There comes to pass an ethical or proto-ethical 'letting-be' of the letting-be of the Heideggerian thinking of being and of thinking as such. Therefore, if the production of economy as face to face ethics is indicated by 'that is to say', that is not to say that the equivalence is without ambivalence. If beyond the amphibology of being and beings an ultimate metaphysico-ethical event of being is traced, then the logicality of the deduction of the latter is proto-amphibological. The verb-noun ambiguity of Aristotle's *on* and the multiple sense of being, including the sense and history of being pursued in *Being and Time* and Heidegger's later works, are multiplied by an ambiguity of *logos* as 'saying' and *logos* as 'said'. Unavoidably if, as the author of that book says, *logos* is being's house.[8]

In other words, what one may risk calling Levinas's 'other thinking', the *andere Denken* and *Andenken* of his 'humanism of the other man', is a thinking otherwise of the 'productive logic' of which Heidegger writes in the Introduction of *Being and Time* that it 'leaps ahead' (*vorspringt*) (*SZ* 10), and of which he writes in the opening sentences of his 'Letter on Humanism':

> We are still far from pondering the essence of action [*Handeln*] decisively enough. We view action as causing an effect. The actuality of the effect is valued according to its utility. But the essence of action is accomplishment [*Vollbringen*]. To accomplish means to unfold [*entfalten*] something, into the fullness of its essence [*Wesen*], to lead it forth [*hervorgeleiten*] into its fullness – *producere*. Therefore only what already is can be accomplished. But what 'is' above all is Being. Thinking accomplishes the relation of Being to the essence of man. Thinking

brings this relation to Being solely as something handed over [*übergeben*] to it from Being. Such offering [*Darbieten*] consists in the fact that in thinking Being comes to language. Language is the house of being. In its home man dwells.[9]

But, it must now be asked, what is a house? What is a home? What is it to dwell?

7 Before and beyond the face

PREFIGURATION

The reader of chapter 6 could be forgiven for thinking that home (*oikos*), is what that chapter left before it was properly lodged in its economy. But the experience of not being quite at home is induced too in the reader of Levinas's own discussion of the home or dwelling. What he names the *demeure*, 'where one stays', appears to be where one never stays still. At least this is the impression one gets from the paragraphs of the subsection 'The Dwelling' that appear under the title 'Habitation and the Feminine'. Although they occur in the section on 'Interiority and Economy' and this precedes the section on 'Exteriority and the Face', they give reason to suspect that one is already, already before reaching the face, well on the way to being beyond it, assuming that when one is beyond it one is not still face to face. But in order to understand how the feminine appears to lead one on it is necessary to follow how Levinas leads his reader up to the feminine from enjoyment.

ENJOYMENT

On Levinas's reading of Husserl the pattern or matrix of being in the world is one of noesis and intended noema. This noetic-noematic structure is not committed to representative idealism. That is to say, it does not postulate ideas as a screen or medium through which one has dealings with the world. And although after the *Logical Investigations* Husserl defends a form of transcendental idealism, the intentionality that the hyphenation of the noetic-noematic stands for does not entail idealism. It does however entail a representativism or presentativism. That is the butt both of Levinas's and of Heidegger's disagreement with Husserl. Care (*Sorge*), is the matrix or pattern of Heidegger's conception of a human being's being in the world or, as he would prefer that we write, being-in-the-world. And the structure of care is not primarily presentative. Handling (*Handlung*), and readiness to hand are prior to presentedness. Levinas approves of Heidegger's denial of primacy to the theoretic and thematic which persists even in Husserl's descriptions of practical, evaluative and axiological ways of being in so far as the latter are analysed as modifications that retain the noetic-noematic core. But, Levinas maintains, even if Heidegger's way of subordinating the theoretical by demoting presence to hand does not simply reverse the order of priority of theory and practice, it does conceive being-in-the-world as possibility or power within a referential whole. This not only neglects a certain presence which is not the presence of theory as opposed to practice. It pays no heed to enjoyment and pain. As Levinas famously says, Heidegger's *Dasein* is never hungry (*TEI* 108, *TI* 134).

Because hunger is also *par excellence* privation and because it is need of that from which we live, it is not simply consciousness of that by which that need is fulfilled. It is the transitive living of that by which living is nourished. The transitivity of the verb 'to live' envelops the transitivity of the verb 'to exist' where what is existed is the instrumentality of, for example, a hammer, a pen or a source of energy. Everyday existence is more than the gearing of wherewithal to the achievement of a preconceived end. For that existential relation with a means is itself existed in enjoyment. We enjoy our daily bread, but we also enjoy the work that enables us to buy it. Even if we find the work irksome. For although Levinas distinguishes joy (*joie*) from distress or trouble (*peine*) and denies that joy is the cessation or antithesis of suffering (*TEI* 220, *TI* 242), he includes all of these under the happiness (*bonheur*) of enjoyment (*jouissance*), so that enjoyment in his sense covers the 'defective modes' of what one ordinarily counts as enjoyment. In this respect Levinas's notion of enjoyment resembles that of Samuel Alexander who in *Space, Time and Deity* adopts the word enjoyment 'to include suffering, or any state or process in so far as the mind lives through it', so that feeling, understanding and any other state of mind is enjoyed.[1] Levinas too ranks contemplation or theoretical representation within the scope of non-reflective, non-representational enjoyment. Not only are the objects of contemplation and the contemplation of those objects enjoyed. So too is the labour without which I might not have the time to sit or stand and stare. Furthermore, these enjoyments, be they the simple bodily or the more complex pleasures by which life is nourished, may mean more to me than survival without them. Occupation with my *nourrir*, my being fed, may take priority over preoccupation with my *mourir*, my being dead.

'Life is not naked will to be', Levinas writes. It is not 'ontological *Sorge* for this life' (*TEI* 84, *TI* 112). Whether or not Heidegger, the target of these remarks, would recognize his description of everyday life in the first of them, given his questioning of the centrality allocated to the will by, for example, Kant and German Idealism and Nietzsche, an accurate indication is given here of the place that is to be taken up in Levinas's thinking by the notion of nakedness. Nakedness *par excellence* is the nakedness of the face. But life is not naked existence. 'The bare fact of life is never bare.' Life is love of life. Returning us to the difficulty we have already encountered over where *Totality and Infinity* stands with regard to the question of being and ontology as treated in *Being and Time*, Levinas says that thinking, eating, sleeping, reading, working, and warming oneself in the sun are not my being but are more dear to me than it – *plus chers*. They are cherished and cared about more than the being that according to *Being and Time* owes its integrity to *Sorge*. Their being prized (*carus*), takes precedence over care for my being (*cura*) (*SZ* 197–8). Here 'being' is the naked or mere existence to which he has earlier referred, sheer substance, he goes on to say, as distinguished from what makes up the content or essence of that substance or existance. With this distinction and with Heidegger and Sartre in mind he considers himself entitled to say that life is an existence which does not precede its essence. In giving this twist to the declaration that existence precedes essence Levinas takes into account the human being's that-it-is and what-it-is, rendering otherwise naked *Dasein* concrete, contentful and capable of contentment by reconnecting it by its umbilical cord to love of life. In doing this, however, does he not leave open the question of his position with regard to the question of being, *Sein*, that is for Heidegger not limited to the *ti esti* and *hoti esti* of *Dasein*? When Levinas says 'The reality of life is already at the level of happiness and, in this sense, beyond ontology', is it beyond ontology in every sense?

Later on he says: 'The love of life does not resemble the care of being reduced to the understanding of being or ontology' (*TEI* 118, *TI* 145), and he puts in apposition references to the 'oecumenia of being' and 'the ontological order' (*TEI* 124, *TI* 150). If, on the basis of this confirmation of what etymology would appear to justify, references to ontology in some sense are taken to be references to being in some sense, then it may be justifiable to take Levinas to be saying that happiness and love of life are beyond being where by 'being' is meant the anonymous there-is. Substantial, instantial or what was earlier described as existantial being is already beyond that. Such being is the being of a being that bears a name. But does there not remain a sense of being that prevents us from claiming that we are beyond being and ontology when to sheer existantial being happiness and love of life supervene?

When questioning Heidegger's treatment of moods and the passions of the soul as *Dasein*'s existential disposition-in-the-world, and when arguing for an independence that exceeds that of bare substance, Levinas writes that enjoyment or happiness is not maintenance – *main-tenance*, holding oneself – in being; it is the surpassing of being. That the genitive here means being's surpassing is indicated by his comment that to one who is able to seek happiness being itself 'happens' as a new glory over and above substantiality, where the French word *arrive* is placed in inverted commas perhaps in order to signal a parodial connection with Heidegger's *ereignet*. So although it is happiness or enjoyment that is said to happen or advene, what is surpassed is not being. What is surpassed is the plenitude of being of substance. The independence of substance, he says, is accomplished by the happening of happiness. This is an accomplishment beyond that of the act or activity (*energeia*), that is the realization of a potentiality (*dunamis*) in Aristotelian ontology. For, although what Levinas says about the advenience of enjoyment reminds one of what Aristotle says in the *Nichomachean Ethics* (1174b) about the supervenience of pleasure, and although his 'accomplishment' echoes Aristotle's statement that pleasure completes (*teleioi*) an activity without being itself an activity or passivity, what is enjoyed is not the substantial thing, but quality *qua* quality and quality of life. What is enjoyed is an '"adjective" without substantive, a pure quality, quality without support' (*TEI* 135, *TI* 161). Yet it is precisely my enjoyment of what is dependent on substance for support that gives independence and self-supporting separateness to my life despite the fact that I am dependent on nutrients to keep myself alive. I have needs, there are things that I lack. Whereas desire is lack or, as we say with ambiguity, want (*penia*) of plenitude or resource (*poros*), human need is lack as source of plenitude in the sense that one can be satisfied or contented with one's lot, happy with one's needs and the task of fulfilling them. This fact of independence through dependence provides an opportunity to put a finer point on what Levinas means when he says that happiness is outside the categories of being. A minimal requirement of whatever is subsumable within the categories of being is that it cannot be such and such and not be such and such. Whereas the structure of happiness seems to imply both independence and dependence. And this is the structure of the ego.

Other classical ontological structures are the pair same and other. If happiness or enjoyment breaks with the logic of non-contradiction, so too does it break with the logic of contradiction according to which the same or self is opposed to the other as *its* other. *Totality and Infinity* aims to find in the interstice of being a place for an alterity that is neither the alterity of not-A over against A, nor the alterity of dialectical contradiction or contrariety in which opposites are reconciled within a higher systematic whole. Neither analytic nor dialectically negative alterity functions as the 'motor' of the genealogy of ethics described in that book. So although the dialectic of Hegelian genealogy is sometimes compared to digestion, Levinas questions whether that dialectic holds for the taking in of food. If the fruits of the earth, that from which I live and which I enjoy living from, are other in relation to myself as the Same, they are not in logical or ontological opposition to me. They are the habitat in the enjoyment of which is constituted my own autochthonous selfhood, not a sameness in which the Sameness of my selfhood loses its separate identity. The bread I put into my mouth becomes me. This is a fact that takes on special significance whenever Levinas has recourse, as he frequently does, to the image of giving the bread from my mouth to the other. Further, the enjoyment of meeting a need by seeking and eating the bread is the ego's unique ipseity, saving it from absorption into a higher unity, enabling it to be at home atheistically with itself, that is to say without cause for petitioning gods of a pagan mythology to come to assist in keeping together its body and soul. And that is to say further that need is the first motor of the ego's genealogical descendence and ascendence.

The ego's happiness is already an ascension. It is an exaltation 'above being', Levinas writes with inverted commas that acknowledge allusion to the *epekeina tês ousias* of Plato's Good. After all, *bonheur* is *bon*. So it is an elevation of the human being above its substantive being. And, Levinas therefore adds unsurprisingly, it is an elevation beyond ontology to axiology. One may therefore find surprising his earlier remark that the 'I can' – the ability to cope with my material needs, the ability that according to him gives concreteness to the bare ability to be, the *Seinkönnen* of *Being and Time* – proceeds from a certain elevation (*hauteur*), and that this procession is a *production ontologique* (*TEI* 89, *TI* 117). This ontological production is distinguished here from what might be mistaken for an empirical illusion. This is not a contrast of the ontological with the empirical, as it would appear to be if by the empirical Levinas meant what Heidegger means by the ontic. That he does not is clear from one of the most explicit and comprehensive statements Levinas makes in *Totality and Infinity* about the method followed in that work:

> Our work in all its developments strives to free itself from the con-
> ception that seeks to unite events of existence affected with opposite
> signs in an ambivalent condition which alone would have ontological
> dignity, while the events themselves proceeding in one direction or in
> another would remain empirical, articulating nothing ontologically new.

The method practised here does indeed consist in seeking the condition of empirical situations, but it leaves to the development called empirical, in which the possibility is accomplished – it leaves to *concretization* – an ontological role that specifies the meaning of the fundamental possibility, a meaning invisible in that condition.

(*TEI* 148, *TI* 173)

The suggestion is that ontology as pretheoretical understanding of being or as the philosophical analysis of that understanding, the two senses of the term distinguished in the Introduction to *Being and Time* (*SZ* 12–13), falls short of itself if it remains fundamental as distinguished from regional. Put otherwise, unless fundamental ontology learns from regional ontology it is not fundamental enough. If it is to follow what may be referred to as Levinas's method of empirico-ontological concretization, it must not remain at the level of the common root, before it ramifies into, for example, epistemology, aesthetics, axiology or – of especial significance for Levinas – ethics.

But since regional ontology is still ontology, and if axiology is ontological in a broadened sense, how can Levinas say that happiness falls within the scope of axiology but not within that of ontology?

Certainly, it does not fall within the scope of ontology in one of the senses Heidegger distinguishes in the Introduction of *Being and Time*, namely ontology as the theoretical description and analysis of being. But what about the sense in which ontologicality belongs pretheoretically to the bare being of *Dasein* in its projective understanding of being, *Verstehen*, interpreted as an existential or way of being of *Dasein*? Levinas's point is that in happiness the human being, while still dependent on the world for the goods thanks to which it may survive, is independent and autonomous. Although the human being remains a being, it can be said that in enjoying itself within the precinct of its abode it breaks with the categories of being. It breaks too with the Heideggerian existentials, namely, understanding, disposition, discursive articulation, and so on, for these, no less than the Kantian categories, and the Heideggerian categories of readiness to hand and presence to hand subsumed by *Dasein*'s existentials, are ways of anticipatively assuming being, predigesting it. Both anticipation of and participation in being are interrupted by enjoyment. Enjoyment exceeds the projective ecstasis of *Dasein*'s care with regard to its own being and other beings in its world. It ruptures the very way of being that distinguishes the way of being of *Dasein* from that of un-*Dasein*ish beings according to the radical doctrine expressed in §4 of *Being and Time*.

It is significant that Levinas speaks here of 'rupture', a word he employs for the ethical or proto-ethical moment of his genealogy. His use of it here draws attention to the way in which the subject's exaltation in happiness already stops projective intentionality in its tracks. Incidentally, this is something that could also be plausibly said of Being in Heidegger's later thinking of Being, where Being as such ebbs back upon the flow of *Dasein*'s care for its own being. The uncanniness of Being, Being's *Unheimlichkeit*, may well be a progenitor of the threatening *contretemps* presented by the *il y a* and indeed by illeity to the ecstatic temporality of the **?** 'I can'. This is why we asked earlier in this section whether Levinas gives a one-sided account of Heidegger's ontology. Admittedly, Levinas often says that when discussing Heidegger he is concentrating on *Being and Time*. The strength of that defence will depend on what we take to be the import of the statement made in that book that the analyses it carries out are provisional. We shall not pursue that question here.

Concretely described, the being of the subject is neither the metaphysical substantivity and permanence of the transcendental ego nor the existential-ontological constancy of *Dasein*. It is the autonomy that happiness brings to the human being which in its exaltation is, as Levinas writes, the *étant, par excellence* and – for what he also writes in the same paragraph licences the omission of the comma – the being *par excellence*, the being that excels being.

THE HOME

In excelling being the human being accomplishes autonomy by accomplishing its happiness. Happiness is not accomplished by the Epicurean, Stoic or Buddhistic suppression of desire and need. It is the accomplishment of need. Nor is it a pastime or *divertissement* in the sense of Pascal, or, in the sense of *Being and Time*, an inauthentic recourse by which I would render myself oblivious to my mortality. Nothing could be more authentic than happiness or enjoyment. In enjoyment I am most self-possessed, ownmost, *eigenst*. Not that in happiness I turn my back on the passing of time. But although, as the enjoyment of need, *bonheur* shakes off the burden of being-in-the-world, it retains a connection with time. Although, appearances notwithstanding, the word *bonheur* may have no etymological connection with *hora*, *heure*, 'hour', such a connection with *augurium*, *heur* and 'augur' reflects a connection with future time. Unlike the futurity of being towards my certain but temporally indefinite death on which *Being and Time* lays more weight than it does on the other temporal ecstases which are however said to be equally original with that to-come (*SZ* 329), the futurity of my happiness with my needful lot reveals itself as a kind of mastery (*maîtrise*) of what is to come. In due course this mastery will reveal itself as the antecedent, prototype or schema of a mastery of another kind. Meanwhile, overcoming the to-come of the nameless menaces that haunt purely instinctive life and are represented by the faceless gods of ancient mythology and the modernized mythology of psychoanalysis, the to-come of need is the to-come of the postponement of dependence on the other. This postponement is what labour and housekeeping buy. With them I buy time in which to prolong the happiness which the lapse of time itself puts at risk. Embracing what in *Being and Time* is called disposition (*Befindlichkeit*) and the moods (*Stimmungen*) such as the anxiety that is paradoxically constitutive of the indefiniteness (*Unbestimmtheit*) of the time of my death, enjoyment places the world within its disposition by holding at arms length the material alterity on which it depends.

This postponement of dependence is accomplished through my body as ambiguously master and slave. My body is that through which I am vulnerable to threats and possession but at the same time capable of sheltering myself from threat and achieving self-possession by the labour of my hands. In this way is remedied, at least for a time, the thrownness or dereliction (*Geworfenheit*) that is the respect in which, according to the analysis of *Being and Time*, *Dasein* is no more fully in control of its being-in-the-world than it is in control of its birth. In this way the subject protects its autonomy.

Evidently, this autonomy through felicity is not autonomy in Kant's sense of the word. Nor is it Heidegger's 'resolution'. Yet its character can be explained in terms of certain features of their thinking. If autonomy were defined within the limits of reason alone it could not be the autonomy of members of a society. It would be the autonomy of disembodied reason as such. For there to be a plurality of autonomous beings a principle of individuation other than pure reason is required. As Kant, followed by Levinas, recognizes, this is made possible only by the sensibility and affections, by the interest in the happiness human beings seek for themselves in manifold ways that vary from person to person. Sensibility and affection imply a certain exposedness, as too does what translators of *Being and Time* call 'resoluteness', 'resolution' or 'resolve', terms that suggest a closed-mindedness, whereas it is unclosedness that is implied by the word *Entschlossenheit* they thus translate. Nevertheless, *Entschlossenheit* does mean 'resolve', and resolve is not an exposedness to every passing whim. It is an openness that has a determined scope.

Similarly, the enjoyment of the self by itself in its home, *bei sich, chez soi*, is the isolated self's secret, the se-creteness by which it accomplishes dis-creteness from the generality of the concept, but also from the particularity which is merely that of a case falling under the concept.

Enjoyment or happiness is the rupture of participation, a difference from the ontological difference as such, a difference from the as such. Even so, this interiority is not separated from exteriority as though spatially by a simple cut or line. For even if its enjoyment is the enjoyment of quality, quality is adjectival of things, the things one must handle, like knives and forks or hammers, to secure one's happiness for the future. In my domestic bliss then I am not only dependent upon the other as the material upon which and with which I work, upon *Zeug* as raw material and *Zeug* as instrument, tool or device. Through the 'malediction' of having to work to satisfy my material needs I am dependent on the Other as Autrui, the other human being who cooperates with me and with whom I cooperate, not least in working with the words through which bread and water and bricks and mortar and slabs and planks and hammers and nails are told apart. So that what I can do with these entities and stuffs proceeds, as we noted earlier, from a certain *hauteur* or uprightness, that of the body of a being that speaks. The Other is an *haut parleur*. As we were on the point of explaining then, but are in a better position to explain now, the empirical fact of the human body's posture by which two persons are face to face, is not an empirical illusion or metaphor of human spirit. Here the empirical facticity is the ontological production. It is an ineffacable testification of the face, its *Zeugnis* or *Bezeugung*, as we could say, borrowing another word from *Being and Time*.

The second chapter of the second division of *Being and Time* is concerned with resoluteness and the search for an attestation of an authentic ability of being for *Dasein*. An attestation is said there to be an existentiell, that is to say, in the sense appropriate to *Dasein*, an ontic certification that can be shown to have its origin in *Dasein*'s existential-ontological constitution. It therefore meets some of the specifications of the method of empirico-ontological concretization set out in the paragraph from *Totality and Infinity* reproduced above in the second section of this chapter. Admittedly, Heidegger warns that the attestation that he finds, the voice of conscience, is not to be confused with empirical experiences (*Erlebnisse*) such as might be described by the psychologist, sociologist or biologist. Nor is it to be understood as what a theologian might take as immediate or indirect evidence of God. But the same is to be said of Levinas's equivalent of this voice, the call of the Other, the command of *Autrui*. Yet he is willing to say that this is 'experience *par excellence*' (*TEI* 81, 170, *TI* 109, 196) and, under the heading 'The idea of infinity and conscience', 'experience in the strongest sense of this term' (*EDE* 177, *CPP* 59). If experience is *empeiria*, this puts a new face on the empirical. The empirical with this new look is the empirical *par excellence*.

Already in the first section of our first chapter we began to learn why newness is one of Levinas's principal themes, and why therefore in the wake of Bergson's *Creative Evolution* the topic of creation surfaces in Levinas's work from time to time. It lies only just below the surface in the very words 'testification', 'attestation', *témoinage* and *Bezeugung*. When Levinas writes of 'ontological production and ineffable testification' (*TEI* 89, *TI* 117) the meaning of the first noun is repeated in that of the second. For to testify is to produce evidence. The idea of production is also implicit in *Zeug*, for *Zeug* as equipment, tool or material is something that is either artificially or naturally produced, *erzeugt*: generated, created. But creative production is not causation, neither in the sense in which Levinas uses the word 'creation' nor in the sense that the word commonly has in ordinary speech. Causes and effects are related within systematic wholes. Levinas seeks a kind of production that allows newness in the sense of ab-solution from totality. And this 'new triumph' is already achieved by the ego's self-centred domestic felicity.

Self-centredness is its own defence, at the very least in so far as the ego's felicity calls for it to protect itself against that by which it would be hurt. This is what might be called the ego's first apology. It explains and justifies its stocking its larder, furnishing its rooms and, when necessary, boarding up its windows and barring its doors. This first apology is apology that appeals to the *bon* of *bonheur*, the axiologically good. But there are manifold meanings of goodness as there are manifold meanings of being, and the value of prudence and of the satisfaction of need are not yet the goodness of ethics. Ethical goodness (*bonté*) demands that the first apology be emphasized or complicated into 'apology, in which the I at the same time asserts itself and inclines before the transcendent' (*TEI* 10, *TI* 40). While retaining the first moment of apology, the ego is called before a higher tribunal at which its mastery over its independent domain becomes subject to a mastery of a radically other kind, a kind outside kind as genus, as, it should not be forgotten, the ego's own happy egoity was not one of such a kind, not one of a such, but *Jemeinigkeit* described otherwise than it is described in *Being and Time*.

MASTER AND MISTRESS

Mastery (*maîtrise*) has a masculine ring to it. Biological and grammatical masculinity and femininity define the species of genus called gender. But Levinas draws upon the vocabulary deriving from that of gender, sexuality and family relationships in order to create room for relations alternative to those by which distinctive features are compared from a third-person lateral point of view in order to be granted membership of this or that class. Sexuality and, in the most concrete sense of the expression, sexual relations have a dimension of depth that is not captured by reflective comparison of the sexes. In all its versions it retains a frontality that no sexless self would experience. And so too does mastery or *maîtrise*. This last, be it noted in passing, is a feminine noun that may be derived no less, if less directly, from *maîtresse* than from *maître*. It covers as much the dominance of a woman as the dominance of a man. And dominance in its neutrality may include *domina* as much as *dominus* in its genealogy, while both of these may be included within the genealogy of *domus* ('dwelling', home). Notwithstanding the neutrality shared too by the conception of sexuality – and by the sexuality of the conception of the concept – sexuality is, as Levinas says, accomplished non-reflectively. Although when he says this he makes no explicit mention of homosexuality, which might be thought to weaken his case, he could have cited it to strengthen the case he makes out for the claim that a radical asymmetry inflects one's experience of sexual alterity. It is arguable that whatever biological symmetry or asymmetry obtains, the personal experience of a homosexual sexual relationship is asymmetrical. In a non-biological sense it remains heterosexual.

Asymmetry and heterologicality are also of the essence of the experience *par excellence* of 'emphasized' mastery, the magisteriality of the Other without which the experience of sexual relationship is not a fully personal relationship. This mastery is teaching (*enseignement*), that intervenes between slavery and the seigniory of the master, disturbing the order of the totality of projective assignments – the *Verweisungsganzheit* of *Being and Time* – in the context of which I point ahead, by pointing the finger at me and interjecting the ensignment that I should take care not to kill. Levinas employs the masculine pronoun *il*, he, for the Other (*Autrui*), who utters this first commandment of proto-ethics. But the word *Autrui* is indeterminate as to gender. Indeed the first presence of the Other is announced in a feminine voice whose first word is a word of welcome, welcome home. Whereas the voice of him who says 'Heed' comes from above, not from outside, not from the exteriority from which I take the other, other things, *l'autre*, into my mouth or my home, the voice of her who says 'Come' comes from inside, from the interiority of the home.

It cannot be too often repeated that the language of gender and family relations is being produced and emphasized by Levinas and that provided it is not reduced to the biological discourse in which it may appear to have its natural home, certain avoidable difficulties, though by no means all difficulties, will be circumvented. He himself would probably challenge this notion of the natural home. He elsewhere mentions with approval Bruno

Snell's thesis that instead of thinking of the extended or metaphorical as opposed to the literal or natural we should think of each use as an extension or 'metaphor' of the other.[2]

> In a study of Homeric comparisons M. Snell (as quoted by Karl Löwith) points out that when in the *Iliad* the resistance to an attack by an enemy phalanx is compared to the resistance of a rock to the waves that assail it, it is not necessarily a matter of extending to the rock, through anthropomorphism, a human behaviour, but of interpreting human resistance petromorphically. Resistance is neither a human privilege, nor a rock's, just as radiance does not characterize a day of the month of May more authentically than the face of a woman. The meaning precedes the data and illuminates them.[2]
>
> (*HAH* 23, *CPP* 78)

The very home where we are inclined to think that the word 'home' is most at home is extended beyond its walls. It is extended through the manner in which the feminine welcome extends toward the masculine demand. Both of these are addressed to the ego, so they both already divert the ego's centrifugal intentionality. Their centripetality crosses the ego's centrifugality in a manner that dislocates both centrality and the great out-of-doors, resiting or rather desiting them at the threshold that is neither unambiguously out nor unambiguously in, but metaphorico-literally both at one and the same time. Except that sameness of time will turn out to be just as altered as sameness of place. For the same is othered, whether the same be a what or a who. And the other as *autre* is othered by the Other as *Autrui*. As follows.

8 The manifold of alterity

THE SAME

Thoughts of something other as the same thing perceptible at different times imply the thought that those thoughts and this thought are the thoughts of a thinker that remains the same. To distinguish the sameness of the other thing from the sameness of what Descartes calls 'the thinking thing' Levinas refers to the self as 'the Same', *le Même*, with a capitalized initial.

Representation of the other as same is representation of the representing ego as Same. The representation of the self as the Same is represented by Plato as a dialogue of the soul with itself. But it is as though in this dialogue of the soul with itself the sole self is, Levinas writes, using a word he will use again with an emphasized sense, surprised. It is as though its mastery over itself is shocked to discover itself overhearing its thought, as though the thought were the thought of another. Its particularity is overcome when the distance between itself and its thought is reduced to the zero distance between itself and what it hears itself speak, and the self becomes indistinguishable from universal thought. The singularity of the first-person singular is taken over by the impersonality of an It, an indefinite One and the Same. As when the ego in Kant that asserts its power over things by assuming their form in advance is thereby resumed within an Ego that transcends particularity and could as well be called a transcendental It, like the *es* of Heidegger's *es gibt Sein*, or a transcendental She or/and He, like the absolute knowing of Hegel on the French reading of it as *Savoir absolu*, as the feminine adjective *Sa* that happens to be also an abbreviation for 'Saussure' and for the *signifiant*, the signifier that in conjunction with the *signifié*, the signified concept, makes up the sign.[1]

This movement from surprise toward the suppression of my mastery is a movement from my domain toward the threshold where my welcome of the other thing is met by my welcome by the Other – by the Mother, perhaps it could be said, but at any rate by a feminine Other or the femininity of the Other that (on the threshold, we shall see, between accusative 'me' and pronominative 'I') saves me from total absorption in depersonalized and timeless general thought.

The saving is effected through sensibility which saves time. For time is lost in eternity when the erstwhile ego synthesizes under universals the instances of them that it imagines or recalls having perceived. Time is regained when I am sensible to the fragility of my enjoyment of the present moment – enjoyment, it will be recalled, that includes the enjoying of contemplative thought and even the thought of my enjoyment's fragility against which I attempt to secure myself by building or buying a home. The home may be represented either as a collection of objects present at hand or as a 'machine for living in', a functional system of handy furniture and other such possessions of which I can dispossess myself if they cease to perform their job efficiently. But my enjoyment of my house and its environs, of my garden, the town and the country round about is not thus representable. Enjoyment and living-from are the unrepresentable conditions of representation in which I am in my element. The element is the background and earth presupposed by what already in his earlier writings Levinas calls position, the earth not viewed Copernically, as though from outer space, but the earth not viewed at all; the earth rather as the Ptolemaic place in which I stand that is for me an unviewed point of view view.[2] The earth as element is where I am standing or sit, posited, *gesetzt*. As described by Husserl, it is the proto-archic earth that does not move when I move the furniture, the *meubles*, that is to say, the movables in my sitting room or when I move myself when there is a removal from one house to another. For although my domicile may be where I sit, the good life is not the sedentary life.

ALIMENT AND ELEMENT

How is the element related to what Levinas calls 'the aliment'? Because he uses the term 'milieu' of the element (*TEI* 104, *TI* 130) and a few paragraphs earlier uses the same term (though within inverted commas) of the aliment, it might be thought that he intends the latter to be understood as an example of the former. He writes of the element as that into which one plunges, in which one bathes (*on y baigne*), and of the world that nourishes me as the aliment and 'milieu' that soaks me (*me baigne*). Perhaps it could be said that an element becomes an aliment when it is not only the milieu as place in the midst of which I live but the medium or means (*Mittel*), from which I live, the *Lebensmittel*, not however grasped simply as means or staff of life, but enjoyed.

More exactly, my nourishment by the aliment is my relishment of the element. For the elemental is precisely the quality thanks to which the enjoyment of what I live from is recalcitrant to representation. The food on my plate can be an object of scientific analysis and can be correctly perceived as a means to keep myself alive and healthy. These representations of the food constitute the food as object or means, and this constitution can be described in the manner of epistemological idealism and noetico-noematic phenomenology as analytic and synthetic operations of the mind. But this projective constitution constitutive of representation presupposes a non-projective, non-representational constitution which is the constitution of the body and the world not as *vis-à-vis* but as that which and in which I live, in which *je vis* (*TEI* 102, *TI* 129). The world understood as a systematic totality of operational signification and the world understood as a totality of facts presupposes an 'underworld'. Descartes glimpses this when he distinguishes clear and distinct ideas that are objects of theoretical knowledge from the obscure and confused data of sensibility. Implying perhaps that the former are teachings of God, he describes the latter as teachings of nature. But when one listens to the Cartesian lesson that the teachings of what is useful, one must also listen to the Humian lesson that the utile is to be distinguished from the agreeable, from the *agrément* that seems to Levinas to be left out of the *Seinlassen* and *Seinkönnen* of *Being and Time*. If my death is an end, so too is enjoyed satisfaction, where to say that it is enjoyed is to say that it is not just a targeted *telos*, but is subtracted from teleologicality and puts an end to means and ends.

The elemental quality thanks to which enjoyment is recalcitrant to representation is that pure qualitativeness prior to property: pure adjectivality without nominality, the anonymity of the *il y a* of the existentless existence described in Levinas's earlier works as both pleasure and fearful for the future. *Totality and Infinity* articulates further in terms of enjoyment and sensibility the temporality of basking in enjoyment and the worry, that is to say *Sorge* and *souci* in an ontic or 'empirical' sense, care for the morrow that attends the there-is today. The apparently present-tensed there-is is now said to be the nocturnal dimension of the future. Nocturnal in contrast to the future dimension of the every*day* being-in-the-world as analysed in *Being and Time*. A future that is indeterminate not because of the indeterminacy of death, but because it comes from no Where. Therefore, although one can say that enjoyment in my home is enjoyment at the threshold of homelessness (*Unheimlichkeit*) and although there would seem to be no reason why this disturbed enjoyment could not be described as a way of being – after all, we have seen that Levinas frequently writes that the *il y a* is anonymous being – this being's to-come that arrives from no Where is differently construed from the being that comes from No-thing-ness as described by Heidegger in 'What is Metaphysics?'[3] and *Being and Time*, not to mention the *Logic* of Hegel.

And the same must be said of its past. 'What the subject contains as represented is also what supports and nourishes its activity as subject. The represented, the present – is *fact*, already of the past' (*TEI* 103, *TI* 130). But the facticity of this *fait accompli* of elemental enjoyment is not to be conceived in the manner sometimes described by Husserl, though not without reservation, as a level superimposed upon that of an alleged purely theoretical presentation or representation. The present and representation are anteriorly supported and nourished by the interiority of the ego's enjoyment. The past and future of this enjoyment are connected in a manner quite different from the manner in which the ecstatic future and past are conceived in the Heideggerian schematism. Whereas Heidegger's conception purports to be one that rises above the notion of life and therefore above the notion of the enjoyment of life, it is precisely in terms of life that Levinas construes the complication of future and past.

> Intentionality directed to the exterior changes direction in its very directedness in becoming interior to the exteriority that it constitutes; it somehow comes from the point to which it goes, recognizing itself as past in its future; it lives from what it thinks.
>
> (*TEI* 102, *TI* 129)

The fact that although what I enjoy can be represented the enjoyment is not representable leads Levinas to say that the elemental world I enjoy belongs to an irrepresentable antiquity that is as an absolute (*comme un absolu*) (*TEI* 111, *TI* 138). He uses the same phrase of the I that takes its stand in the world. I find myself in it as being an absolute (*comme étant un absolu*). Two paragraphs earlier he refers to the quasi-eternal *ancienneté* of the element, explaining that it is quasi-eternal because of an insecurity that disquiets it as the (emphasized) *other*. All these occurrences of the word *comme* are in principle translatable by 'as' and this may be an 'as' of identification. It is worth asking, however, whether Levinas is intending the word in the sense of 'as if' or 'like'. The implication of this could be that for a radical absolute we shall have to look or listen elsewhere – supposing there is a where, for he has told us that the elemental comes from nowhere. In conformity with this reading, the implication of his phrase 'as the *other*', where the stress is also his, may be that what really and absolutely disquiets is not the *autre* of the element but the call of *Autrui*, the Other human being; not the demonic strangeness of ilyaity, but the illeity of the stranger. Yet the structure or structurelessness of the *apeiron* of the *il y a* will be creatively pro-duced or elevated by the infinity of illeity; the pure loss without utility and the pure expenditure without afterthought, *pure dé-pense*, of enjoying the elemental will be picked up by a general, unrestricted economy in which exchange gives way, if not to generosity, to a giving in responsibility that may appear to be more like irresponsibility in that the donor does not reckon to save itself;[4] and terror before the menace of the waning of worldly enjoyment, enjoyment of *nourritures terrestres*, will be reflected in the structure and destructuration of my world when I am no longer innocently deaf to the Other, no longer neither for him or her nor against.

The pronouns here must be distinguished because in the order of exposition of the second section of *Totality and Infinity*, *Autrui* as stranger is approached through *Autrui* as the familiar and feminine presence that is not only not an unwelcome disturbance, but welcomes me in the house.

And dare one ask whether the approach to her is being made already when three times within little more than three pages (*TEI* 101–5, *TI* 128–32) Levinas refers to the elemental world of earth, sea and sky from which I draw nourishment as the world in which I am *au sein*: in the midst, in the milieu, at the heart, but also maybe at the breast? What nourishment could be more elemental than milk?

WORDS OF DISCRETE AND INDISCRETE WELCOME

True birth is domiciliary, when the newborn is separated from its instinctive nature and no longer umbilically attached to its cause. Levinas says at one point, as we have earlier observed, that innocent enjoyment is a halfway stage, a milieu between the system of natural causes and the system of reason where meeting the Other (*Autrui*) opens infinity (*TEI* 107, *TI* 133–4). How can he say a few pages later that the full description of enjoyment must acknowledge that in enjoyment the human being already has the idea of infinity? He says this because although enjoyment in separation is enjoyment of qualities as qualities, these are qualities of nameable things, for example furnishings and, maybe we should now add, the breast. Entities become fixed in their identity by being represented by names. By being so named the pure quality that is enjoyed gets superseded by common property. To say that common naming language makes things shareable is to say that it is social. So is not the enjoyment of represented things already open to *Autrui*? If so, how can the egoistic enjoyment of represented things be intermediate between the instinctive and the rational?

In being through language in relation with other people, how can it fail to belong to the system of reason?

It is not simply to the system of reason that Levinas refers, but to the opening to infinity through the system of reason. That opening would disrupt the system of reason and the system of common linguistic exchange. That language is where one is at home with others, the others who initially share one's mother tongue, initially with one's mother at whose knee one learns one's mother tongue. It is therefore at her *genou* that, as Derrida would say, we enter the community of *je-nous*. That community, however, is the community of a family scene. It is an intimate community. And it is a com-unity, a being-with. To link the feminine with the mother or the nurse as we have done is to articulate Levinas's text in a manner that accents what he himself does not make as explicit at this stage of his geno-phenomenological description, the stage of habitation, the 'first con-cretization' of the *ich bin* which the onto-phenomenological description of *Being and Time* connects with the idea of dwelling-place through Germanic *bei* ('at home'), *bu*, -by as in Whitby, and, according to Grimm, *bauan* ('to build or cultivate') (*SZ* 54). This articulation, however, in linking the feminine as mother to the articulation of discourse, which under the title *Rede* (*logos*) is the articulation of intelligibility in the existential-ontological analysis of *Being and Time* (*SZ* 161), suggests a feminine–masculine articulation of discourse itself into what in speaking I give another to understand and the uttering that is the donation, expression and exposition of myself. At the risk of exceeding Levinas's express intention, the feminine as welcoming presence in the home may be taken to correspond with the universe of discourse that Levinas will distinguish in *Otherwise than Being* (but the distinction is already made less explicitly in *Totality and Infinity*) as the system of the said, the *dit*, from the counter-systematic to-say, the *Dire*. The latter, on this reading, will carry a masculine inflection.

The feminine presence of the Other relates to the masculine as the discrete to the indiscrete. The reference made earlier to discreteness was a reference to the gap (*décalage*) between totality, for example that which Heidegger claims is enabled by *Dasein*'s being toward its death, and the enjoyed affectivity of the secret, concrete ego. This discreteness is not disrupted by the feminine welcome, whether that be maternal or not. And, at the risk of introducing the categories of the mythologies of psycho-analysis that Levinas himself might not object to as long as they are confined to this early stage, it has to be said that the femininity of the maternal may be ambiguous, retaining traces of the femininity of an in-timacy that is its genetic and perhaps geno-phenomenological antecedent.

Clearly, we are on the brink of the trans-generational questions that are to be considered in the fourth section of *Totality and Infinity* under the heading 'Beyond the Face'. Restricting attention for the time being to the second section, we find Levinas writing there of 'the gentleness [*douceur*] of the feminine face' (*TEI* 124, *TI* 150). When he says that it is in this gentleness that the separated being can recollect himself and that it is thanks to it that it *dwells*, *habite*, is the underlining of this last word meant to signal a lexical derivation from *habere* ('to have'), and perhaps through this a geno-phenomenological derivation from the *avoir* of the *il y a*? Or – or and – is the underlining meant to draw attention to the fact that a habit is a manner of being, a *manière d'être*, as Littré's dictionary says, in the phrase Levinas uses almost as often as he does *façon d'être*? The word *façon* is used in this very same sentence, asserting that the self-recollection (*se recueillir*) in interiorization (*Erinnerung*), which is also recollection in the sense of memory, is an original way by which is produced the welcome (*accueil*) of the face. Here, note, the ego is welcomed. This welcome is said to be the first revelation of the Other. Immediately after this it is said that the idea of infinity reveals itself in the face. If this means that the idea of infinity reveals itself in the gentle feminine face, does it not mean also that the connection made above between the feminine and the *dit* as opposed to the *dire* has now to be unmade? No. What does follow is that the complexity of the connection must be recognized. The interior and the exterior of the human condition are not regions of a homogeneous space, anymore than human time is ultimately the time that is given by clocks. 'Simultaneously without and within', the human being 'goes forth outside from a privacy [*intimité*]. On the other hand this privacy is opened in a house that is situated in an outside' (*TEI* 126, *TI* 152). To cite again a reminder from Derrida, the *for intérieur* is at the same time a *fors* that goes outside. And the archaic *fors* which means 'saving' or 'save for' in the sense of 'except' is crossed with 'saving' in the sense of 'economic security'. As the content of something that is said is levered open when someone holds forth to another. Discourse is the first donation. Expression is offer of the world to the Other. Exposition, auto-exegesis, is a second dispossession of oneself after the first dispossession, after atheism which frees one from possession by the faceless gods of mythology. It is a destitution of the site accomplished in turning from the discrete presence of the Other as feminine to the Other's face now described as indiscrete.

Why indiscrete? If the feminine presence is discrete because it is presence in the home and the home is extraterritorial, removed, it would seem that the indiscrete face must remove this removal. This simple reversal fails to do justice to the multiplicity of the kinematics of the turn from the discrete to the indiscrete. Having moved from immersion in the elements by taking up residence in a dwelling from whose windows the ego can look out upon nature and through whose doors it can take possession of materials and goods from outside by which to sustain its life inside, the ego, although not absorbed in the pure qualitativeness of the elemental, is still absorbed in proprietorship over the things it now represents to itself as things. It represents those things to itself. Even the linguistic representation this implies, which in turn implies at least the idea of the discrete presence of the Other, is a representation for me which embraces the for-us of my compresence with the presence of the feminine. The language we speak is private, though not in principle private. It is in principle apt for publicness, that is to say, for indiscretion.

THE GARDEN OF EDEN

It is impossible to resist the temptation to turn back here to the story of the Garden of Eden. Public indiscretion in the garden would be misdemeanour in the face of God. In the Genesis narrative Adam gives names to all cattle, and to the fowl of the air, and to every beast of the field (though apparently not to the serpent, who is contrasted with the beast of the field as more subtle). He does this before Eve has been created, but not before God has conceived the idea of her as Adam's helpmeet, an idea that is mentioned before mention is made of the fowl of the air and the beasts of the field. When Eve is more than an aspect of an adrogynous Adam, more than present only as Adam's rib – or side, or tail, or face! (see below, the fifth section in chapter 10) – her discrete presence would be contemporaneous with the indiscrete presence of the God of monotheism in terms of whose law indiscretion is defined. Her retiring discreteness, represented by the hidden rib from which she later comes forth, is already one side of indiscretion, according to an 'extremist' text to which Levinas refers (*DL* 59, *DF* 38). That text goes as far as to say that with her was created the Devil. But this 'her', Levinas would add, must be understood as coordinate with 'him', both being denoted by 'Adam' understood as the name of the human being prior to any separation of woman from man. Levinas could add further perhaps that 'Devil' should be understood as a metaphor of evil more radical than original sin and that 'Satan' should be understood as a symbol for the accusation that one is one's own worst enemy (see the end of the third section of chapter 5 above). And does the original so-called first disobedience in the garden represent an original disobedience and deafness presupposing the pre-original obedience given to a call before the call is heard and understood?

To turn to the Genesis story is not altogether a digression here if it bears witness, as Levinas would claim that it does, to an ethical deep structure or destructuration that admits of abusive expression in philosophical Greek. It is especially relevant at this stage in the narration of the genealogy of ethics, at the moment in the kinematics of the turn from the discrete to the indiscrete presence of the Other, a turn which is always exposed to the risk of a turning back.

Levinas marks the directions and forces of this kinematics by the notions of welcome (*accueil*), approach (*abordement*), opposite (*en face*), and from above (*de haut*). The discrete presence welcomes me privately. I welcome the indiscrete face that approaches and commands me from above. Here the face is indiscrete because public, not because it overcomes my separation from elements or things. Without overcoming the separation constituted by my privacy, it calls that privacy into question from a point of view that is separate in the dimension of height. Its approaching or accosting me from above is contrasted with my approach to things outside and opposite my windows and doors. From within the privacy of my house I can, like Gyges in Plato's *Republic*, look out on the world and assume mastery of things without being seen. That appropriative mastery is challenged by mastery as non-appropriative teaching. The lesson taught by the indiscrete face of the Other is 'Thou shalt not kill', where killing is to be understood in its widest sense as the ethically impossible suppression of the Other's alterity, the reduction of the Other to the same. The only ethically appropriate response I can make to the Other's 'first word' is non-appropriative welcome into my home. This is how 'second donation' can take place. Above and beyond the first donation which is that of giving names, beyond the linguistic representation that being with the feminine Other entails, is the re-presentation of these named and appropriated things to the guest. The thinghood of things is their presence as presents, their aptness for being disappropriated to the Other.

The ego as for-me is enabled by the between-ourselves, *entre nous*, and the for-me and the between-ourselves are accomplished as the self's for-you. But without the self's losing its ego's identity as selfsame. Without that identity it could not cooperate with others in an economy of gathering, manufacture, barter or exchange where goods have a monetary price; it would approach the Other with empty hands and its promises would be empty words. Nor must the ego lose its separateness, for without that it becomes identical with what transcends it, immanence becomes indistinguishable from transcendence, so that it risks identification with the gods of pantheism. The ego must be so abruptly isolated that it runs the risk of atheism. Only so can it run the risk of forgetting the idea of the infinite.

If the idea of the infinite were necessary to its essence as ego, remembering it would be an anamnetic return to itself. The infinite is only truly transcendent when the idea of it is always inadequate to it, and the instruction of an absolute Other is necessary to reawaken it. It is teaching that is necessary here, not midwifery. And if I as pupil am *élève*, the elevation achieved at the sound of the master's voice that hails me from above is not a raising of consciousness through explicitation that merely follows the laws of formal or dialectical logic. 'In order to pass from the implicit to the explicit there has to be a master who appeals for attention' (*TEI* 112, *TI* 138). 'Spirit' here is Cartesian, not Socratic or Hegelian. In this way alone can spirit be creator of the new. Spirit not as consciousness, but spirit as conscience, inspiring shame over my complacent egoism. Spirit otherwise than as that of spiritual idealism. Spirit as *je ne sais quoi*, spirit as I do not know what: absolutely not knowledge, absolutely not what.

Nor who, if the question 'Who?' is in principle answerable by giving a proper name. For although Levinas speaks of the Other, *Autrui*, as master, and although his reference to the feminine presence may seem to imply the presence of a female, he expresses the hope that it goes without saying that his reference to the feminine presence in the house is consistent with there being no female at all present in the house (*EEI* 73, *EI* 70–1). Also, Levinas frequently says that the indiscrete Other, the Other with which the feminine presence of the Other is contrasted, is the stranger, the orphan and the widow. So that if the feminine presence is the presence of *Autrui* and the master is also *Autrui*, it does not follow that *Autrui* is a pronoun replaceable in the first case by the name of a woman and in the second case by the name of a man. The feminine presence and the masculine presence are the presence of *Autrui* in its infinity but with that infinity respectively forgotten and remembered. To say that in the welcome by the feminine presence of the Other infinity is forgotten is to say that my welcome of the infinity of the Other is presupposed as 'the first revelation of the other, supposed in all other relations with him' (*TEI* 171, *TI* 197).

This assertion is repeated in an interview that took place in 1982 and is included in Levinas's *Entre nous*. Asked to explain how he distinguishes *Erôs* from *Agapê*, Levinas now insists that the latter cannot be derived from the former. He says that he once held (*Autrefois, je pensais*) that alterity begins in the feminine. This could be taken to imply that he once held that *Agapê* can be derived from *Erôs*. He attributes to *Time and the Other* the claim that the feminine is alterity itself. He adds that he does not deny this claim now and reminds his interviewer that in *Totality and Infinity* there is a chapter that describes *Erôs* as love which becomes enjoyment whereas *Agapê* springs from responsibility for the Other. Whether or not his reference to what he once thought is an admission that he now thinks otherwise, it is clear that his chief aim at this stage of the interview is to distance himself from what he takes to be the Freudian position that *Agapê* is derived from *Erôs*. This is consistent with the latter being prior to the former in the order of exposition of *Totality and Infinity*, and with Levinas's holding in this book that just as there can be violence only to a being with a face, so too there can be erotic love only of a being with a face, and that *Agapê* is found already bound up with the phenomenology of *Erôs*. The interpretation of Levinas's reply to his interviewer turns on whether it is only to a beginning in the order of exposition that he is referring when he says that he once thought that alterity begins in the feminine. Especially significant for our present purposes however is what he goes on to say immediately after this. The alterity to which he has just referred, he says, is very strange: 'woman is neither the contradictory nor the contrary of man, nor like any other difference. It is not like the opposition of light and shade' (*EN* 131). At the very least this allows for the possibility that the feminine and the masculine are aspects or moments when understood not biologically, but philosophically.

That it would be mistaken to suppose that Levinas's references to the feminine and masculine are references to the biologically female and male is underlined once again when in the fourth section of *Totality and Infinity* the Other is identified with the son in relation to the father and he explains that this relationship is exemplified by that of a pupil to the teacher, where neither term is specifically gendered. As the title of that section states, however, these are relationships 'Beyond the Face'. Because the feminine is treated once again there, it would be relevant to pass directly to an examination of what else he says on that topic in that section now that note has been taken of what he says concerning it in the second section. However, to skip the third section of the book in order to proceed immediately to what is said in the fourth concerning genealogy in the sense of family relationships would run the risk of missing the explanation that the intervening section gives of how the concern with genealogy in that most determinate sense is generated within the genealogy of Levinas's argument. The next chapter will therefore delay the discussion of the topic of the family of man and woman by first reintroducing a topic that has emerged in earlier chapters: the topic of the dynamics of delay.

9 From sensibility to sense

A NEW DIMENSION

Visual representation and enjoyment, touch and work, facilitate a forgetting of the horror of the there-is by enabling separation. The amorphous is succeeded by form and comprehension. But the space across which objects are seen or grasped is not absolute exteriority. That space is the space of the interiority of the Same in which depth is a dimension of being side by side, a third dimension equivalent to laterality perceived from a different point of view. It is the space in which the ego exercises power. Absolute exteriority is a new dimension where depth has no lateral equivalent and where there is no comparison of depth; a dimension beyond measure. Not the interval between a viewpoint and a phenomenal surface or façade, the absolute interval is the face to face.

The face is the place where sight is intersected by speech. Discourse, dis-course, breaks the continuum of the space in which visible and tangible objects are in relation (*rapport*) one with another and can be carried (*rapporté*) within mutual proximity. The proximity of one face to another is one of infinite distance. It is a relation that preserves the separateness of the terms from each other and from the relation itself. This relation of locution dislocates power, despite the fact that it is a relation of orientation, that is to say, a relation in which I look up to the Other rising above me. Orientation, presupposed by occidentality, where language sets into concepts, paralyses the very power to power, Levinas says. It disempowers, one might add, the will to power, the *pouvoir* of *voir*, the faculty of sight, the faculty of light, the faculty of clear ideas. Senseless by the standard of formal logic, it is yet rationality *par excellence* penetrating form: *ratio* in the sense of the ethical regard that one interlocutor must have for another as interlocutor, whatever the message conveyed.

But if this superlative reason is incarnate in a phenomenal face, is not

Levinas confronted with the problem of schematism that confronted Kant, the problem of the union of reason and sensibility that Descartes failed to overcome when he appealed to the pineal gland? Is this problem not posed by Levinas when he says that the face is at the limit between holiness, implying separation, and caricature, implying phenomenal representation? One way of attempting to circumvent this problem is to argue for the irreducibility of the *corps propre*, the body lived as one's own, from which body and mind are unreal abstractions. This is a solution favoured by, for example, Merleau-Ponty.[1] Levinas considers that although this carnative account covers more than the self as 'I think', it does not extend beyond the self as 'I can', the self of possibility, ability, activity and will, the self which on his account is the self of enjoyment, work and perseverence in one's being. It leaves out of account the non-phenomenal face. Instead of saying that the face as expression is incarnate, he prefers to say that it is that by which the self is disincarnate. Like Merleau-Ponty, Levinas is objecting to the typically idealist identification of reason with will, an identification that entails the identification of ethics with politics (*TEI* 192–3, *TI* 216–17). This is already typical of Kantian idealism. For Kant the reason that is architectonic of the mind, reason as faculty of Ideas, is one with the good will. Levinas holds the two apart by grounding will in the lived body of the free agent while positing a reason beyond even the infinite rationality of the Kantian Ideas. Levinas's rational Desire of the Other exceeds Kant's rational will because it is positively infinite, whereas the infinity of the Kantian Ideas is only the negation of finitude. It is positive infinition. Descartes's idea of God is an idea that cannot comprehend infinity because infinity is not its object. It exceeds objecthood, including the noematic objecthood within which it is confined in Husserl's theory of ideas. It exceeds theory and thematization in the Husserlian sense of the word – though not in the emphasized sense given to the word when Levinas writes that a thing is thematized not when it is simply made an object of contemplation but when it is placed at the disposition (*thesis*) of another. That alone is true objectivity, objectivity in which the reference to others that objectivity implies is achieved only through my ability to distance myself from my possessions by offering them to the other through speech (*TEI* 184, *TI* 209). Language is the door through which the other comes in. And indeed Levinas applies the metaphor of the open door to Descartes's positive account of infinity. It is a door through which he himself passes on his way toward his account of infinition. Infinition is the infinition of Desire for the Other, and the infinition of Desire for the Other consists in the increase in responsibility that comes with my response. So that, as distinguished from need, ethical Desire cannot approach satisfaction even asymptotically. The anasymptotic infinition of Desire for the Other means that there is always time for my response – even though my response is always too late.

Yet non-ethical desire or will (*vouloir*), while grounded, as we put it, in the economic self concerned with its own survival and happiness, has an *Abgrund*, a disground, in ethical Desire. For the desire to preserve oneself implies in principle that I may want to kill someone who puts my life at risk. I can want to kill or murder (the distinction seems not to matter here) only a being over whom I can exercise power. I can exercise power only over a being that belongs to the sensible world. But a being that belongs entirely to the sensible world, although a being I can exterminate or destroy, is not one I can want to murder or kill. I can want to murder or kill only a being with a face that expresses itself phenomenally, that is to say, in the physical countenance, while at the same time escapes my power through resisting it not with force but by the first and original expression of the face commanding 'Thou shalt not kill'. This says the same as 'Peace be with you', 'Shalom'. Therefore war presupposes peace. The dialectic of master and slave presupposes the relation of teacher and pupil. It is in the teacher's weakness that resides his or her strength: in the vulnerability of the Other's face which is indeed sensible, but in a manner that permits the Other to preserve his or her independence from my power to slaughter or enslave.

In appealing to me both as height and in the humility of his un-clothedness and hunger, the Other does not limit my freedom. On the contrary, he sets my freedom free. By imposing on me the burden of responsibility, the Other releases me from the anonymous fatality of the burden of being from which enjoyment and work could bring only temporary relief.

I do not escape that fatality and he does not escape my grasp by each of us testing the other's strength of will. For although I may impose my free will, I am not free to prevent my will being alienated by historical, socio-logical and psychoanalytic explanations that bend the motives of my acts and the meanings, the *vouloir dire*, of what I say. My freedom is taken into slavery. And I do not rise above this slavery by courageously willing whatever the other wills for me. For if courage ultimately means willing-ness to die, that too can be what another wills, so that the outcome of my will satisfies his.

However, in view of the corporeity Levinas ascribes to the will, how can an infinite regress of schematisms be avoided, or an endless proliferation of pineal glands? If my free will is conceived as spontaneous causality, its freedom is already prejudiced by my having been thrown willy-nilly into the circumstances in which I find myself born, the *Befindlichkeit* of the *Geworfenheit* of *Being and Time*. This, it may be said, still leaves me with a finite freedom. But how, if the will is incorporated, does its freedom relate to the embodiment by which that freedom is limited? The postulation of a mediating gland, valve or clutch to explain how the limiting factor can gain purchase upon the limited and how agency can to some degree overcome resistance simply turns into the problem as to how the two parts or aspects of the intermediary relate. For an account of freedom one must therefore turn away from causality as *sui generis causa sui*, to non-causal, ethical creation.

And the interpretation of creation as ethics demands a reinterpretation – an interpretation different from that which *Being and Time* gives – of the deferral of death.

THE DEALING OF DEATH

The sensible world makes sense when what is present in it is not simply present to me and its otherness is, like the bread I take into my mouth, digested by the Same. The world takes on meaning and sense through the 'objective spirit' of institutions, but that meaning remains impersonal and without orientation. The sensible world becomes a personal and oriented world only when I, the Same, represent what is present in it to the Other, when egological position is accomplished as apologetic position, thesis in pro-thesis for the Other.

This turning toward the face of the Other, *virage au visage*, is accomplishment through the ambiguity of the will, through the will's two-facedness. Like the Kantian schema, the will is a fusion of sensibility and meaning or sense. It was stated in the first section of this chapter, after a reference to the Kantian Ideas of reason, that whereas Kant identifies the pure will (*Wille*), with pure reason, Levinas locates will in the lived body. The will is corporeal. From this it does not follow that the will is simply opposed to reason. Its corporeality is not simply that of physical matter. Its 'primary qualities' are not simply quantity, energy, mass and suchlike. Lived corporeality is prone to fall under these categories but has at the same time the power to resist them. It can resist the physical resistance of external forces acting upon it by turning a face to the ethical resistance. Like Kant's ambiguous *Willkür*.

This does not mean that my corporate will can turn its face away from the ultimate resistance, my death, which is the ultimate meaning of violence and the meaning that menaces life and the lifeworld with meaninglessness. But meaningfulness is not secured by resolute being towards my death, in the manner described by *Being and Time*. My death is not something – or the nothingness – which I am simply toward. It too is toward and against me. My mortality is lived as menace. I suffer it. It is untoward. It is against my will, most obviously against my will to survive. It is therefore more or less than anxiety before nothingness. More and less. The death of another may appear to be accommodated by the opposition of being and not being, being there and no longer being there. And in the will to murder, Cain's will to murder Abel, death appears as annihilation. But the opposition of being and nothingness does not accommodate the opposition with which I am faced by my death. Death is against me. Its when and whence cannot be foreseen. Because it is beyond every horizon, it cannot be comprehended. In that sense it lacks every sense. Yet this ultimate absurdity ultimately makes sense because it does not lack direction. It is directed precisely at me. But, contrary to what Heidegger writes in *Being and Time*, it is not that which isolates me in my solitude. It does not leave me alone. It is what reveals that in my solitude the Other already attends. He or she attends me as the source of assistance, as comforting friend, as doctor or as the presence of the male or female nurse who waits upon me. But my appeal for assistance is necessary only because the Other also lies in wait, because I am already, already in my being for myself, delivered over to the Other in the hostility of my impending death. Death is not isolation. Death is interpersonal. Terrifyingly. For it is personified in the threat of an alien will.

Nevertheless, the very violence of Cain's murderous will is the source of peace and the resource of meaning in life despite death. For violence is evidence of a humanism of the other human being. Just as violence can be done only to a being with a face, so too can it be perpetrated only by such a being. The counterviolence that the malevolence of death provokes itself evokes the possibility of an alternative to the prosecution of my *conatus essendi*. It is a chance for the pursuit of peace, for saying which, already as a saying, is already a letting there be peace.

THE DELAYING OF DEATH

To allow peace is to allow time. For the will, like the homophonous English auxiliary verb, spells futurition. It implies a consciousness of what is to come. Therefore will, although the spring of violence, is at the same time a haven of non-violence and peace. The will's first impulse is to rush to its own defence against its oncoming death. It first exercises its power in its own cause. But death escapes its power at the last moment. The gap between it and the last enemy is closed from the enemy's side. The consciousness inherent in will does not know this closure. To its last it keeps open a future. The future tense is the tense of presence to conscious-   √ ness. As discourse is already distance from self-possession and presence to self, the present of consciousness is *détente*, distension, detention and delay. Levinas now uses the word 'preparation' which we used above in chapter 3, it will be recalled, in explaining what Levinas means when in *Existence and Existents* he writes of dilatoriness (*paresse*). Discourse, it should also be recalled, is *vouloir dire*, the expression of conscious will and the will to express. So discursive distantiation is temporization. Its distantiation is temporal, where temporal distance is distinguished from spatial distantiation by what Levinas calls the 'interference' – we could say 'interface' – between the movements of my going to my death and death's coming to me (*TEI* 211–12, *TI* 235). Death comes to me from no where, but it does come from someone or, in the case of what is called natural death, it comes as from someone. However, as was said in chapter 5, this evil translates into *éveil*, an awakening to the 'first word' voiced even by someone with murderous intent, the command 'Thou shalt not kill'. This evil, but without malignity vanishing from the scene, translates into good. And my being ethically unfree to turn a deaf ear to this command is   √ discovered to be the condition of the infinitely difficult freedom of my will.

'Thou shalt not kill' reminds me that the possibility of committing murder is implicit in my will to live. But does it not remind me too that that will is served by a willingness to live by letting live? Does not education, if not already plain common sense, inform us that self-interest is best secured by reciprocity within the framework of public institutions and, above all, the law of the land? It is this 'above all' that Levinas questions. In questioning it he questions the ultimacy of the inference Plato makes in the *Republic* from the appeal to Gyges, whose power to see without being seen is invoked frequently in Levinas's own work. Levinas's questioning of the ultimacy of the State is also a questioning of Hegel. Hegel's philosophy of politics, law and history is no less often present in the thoughts of the author of *Totality and Infinity* than is Rosenzweig's opposition to the idea of totality, for this opposition is an opposition to that philosophy. One place where it breaks through the surface of Levinas's book is the final subsection of the third section entitled 'The Truth of Will'. That is already a Hegelian title, but it would have been no less appropriate if Levinas had borrowed from Rosenzweig's works the title 'Hegel and the State'. If *Totality and Infinity* is a section-by-section dissection of *Being and Time*, it is also a running commentary and critique of the idea of infinite totality that is meant to be replaced by the idea of finite wholeness developed in the latter book. While interrupting in mid-flight Heidegger's revision of Hegel's science of the experience of consciousness Levinas's philosophy of experience *par excellence* brings down the owl of Minerva. A genealogy, an analysis of the genesis and structure of Levinas's phenomenology and meta-phenomenology of ethics,[2] could include a section-by-section comparison in double columns of *Totality and Infinity* and the *Phenomenology of Spirit*. Readers familiar with Hegel's text will not fail to pick up Levinas's signals. In the subsection in which he argues that the truth of the will is accomplished in 'the situation that could be called the judgement of God' explicit mention is made of Hegel and his great meditation on freedom.[3]

What force should be attributed to the words 'that could be called' is a question to which we shall return later in this chapter and in the next. It is enough for the purposes of the present chapter to register that Levinas contrasts this judgement with the judgement of history. We already know that Levinas does not deny that the judgement pronounced by political and legal institutions ensures a certain meaningfulness despite death. It ensures it beyond the death of the individual. It therefore ensures it historically; it ensures it over time. But it ensures it through the death of the individual; and it ensures it through dead time. It remembers the life of the person only through his or her works. This memorial interiorization, *Erinnerung*, is an exteriorization that forgets expression in the sense in which Levinas distinguishes expression as speech inspired by the Other from work in which expression is, in both senses of the word, betrayed. Placed at the mercy of alien wills by incorporation in a historical written text, the will of the subject is objectified 'as one nowadays says' (*TEI* 219, *TI* 242). This qualifying phrase warns us that in the text Levinas is writing an emphasized notion of objectification is to be introduced. It will be brought in, however, not at the expense of the contemporary notion. For the inspiration of speech is sober. There is no scent of strong spirit on its breath. Whether and, if so, precisely in what sense it could be said to be enthusiastic still remains to be seen. But it is already quite clear from what Levinas writes that the breath of inspiration is cool. Noumenal it may be if that term may be used in contrast with the term 'phenomenal' to mark that it is rational and in itself. Numinous it is not. And if by mysticism is meant the identification of the Other with the Same, it would do violence to Levinas's text to read into it the idea that the ethical and the mystical are one.[4] By the ethical is meant in his text the fission that defeats final fusion into one, whether that be the one of *das Man*, the one of the impersonality of the *il y a*, or the One of the logic of Parmenides. This does not mean however that the ethical can divert its face from the oneness of uni-versality. The sobriety of inspiration by the Other means agreement with Hegel's assertion, intended as a criticism of Kant, that the good will or respect on their own cannot be equated with freedom. Levinas's agreement with this is manifest in his insistence that the ego, the Same, must become a participant in a socio-political economy if it is to respond to the Other's call. It is banal to say that without this involvement not even the ego's freedom is achieved. And if, in the manner of the Stoic of Hegel's *Phenomenology*, the ego supposes that he can accept hunger, thirst and death without forfeiting the freedom of thought, it has to be recognized that that allegedly private thought itself has as its condition the public institutions of learning and language that are conditions of each other. To cite a British Hegelian and the words he cites from Hegel,

> He learns, or already perhaps has learnt, to speak, and here he appropriates the common heritage of his race. . . . The soul within him is saturated, is filled, is qualified by, it has assimilated, has got its substance, has built itself up from, it *is* one and the same life with the universal life, and if he turns against this he turns against himself; . . . 'he is a pulse-beat of the whole system, and himself the whole system'.[5]

If he is only that, however, the pulse-beat has stopped. Or more exactly, as Levinas writes, his will exists 'as though it were dead and the only signifying open to it would be that which its heritage would mediate' (*TEI* 219, *TI* 242). In appropriating the common heritage it is appropriated by it. The I becomes indifferently the he, she or one of legality and egality. But this is not the only way of signifying open to me. There is a signifying of myself which signifies that I am not the Other's equal, that the egological self does not fulfil itself in the universal one and all of the Parmenidean *hen kai pan*, but empties itself of its egological self incessantly in response to a command from beyond law to which it owes not unicity of identity, but uniqueness of election that makes me the cynosure of an ethical universe in which I am elected not to be saved, but to serve. To 'serve time', but no longer as a prisoner, and not as a slave. For the incessancy of its *kenosis* derives from its being commanded to command. And commanding is the commanding of time: a mastery beyond that of the energetic virile ego at home or at work; a mastery where power is neither will to power of the ego over what is other than it in a relation of force against force, allergy, nor passive power still within an allergic relation. The passive power of this mastery is otherwise passive, non-allergically passive, passive like the patience of Job. But because non-allergic patience is waiting in the sense both of waiting for and waiting on, it is summoned to summon up the resources of its energic ego as gift without gratitude in return. Even without the expectation of forgiveness, for the exigency of its obligation to apologize increases in direct proportion to the degree to which it takes that obligation on. 'The better I accomplish my duty, the fewer my rights; the more just I am, the more culpable I am' (*TEI* 222, *TI* 244). But the tribunal according to which the duty, rights, justice and guilt here referred to are defined is not that of a system of ethics or law or custom (*Sittlichkeit*). It is that of 'what might be called the judgement of God'.

EXPERIENCE *PAR EXCELLENCE*

This so-called judgement of God is Goodness. The incomparability of this judgement, of this primary separation (*Ur-teil*), the incomparable condition of all comparison, grading and value, Height beyond heights, like Plato's Table beyond tables – and like the Table of which even the tablet of Moses is one among other codifications? – may be compared with the incomparability of the veracity of God in the *Meditations* of Descartes. Metaphysical, beyond being and being's truth, veracity is the condition of all truth. But in the meditations of Levinas at least, veracity is a condition both as a *sine qua non*, and a condition in the sense in which one speaks of the human condition. It is a condition in both senses because, to apply to him a phrase Rosenzweig applies to himself, it is a condition of Levinas's 'absolute empiricism'. Levinas is concerned that his reader should not mistake the status of his claims. Like Heidegger and Husserl and Frege, he insists that they are not to be taken as psychological, sociological, biological or even anthropological remarks in so far as these adjectives define areas of purported scientific factuality. That is why in *Totality and Infinity* he asserts repeatedly that he is distinguishing ontological structures or ways of being. Unless one grasps that when Levinas asserts this he is continuing a tradition to which Heidegger belongs, one will be perplexed as to how that book can be so critical of ontology. There is no reason why Levinas should not make ontological criticisms of fundamental ontology. But the ontology he defends in that book is not fundamental ontology in what he takes to be the sense ontology has in *Being and Time*. Levinas's ontology calls into question the fundamentality of the 'ontological difference', the distinction between being and beings, between the ontological and the ontic, upon which *Being and Time* takes its stand. As previously noted, Levinas's ontology stands for the ontological significance of concrete empirical, hence ontic, experience. Whether or not Heidegger does too is not a question we shall reopen here. We touched on that question in chapter 7, where we also observed that in *Totality and Infinity* and some of his essays Levinas writes of what he calls contextless experience and experience *par excellence*. This would not be experience in the usual sense of empirical experience. It would be, we might say, the quasi-transcendental condition of such experience. Quasi-transcendental if a transcendental condition is an analytic or synthetic a priori formal presupposition. What Levinas counts to be experience *par excellence* subverts formality while making it possible. Absolute *empeiria* does not fall without remainder within the empire of eidetic universality or form. It rends form and renders it impossible as *virgo intacta* or *vir intactus*.

The face that accuses cannot, as accusing face, be cast into the accusative, cannot be categorized or objectified, for it is the quasi-transcendental condition of objectivity. Yet its force as a quasi-transcendental, ontological or quasi-ontological condition of the ontic depends on my experience of the ontic for its concreteness, since it is affection, sensibility, and a posteriori in its apriority. Its way of being, its ontological status, is that of the ontic. That is its condition, in the sense the word 'condition' has in the phrase 'human condition', as mentioned a moment ago. It *is* the human condition. And it is the condition of God de-picted in Exodus 33:23 as one who exits, one whose face is invisible, one who leaves only a trace, one who has already gone before, one of whom we see only the back parts, a posteriori. This condition of God without divinity, without the imperialism of *eidos*, genus and universality is the human condition. Not in the sense that the human being fulfils its being only when that being is increased in mass – or in Mass – by the being of God. It could be said (and more will be said about this in Part III) that in Levinas's ethics without divinity the name of God is invoked as a metaphor of the infinite metaphorization to which the other human being calls the self, as God called to Adam 'Where art thou?' and to Abram 'Get thee out of thy country.' The first time I call something by a name I already distance myself from my self in the generality of genus and species. But in responding to the call of the other human being I am calling time itself into being. I have already taken another step, the *pas encore* of a 'not yet' that is not a promise of progress toward a greater being or Being, not fulfilment, satisfaction and repletion, but a vocation from the other side of an infinite vacancy, e-vidence, opened up in my being and my being toward my death. Being toward being or nothingness, becoming myself and passing away, being, nothingness and becoming are suspended by the to-come, *à-venir*, *Zu-kunft*, the arrival from the other shore (*de l'autre rive*), of *Autrui*, the Other who will always have not yet arrived.

The Other will always have not yet arrived because my responsibility is never fulfilled. The ultimate reason why my responsibility is never fulfilled is that my absolute responsibility is inclined to become confused with relative responsibility determined by the law that defines my station and its duties. So it is not enough to say, as we said earlier, that the reason why my responsibility increases is that each time I meet an obligation to one person I incur obligations to the many others in whose lives my action has repercussions. The infinition of relative responsibility, the responsibility of plural responsibilities, is indeed the concretization of the infinition of absolute responsibility – and it deserves to be repeated that concretization (*con-crescere*), means 'increase and growth'. If the Other is responsible for me and other Others, and I am responsible for his responsibilities, my responsibility waxes greater than his. But absolute responsibility is responsibility before the law. It is responsibility not directly to law, not even to the moral law, but responsibility to law – the law of law – only because it is responsibility to the face, responsibility to face a face, to save it from effacement in (l)egality. It is responsibility to save the face from becoming only a case. This always impending danger is exemplified in the difficulty touched upon above of avoiding a sort of type-fallacy with regard to the Mosaic law. How can the Ten Commandments of the tablets of Moses be only an ectype of the archetypical command when one of those ten, 'Thou shalt not kill' (or 'Love thy neighbour'), is cited by Levinas to express that archetypical command? Even the sanctity of expression seems to be put at risk here, in that it appears to be in danger of becoming identified with the expressed. It appears, apparently, and becomes phenomenon, a graven image such as another of the Commandments on the tablet self-referentially forbids. This Levinas does not deny. On the contrary, it is part of what is affirmed in his notion of the enigma, the ambivalence by which a trace may masquerade as a sign and by which the He of illeity may be taken for an It. It is precisely the predicament of citation, a predicament from which the only chance of exit is recitation, going out to the face of the Other, welcoming exile, saying 'Here, send me', obeying the law of the endless deconstrual and reconstrual of law, moving from place to place time and time again.

This again is the again of 'the agenbyte of inwyt'. Conscience is the spur to follow the primal trace, the *Spur*, to borrow Heidegger's word, of the Levinasian trace that 'remains preserved' less in 'the language to which Being comes' than in the appeal with which the face of the Other comes to me.[6] Absolute conscience, that reminds me that though I cede my place to others, I still keep a place in the sun for myself, so that I can never apologize sufficiently.

And again, I can never apologize sufficiently because each and every other is the Other, *Autrui*, so that the Other will always have not yet arrived. Every day he and she will be on the way, *immer unterwegs*. The party to end all parties that will welcome him and her into my home, the time of the goodness of welcome (*bienvenue*), and the moment of the goodness of time (*kairos*), will be adjourned from day to day.

Further, is not a peculiar difficulty presented by the call that Abram hears? Is not his difficult freedom exposed to the specific difficulty that absolute empiricism, in requiring absolute experience and absolutely non-literal veracity to be verified by the evidence of which it is the condition, must run the risk that the evidence will falsify that absolute experience, render it null and void? Otherwise put, if ontological metaphorization owes its concreteness to its onticity, must not some of its metaphors be bad? This is a question that some of our later chapters will treat in general terms. But it is raised specifically by the example we have taken to illustrate and concretely produce what Levinas calls 'what might be called the judgement of God', the absolute call of the Other. For when we read on in Genesis 12:1, 2, we learn that Abram, the lofty father, was commanded to depart from his father and the rest of his kin, and was in the course of time to become the leader of a nation and renamed Abraham, meaning 'father of multitudes'. How can Abraham's turning his back on his own family be a metaphor of the obligatoriness *par excellence* that in the fourth section of *Totality and Infinity* Levinas goes on to describe in the language of family ties? And how will Levinas show that the time of national history and the time of face-to-face presentation must be taken another step back, a *pas encore*? How will he show that those times have to be taken back to the 'not yet', to the *pas encore* of the 'first phenomenon of time' in which the time of history and the time of the face to face have a common root in paternity beyond the face without which time – even the time of the face to face! – would be no more than the image of eternity?

10 Generations

ABSOLUTE EMPIRICISM

The most profuse apologies are never enough. Not only because my apology is an *apologia pro vita mea*, as though what mattered most was my achieving a clean slate; or because there is another stranger alongside the stranger to whom my apology is made and to whom I give the bread that was on the point of becoming a part of me. But also because there is a stranger beyond the stranger, beyond his face, and beyond the feminine presence by which I am welcomed in the home before I leave it and go abroad. This is the face of Adam's helpmeet, and of the wife of the nomad Abraham, who asked in the tent 'After I am waxed old shall I have pleasure, my lord being old also?' (Genesis 18:13). It could be said that femininity is habitation itself (*DL* 54, *DF* 33), that Eve *is* the fruitful garden and Sarah *is* the tent, and that the garden and the tent are metaphors of the home from which metaphor takes leave, metaphors of metaphors therefore, and of metaphor as such, if home is a metaphor for the zero point of origin, absolutely literal or, in the case or non-case of the face, absolutely non-literal, away from which the metaphor is said to range. But lest it be said that these metaphors themselves are too homely, and that ontic concretization should range further abroad than the history of Judaism if it is to sustain its claim to ontological force, an illustration from a different culture should be risked.

Consider the Tibetan Paramasukha–Chakrasamvara painted cloth icon (*tangka*) of the late fifteenth to early sixteenth century in the Robert Hatfield Ellsworth Private Collection. This icon represents the Buddha as the union of Father and Mother, which is to say, the union of Compassion and Wisdom. One commentator writes:

> Wisdom comes through experiencing the perfect 'transparency' of the self, which leads to utter freedom from self-concern. Such transparency

of self gives a clear view of others; such freedom from self-concern makes room for concern for others. Wisdom is the bliss of seeing through the delusion of self-preoccupation to reveal the underlying dimension of freedom. Compassion is the expression of such bliss to others. Compassion is also sensitivity to others' suffering. It sees them imprisoned in self-involvement, and reaches out to show the way to freedom.[1]

This reaching out is most characteristic of Mahayana Buddhism with its idea of the Bodhisattva who postpones his own liberation in order to help others to obtain theirs. It may well be that this conception of social messianism is in significant respects different from that on which Levinas will touch at the end of the section of *Totality and Infinity* that our survey of that book has now reached. It may well be doubted whether the notion of the loss of self is compatible with Levinas's notion of the wisdom of love in which the self or Same remains separate from the Other. It may however be pleaded that such lack of correspondence can be tolerated and set aside. With any analogy there will be some failure of fit. One has to pick and choose. And where one metaphor breaks down it will have to be mixed with another. When it is asked by what criterion this picking and mixing is guided, one may begin to wonder whether ontic concretization of the ontological need take the form of appealing to narratives or myths at all, whether these be drawn from the Far East, the Near East, the West or the Near East-and-West of which Greece is one among other hubs – always supposing that the analogy of the hub is not here an oversimplification, and there would certainly be an oversimplification if this analogy were applied to the idea of Israel. To the question 'How do you reconcile the phenomenological and religious dimensions of your thinking?' put to him in a dialogue with Richard Kearney Levinas responds:

> I always make a clear distinction, in what I write, between philosophical and confessional texts. I do not deny that they may ultimately have a common source of inspiration. I simply state that it is necessary to draw a line of demarcation between them as distinct methods of exegesis, as separate languages. I would never, for example, introduce a Talmudic or biblical verse into one of my philosophical texts, to try to prove or justify a phenomenological argument.[2]

Levinas is not saying here that he would never introduce a Talmudic or biblical verse into one of his philosophical texts. He does that often, though often in parentheses or footnotes. He is saying that he would never do so in order to try to prove or justify a phenomenological argument. Although this would leave room to introduce such verses to prove or justify any non-phenomenological arguments his philosophical texts might contain, that he wants to say that he would not do that either is put beyond doubt by his statement earlier in this reply that he makes a sharp distinction between confessional and philosophical texts, not just philosophical texts of the phenomenological kind.

What about the mythological and literary references that Levinas makes, for example the references to Ulysses, the symbol of homecoming, as contrasted with Abraham, to Deucalion, to Antigone, to Dostoevsky, to Shakespeare's Hamlet and Macbeth, to Rimbaud, who provides the first words of the first section of *Totality and Infinity*, and to Baudelaire, who provides some of the words of the concluding sentence of the book's conclusion? Various functions are performed by these references and citations. For example, 'The true life is absent', from the first of Rimbaud's 'Délires' entitled 'Vierge folle. L'époux infernal', gives voice to the indeterminate sentiment of the meta- of metaphysics that the metaphysics of Levinas will determine as the 'beyond the face'.[3] The couplet from one of Baudelaire's poems entitled 'Spleen', 'tedium, fruit of the mournful incuriosity that takes on the proportions of immortality', makes vivid the reason why the heroic pursuit of salvation for oneself is as deceptive a response to the malaise Rimbaud puts into words as is the self-destruction contemplated by Macbeth. But voicing, making vivid, illustrating, symbolizing and so on, are ways of justifying, if not proving, by making concrete the psychological and other empirical facts of which Levinas aims to bring out the ontological significance. It is because ontological significance is presumably of wider scope than significance confined to one culture that variation of the cultural sources from which the illustrations and symbols are drawn increases the probative force of the argument into which the latter are introduced. Not simply on account of the increase of the scope of the evidence, but also because in increasing the scope of the illustrations one increases the risk of disconfirmation. This is one reason why the Paramasukha–Chakrasamvara *tangka* was introduced into our exegesis of Levinas's argument. However, the increase in the scope of the illustrations entails too an increase in the possibility that although the author may succeed in making only non-evidential and non-argumentative references to what are for him confessional texts by 'mentioning' them only rather than 'using' them, and by mentioning them only parenthetically and in passing, for some of his readers the illustrations that for him are deemed purely literary, therefore allowed to have at least indirect evidential force in his philosophical argument, will be confessional and holy. Hence by Levinas's embargo they will be disqualified from having such force in their judgement of the validity of his argument. For a Tibetan Buddhist the Paramasukha–Chakrasamvara *tangka* is likely to carry the religious significance that would disqualify it from functioning as phenomenological evidence for him unless he could neutralize the religious significance. He would have to neutralize it however without naturalizing the *tangka* or its description, that is to say, without adopting toward it the so-called 'natural attitude' of objectivating science. The phenomenological attitude, assuming there is only one, lies between these extremes. This is the interval where Levinas's absolute empiricism is accomplished, absolved both from matters of confessional faith and from matters of naturalistic fact. This is the space which allows eidetic phenomenology to claim to be more empirical than classical empiricism for which synthesis is purely psychological association. This is the 'everyman's land' by occupying which Levinas's empiricism can claim to be truer to the Facts Themselves (the *Sachen selbst*) than eidetic phenomenology because it faces the non-phenomenological presentation of the face of the Other. Its genealogy of ethics is as terrestrial as Nietzsche's genealogy of morals.

> The face in which the Other – the absolutely other – presents himself does not negate the Same, does not do violence to it as do opinion or authority or the thaumaturgic supernatural. It remains commensurate with him who welcomes it; it remains terrestrial.
>
> (*TEI* 177, *TI* 203)

The 'noumenal' face is not faced in numinous fear and trembling. Its traumatism is without thaumatism. It is not the face of a being behind the scenes. It is on the scene, as much a family scene as the Freudian scene – though another scene (to which we shall return below in the last 'scene' of our last 'act'). The Paramasukha–Chakrasamvara *tangka* presents the trauma and the drama of the domestic down-to-earth scene to which Levinas's genealogy beyond the face owes its birth.

PRENATAL CARE

According to the analysis of *Dasein* in *Being and Time* the anxious care for being that is a possibility of *Dasein*'s being toward its death is not care for a determinate object. Nor is it a determinate object that troubles voluptuousness according to the genetic analysis of the erotic in *Totality and Infinity*. The exotic in the erotic is unformalized and unformed. Its pre-conceptuality is represented in the temporality of the fatherhood–motherhood of the Ellsworth painting. For what this icon most strikingly displays is sexual union, not birth. She, Vajravarahi, is all red except for her hair, which is black, and black is the predominant colour of her consort Shamvara, as though wisdom is penetrated by compassion. She has her back to us, but she looks upward to his face and above. He, all hands, embraces her with two of them, but he has five other pairs with which to indulge in 'a mere random groping' after wisdom, like Kant's searcher after knowledge before the sure path of science has been found and search is *ein blosses Herumtappen*.[4] However, he is four-faced. One of his faces is red, as though compassion takes on the colour of wisdom. It could be said that his lateral faces look to the other Others, that the face at the back looks to his progenitors, and that his frontal face looks through her and us to posterity. All the faces of Father Shamvara have a third eye, 'an eye too many', like King Oedipus.[5] What is the meaning of that? Is it the eye of patient, passionate, compassionate conscience that, like the eye of wisdom, looks up? To ask this is to speculate about speculation. It is to perform an imaginative variation – but remembering that for Husserl imagination is the motor of phenomenology. It is iconographic play, the random groping of foreplay. And it gives a second reason for invoking a work of plastic art: to provoke the question whether its rhythmic plasticity is plastic enough to take the imprint and impregnation of ethics; to probe Levinas's non-confessional texts to try to extort from them the confession that the work of art as interlude can be at least a prelude to the 'serious matter' of ethics. Is it not Levinas himself who tells us that the erotic prefigures or mirrors the serious face of ethics when he says that voluptuousness, as distinguished from the enjoyment of things and their disembodied qualities, is possible only where there is a face? So whether the aesthesis of the work of art is ethical sensibility – aesth-ethical, whether the beholder of it is beholden by it, will turn on whether the work of art turns a face to him or her, whether it can be an expression of ethical welcome, as Levinas seems to allow when he agrees with Paul Celan that there is no difference between a poem and a handshake (see the fifth section of chapter 14 below).[6]

Levinas seems to allow also that although there is a difference between the handshake and the caressing hand, the latter is not opposed to the former, but pre- and post-supposes it. The straight face of ethics is pre- and post-figured in the playfulness and laughter of voluptuous *jouissance*.

The joy of this voluptuous *jouissance* is not to be confused with the joy that has been referred to a few pages earlier (*TEI* 220, *TI* 242) before mention has been made of the sensual and sexual relations with the other. That would be to confuse the more confused joy of sexual fusion with the joy of religious sensibility where the fission between my singular self and the Other is more sharply defined because religious sensibility affirms itself against the tyranny of universal law in which the singularity of the subjective will would be dissolved. A stay of this perdition is accomplished through the maintenance of my separateness from the Other that nevertheless maintains my communication with the Other in apologetic discourse addressed to him under 'what might be called the judgement of God' and, thanks be to that, in truth. Joy in apology before the Other's face may not yet be the joy of *felix culpa* that will flow back over apology when apology is answered from beyond the face by forgiveness. One suspects, even so, that of this last felicity and of the pleasure of sensual *jouissance* leading on up to it, Levinas would say what he says of joy in apology spoken before the Other's face: that it is neither the cessation of nor in opposition to pain or grief (*douleur*).

One cannot but wonder, however, about the order of this 'leading on up'. For although we are going to be shown in the last section of *Totality and Infinity*, entitled 'Beyond the Face', how, phenomenologically rather than biologically, sensual and sexual tenderness finds itself with child, this gentleness has already been encountered in the welcome of the feminine presence in the interiority of the home as described in the section entitled 'Interiority and Economy'. It is from the home that the ego goes out apologetically and in due course beyond the face. So that the 'not yet' of offspring beyond the face is in some sense already resident in the home, and perhaps has a place prepared for it before the abode in the foreboding of the *il y a*. So that when *Totality and Infinity* has been read it has to be read again from back to front. This is not an uncommon requirement. It applies, for example, to Kant's *Critique of Pure Reason* and his Critical *Gesamtwerk*, to Hegel's *Phenomenology of Spirit*, to Husserl's *Logical Investigations* and to Heidegger's *Being and Time*.[7] The challenge is to understand the 'already' of *Totality and Infinity* otherwise than it is understood by Kant, Hegel and Husserl, in a wise that marks the reasons why Levinas punctuates the tidal advance of that book by phrases like 'and this is a new dimension', in a wise, that is to say, that explains how his 'already' is compatible with his 'not yet'.[8] Maybe the gesture he makes in the direction of Descartes is the most helpful pointer he gives to a way away from the one followed by those other philosophers, away from the task of breaking into the hermeneutic circle in the right way that Heidegger places on his own agenda (*SZ* 153) and, following Schleiermacher and Dilthey, on the agenda of every reader of every book.[9] In appealing to the *Meditations* of Descartes Levinas is not perhaps proposing the simple alternative agenda which according to Heidegger is never decisive, namely that of breaking out from the circle and out of the book. Yet he is proposing something that has an 'almost absolute proximity' to what the author of *Being and Time* describes as 'a remarkable "relatedness backward or forward" which what we are asking about (being) bears to the inquiry itself as a mode of being of an entity' (*SZ* 8). Whether we judge that Levinas could have used these words of *Totality and Infinity* will depend on which of the many senses of 'being' we attribute to that word. We shall return to that tantalizing question of being yet again in due course, but it is time to say that the question of the question itself is one that is no less decisive.

EROT(ET)OLOGY

The way into *Being and Time* is precisely through the opening of the question, through, as Heidegger here observes, the inquiry or, better, through inquiry as such as a mode of being of *Dasein*. Already in the second section of the first part of the Introduction an erotetic phenomenology is outlined. The formal structure of the question is said to relate a *Gefragtes*, a *Begragtes* and the *Erfragte*. Supported by what Heidegger goes on to say, the translators list these respectively as that which is asked about, that which is interrogated, and that which is to be found out by asking. One might well wonder why no place in this formal structure seems to be allowed for *who* asks or is asked. Admittedly, it is the structure of the specific question of being and hence of *Dasein*, the who, that is the topic of this analysis. And the analysis owes some of the concreteness Heidegger requires of his analysis to the ontic-existentiell relation he as author bears to his reader. The question Levinas would still ask is whether Heidegger's ontological analysis of that relation can do justice to what he, Levinas, means by the face to face. As ontological in one of the senses Heidegger's Introduction gives to that word, that is to say as 'a *theoretical* inquiry which is explicitly devoted to the meaning of entities' (*SZ* 12; emphasis added), the face to face is missed, recycled and metabolized in the hermeneutic intestine.

Another question Levinas would ask, as will become clearer when we go on to consider *Otherwise than Being*, is whether the question that may or may not be followed by an answer is always preceded by a certain response. Before any question has been put a response has already been given. There has already been the offer of an unrefusable gift. It is true that in his lectures of 1929 and 1930[10] and elsewhere Heidegger too treats of address and gift that is not the address and gift of the question. But in his treatment of them the address and the gift are the address and the gift of being. Whereas what Levinas is pointing to, for example when he points to Descartes, is address that is gift of the self, as this is given when, as though lifting his pen from the page and envisaging his prospective reader, he says to him or her: 'Philosophy itself constitutes a moment of this temporal accomplishment, a discourse always addressed to another. What we are now exposing is addressed to those who shall wish to read it' (*TEI* 247, *TI* 269).

This envisaging of prospective readers is a looking forward to persons not here and now present, perhaps to persons not yet even born. Both looking ahead and looking at are *Anschauung*. This is the Germanic equivalent of the Latinate *Intuition* used by Husserl in stating the 'principle of all principles' according to which 'theory itself . . . could not derive its truth except from primordial data' (*Ideas*, vol. I, §24). This would be the test then of the Heideggerian ontological inquiry whose theoretical status we emphasized above. Levinas's testing of that theory 'emphasizes' the theo- retical again by proposing an alternative account of what is primordially given in which *theôria*, *Intuition* and *Anschauung* are traced back from what is speculatively or contemplatively looked at to the regard of or beyond the face. The given is in the first place a giving, and first-order presence is the presence of the Other. This may be a presence across time. Indeed, it is one of the aims of the fourth section of *Totality and Infinity* to persuade its prospective reader that it is generations to come that generate time. Since pupils and prospective readers exemplify what Levinas means by oncoming generations, it is clear that biology functions here as a metaphor or metonym or, more strictly, synecdoche, for although bio- logical generation is not all that is intended, it is not entirely excluded. This is evident from the explanation that 'What we are concerned with is paternity of which biological fecundity is only one form and which, as original effectuation of time, can, with human beings, be supported by biological life but is lived beyond that life' (*TEI* 225, *TI* 247). This *se vivre au delà* of the concept of paternity is itself a metaphor (but more will be said below in chapters 13 and 14 about metaphor) of the survival Levinas mentions a few sentences earlier when he writes that 'The fecundity of subjectivity by which the I survives itself [*se survit*] is a condition for the truth of subjectivity as clandestine judgement of God.' The juxtaposition of these sentences underlines the 'remarkable "relatedness backward or for- ward" which what [Levinas is] asking about . . . bears to the inquiry itself as a mode of being of an entity'. The fecundity and begetting under investigation include that of the discourse in which that investigation is being conducted. This discourse, we must not forget, includes what sur- vives all inclusion, namely the infinity of the giving, forgiving and address offered according to Levinas's reading of Descartes by the absolutely Other who is revealed to have already pronounced to the meditating ego what could be called the judgement of God. If the very expressing of that judgement is expressed through the words 'Thou shalt not kill', that judge- ment owes some of its force to generations to come. For to kill the person facing me is to kill the multiple generations to which he or she might have given birth. This fact immediately engages my will in a depth of responsibility it would not have if the future were that of a historical destiny determined either by the wills only of others or by a general will defined by universal laws which, rational and reasonable though they may be, silence the apology I am still able to make for myself before the face of others up to my death, *fino alla morte.*

But is my defence finally reduced to silence and absurdity by my death? Not if I remember that more fearful than my death is the risk that I might bring death upon the Other. Not if, since the commandment not to kill is embraced by the commandment to love the other as myself, I myself bury my love of my self in a love for the Other that goes on producing itself in truth in the ambiguous phenomenological-ontological sense attributed to production in the preface of *Totality and Infinity* as the accomplishment of something's being and appearing, and, in the light of what is said later in the book, as the accomplishment of something's having its say, its *se dire* (*TEI* 231, *TI* 253).

THE ANALOGY OF LOVING

If production is ambiguous, so too is love. Love is one form of production. How does amorous production have its say? Does amorous production have its say in amorous reproduction? Why is the ambiguity of love referred to in the title of a subsection of the fourth section of *Totality and Infinity* not defined there by the distinction between *erôs* and *agapê* – although, as we saw above in section 4 of chapter 8, Levinas speaks about this distinction when asked to do so in an interview that took place in 1982. It is unlikely that Levinas avoids the word *agapê* in this book because it tends to be used of a Christian concept of love and because he wants to privilege Judaic conceptions. In his philosophical texts, he insists, no especially oriental wisdom is being invoked. He aims to expound their philosophy as far as possible in the concepts of the language from which the word 'philosophy' itself springs. So although the word *agapê* too belongs to that lexicon and is not uncommon in Plato, the risks of its Greek meanings becoming charged with Christian ones are indeed avoided by avoiding the word. But that avoidance is not a precaution which he takes in order to facilitate his speaking Hebrew in *Totality and Infinity*. This is a book in which any gesture that might be deemed characteristically Judaic is to be expressed in 'Greek', that is to say, in the language of the West. Not that no risks are run by love's Latinization as *amour* (or indeed its Germanic Anglicization as 'love'!). At least some of the force of the

Christian conception and the Judaic conception that is one of its roots, for instance, Leviticus 19:18, is preserved in Levinas's notion of the welcome of the Other. And 'welcome' is given by Liddell and Scott as one of the senses of *agapê*. For welcome of the Other Levinas uses the word 'Desire', usually written with a capitalized initial. But in *Totality and Infinity* at any rate this is not identified with *amour*. It is, however, connected with it:

> The metaphysical event of transcendence – the welcome of the Other, hospitality – Desire and language [*langage*] – is not accomplished in love. But the transcendence of discourse is tied to love. We shall show how, through love, transcendence goes at the same time further and less far than language.
>
> (*TEI* 232, *TI* 254)

The true language of love is neither just the serious words of ethical Desire nor just the sweet nothings spoken by Eros, the *doux rien* of Mallarmé's *L'après-midi d'un faune* from which Levinas cites. Paradoxical though it may seem, it is in equivocity that the language of love is true to itself. On the one hand, as love for a friend, a child, a brother, the beloved, one's parents, love is transcendence toward discourse with the Other, transcendence toward the transcendence of discourse where this latter genitive is a subjective genitive referring to the transcendence that belongs to discourse. But love is also transcendence toward the transcendence of discourse where the genitive is understood subjectively. That is to say, the transcendence that is Desire, face-to-face presence and direct speech is opened through love to an ever more future future beyond the face, beyond discourse and beyond Desire: the Desire of Desire which is more remote than the remotest possibility. But it is opened to this transcendence of transcendence because, on the other hand, love's transcendence toward the Other, toward Desire, is prone to gravitate toward an immanence in which the intentionality outwardly directed toward the beloved is inverted inward as if to the lover. Levinas cites the myth recounted in Plato's *Symposium* by Aristophanes according to which the satisfaction of erotic love is the reunion of the separate parts of a single androgynous being. In Aristophanes' version of the myth the parts, once separated, are turned back to back. It is important to note that in the 'judaic' version some commentators see in the story of the creation of Adam and Eve, the partners remain face to face. The two aspects or sides, in French, *faces*, of the original androgynous being are two faces, *visages* (*DL* 56, *DF* 35). Referring to the same myth earlier in *Totality and Infinity* Levinas suggests that Plato's rejection of it may be interpreted as a recognition that the account of love as pure nostalgia overlooks its relation to transcendent Desire (*TEI* 34–5, *TI*

63). Love of a person remains love for a transcendent Other, hence does not allow satisfaction, yet it gravitates toward need, hence toward what allows satisfaction. Since it is the ego persisting in the enjoyment of its immanent being that has needs, the need for another in *enjoyment* of the Other is a quasi-need or, as Levinas says, on the hither side of need; and its immanence is not quite immanence, because it is an enjoyment *of the Other*. From this coalescence of what is on the hither side of immanence and on the thither side of face-to-face transcendence arises what is neither just being nor just not being, but that which is not yet.

Except that this 'that which' is not a this or a that. Light comes, but nothing comes to light. The not yet is essentially secret, essentially without essence and signification. This non-signifying is not simply darkness understood as the absence of light. The non-significance of the secret is not non-appearance. It is the equivocity of non-appearance in appearance, and the simultaneity of appearance and non-appearance is what constitutes profanation and conditions equivocity itself. The equivocal is the erotic, and erotic love is at once immodesty and modesty. The density of the non-significance of the way of being of erotic love – akin to the darkness of the night of the *il y a* in which the insomniac hears only noises that make no sense, where there is no one to be given a name and nothing with a form to be laid bare or disrupted – is lightened by the tenderness with which love responds to the Other's fragility, so that the epiphany of the Other who is loved is the epiphany of the Other as feminine.

Levinas's phrase *l'Aimé qui est Aimée* confirms again that his topic here is the feminine, not the female, in contrast to Nietzsche's topic in the section of *Ecce Homo* entitled 'Why I Write Such Good Books'. But both Nietzsche and Levinas are commenting upon, in Derrida's words, 'the complicity (rather than the unity) between woman, life, seduction, modesty – all the veiled and veiling effects' of truth.[11] However, Derrida goes on, spurred by the opening words of *Beyond Good and Evil*,

> Woman (truth) will not be pinned down. In truth woman, truth will not be pinned down.
>
> That which will not be pinned down by truth is, in truth – *feminine*. This should not, however, be hastily mistaken for a woman's femininity, for female sexuality, or for any other of those essentializing fetishes which might still tantalize the dogmatic philosopher, the impotent artist or the inexperienced seducer who has not yet escaped his foolish hopes of capture.
>
> (*Spurs*, p. 55)

Essentially fetishized truth may be the truth of what is said or left unsaid. It

may be the dis-closive truth of *a-lêtheia* which according to Heidegger lies
under the truth of what is said or left unsaid. Levinas's complication of the
Aimé and the *Aimée* and his statement that the essence of the non-essence
of the 'not yet' is exhausted by clandestinity are in their turn challenges to
the essentialist fetishization of the feminine and truth. One of the remarkable aspects of his challenge, however, is that as well as emphasizing
the equivocity of the said, the *dit*, it emphasizes the equivocity of the to-say,
the '*dire*' – though the appearing–disappearing effect of the inverted commas here must not be overlooked. They signal the appearance–
disappearance of the frank face-to-face *dire* of which more will be said in
the book whose title announces that it treats of what is *Otherwise than
Being*. Whereas *dire* is frank saying, the saying of '*dire*' plays hide and
seek with the truth; the presence of its truth is the presence in absence of the
feminine whose indiscrete and wanton immodesty presupposes discrete
modesty and the tenderness of her welcoming presence in the house.

   In the intimacy of the house the care of the lover's response addresses
the vulnerability of femininity in the indulgent compassion of the caress.
The caress is hungry to express its love but its hunger feeds on its failure. ✓
Once more, the desire that moves it, desire written with a lower-case initial,
is to be distinguished from the Desire that Levinas writes with an upper-
case initial. For it is a desire that can be satisfied, whereas Desire cannot.
The distinction does not however exclude a connection. This is exhibited in
the way that the desire animating the caress is reborn even in its satisfaction, fed by what is not yet, which is not an anticipated possibility nor pure
Desire of Desire, but the to-come of a future to come beyond every future:
ever violable yet inviolate virginity. The flesh the caress explores is not that
of the lived body of possibility, of power, of the 'I can'. Nor is it that of the
physiological body. Nor again is it, in Merleau-Ponty's words, that of the
body as expression or speech,[12] or, as Levinas says, the body as face – for,
as Levinas also says, it is not only to the physiognomy that the face
corresponds; it may be, for example, a hand or the stooping shoulders of the
person in front of you in the queue for water or bread (*TEI* 240, *TI* 262); or
a rib (*SS* 134, *NTR* 169). The flesh of the beloved feminine presence–
absence over which the caress roves is the flesh of the body whose erotic   ✓
nudity is denuded of form in a swooning evanescence foreshadowing the
stroke of death. It is not an entity, then, not a being, that these searching
hands stroke. They are without object, like the enjoyment of pure elemental
quality, and the *apeiron* of the there-is. No thing and no person is grasped.
But these same hands are the hands that offer and receive the handshake of
welcome – the handshake, incidentally, to which a poem may be compared,
not least *The Poem of Poems*, *The Song of Songs*, in which the liaison

between divine and erotic love is explored. And the welcome expressed in the grasp of a hand infinitely exceeds any grasp and calls to be expressed again and again. Between that ethical infinity with its never present, never representable or recollectable past and the ever more future future of erotic aesthesis there is a family connection whose genealogical ramifications are slightly simplified if we say, as we have said on the basis of what is said in *Totality and Infinity*, that they can be marked by the transition from lower-case desire to upper-case Desire and Desire of Desire.

That there is a transition to mark is apt to escape one's notice, for reasons on which Levinas elaborates in the essay entitled 'God and Philosophy' published a year after the year (1974) in which *Otherwise than Being* was published, though based on lectures delivered in the same and preceding years. It is not through lack of vigilance that Levinas there uses both a lower-case and an upper-case initial when referring to the desirability and the Desirability of the eminently Desirable (*DVI* 113, *CPP* 165, *HLR* 178). Nor may it be through lack of vigilance that Levinas's translator uses lower-case initials throughout. The eminently Desirable is in that essay identified with the Infinite and the Infinite is there identified with God. But the eminent Desirability of God in which God is the *telos* of an attraction becomes the eminently Non-desirable (or Non-Desirable) when instead of being the infinitely remote being in which the finite being would make a direct approach to its ultimate well-being, as though one could be face to face with God, that directness is converted into indirectness. This conversion is the interruption of the teleology of the attraction of goods by the superior goodness of response to the other human being, beyond the usual opposition of teleology and deontology. The Good (*Bien*) of God as the eminently Desirable can be approached only via the goodness or kindness (*bonté*) of disinterested love of one's neighbour: 'dés-inter-*essement*' of the nakedness of the face to face in which being undoes itself from its being-ness, as in sexual love nakedness is undoneness of form, not only undoneness of clothes. Desire as *ekstasis* toward the entitive objectivity of divinity conceived as a final Being and a final good, and the idea of God as one with whom I may have direct speech, give way to desire as the unattractive burden of responsibility toward the other human being. I respond in direct speech to this Thou, having been commanded to love the Other from beyond the Other by another other, a third personality, the *Il* of Illeity, not to be confused with the impersonality of universal law, be it the moral law itself.

ILYAITY, ILLEITY AND ELLEITY

Nor is illeity to be confused with the *il y a*. But that confusion is easy to make. For both are disturbances of my complacency. It would therefore seem easy to confuse illeity also with the erotic, for *Totality and Infinity* has told us that the erotic lies alongside the *il y a*. 'God and Philosophy' tells us that responsibility to which illeity binds me is the non-erotic *par excellence*. It tells us also that responsibility for the Other, my egoistic subjectivity's being ethically subjected to the Other, is Love without Eros. How can that be if, as it says only one paragraph earlier, 'Pornography is perhaps that which dawns [*pointe*] in all eroticism as eroticism in all love' (*DVI* 112, *CPP* 164, *HLR* 178)? Does the second clause of this statement not contradict directly the reference to love without Eros? Does this statement not imply that pornography dawns or arises even in the Desire of responsibility for the other human being, the Thou who owes his separateness from being to the Him or He of the illeity that some people call by the extraordinary word God? Does it not follow that if vulgar Aphrodite and celestial Aphrodite are sisters, they have a third sister who is noble upper-case Desire and who is not without vulgar lower-case desire?

The answer to each of these questions is 'No'. Day dawns from night, but the light of day may bear no trace of the darkness of night. Still, there remains the enigma, the ambiguity of sign and trace. The ambiguity in the divine comedy of the temple and the theatre, the equivocity of expression in the face as the *Dire* of *Désirer* and expression on the face as the *rire* and guarded '*dire*' of *désirer*. If pornography is enjoyment of the representation of the beloved to the point where one's attention is absorbed more by the image than by the absent beloved him- or herself, then there could be a celestial pornography of the erotic that might be confused with the illeity of Desire. It would be the idolatry that has not learned that the transcendence of Desire is not the objectively genitive transcendence of an object intended, and is not representable, synthesizable, or reducible to mastery by the 'I can' of the human being's *conatus essendi* or the transcendental ego's 'I think'. To learn this is to learn the lesson of the third Meditation of Descartes, that although the truth of the *cogito* is first in the order of learning, the ego is not altogether its own master; the ego is not self-taught.

But the separateness of the mastery that schools the ego's mastery of itself risks confusion with the separateness of the mystery of the mistress. The separateness of sanctity or holiness (*le saint*), forgets its separateness from the separateness of the sacred (*le sacré*), in the strict use Levinas sometimes, though not invariably, gives to these two words. As affirmed too by the identification of the mother with wisdom in Tibetan Buddhist icons, the feminine, at once interlocutor and collaborator, is *maître supéri-eurement intelligent*, 'so often dominating men in the masculine civilisa-tion into which it enters' (*TEI* 241, *TI* 264) – or into which *he* enters, *il*, who is *maître* but *femme*, as though the separateness of illeity is not cut off from the separateness of elleity, as though the mother were far and unfar from the father, *ent-fernt*, as Heidegger writes, in the near distance, *Distanz*, as Nietzsche writes, *Dis-tanz*, as Heidegger's and Nietzsche's words are re-written by Derrida, under the heading 'Veils'.[13]

As implied by the identification of the father with compassion in Tibetan iconography, in Levinas's genetology the masculine is the principle of ethical responsibility, not, be it noted, of political duties with their cor-relative rights within which Creon's authority holds sway. It is the feminine principle that is the principle of rights (*droits*). If these include domestic rights or sacred rights like the right to bury and be buried defended by Antigone, one wonders whether they would also include civic and political rights. For the sphere of these latter, the sphere associated with Creon, is, although public, still an interiority, still the interiority of a circle or sphere. It is a public interiority with an economy as closed as the regime of the home. True, Levinas writes in *Du sacré au saint*, in the Talmudic reading 'And God Created Woman' – but, it should be observed, in a paraphrase of the last chapter of Proverbs, so not necessarily speaking for himself, and not speaking philosophically:

> Woman is not at the summit of the spiritual life as Beatrice is for Dante. It is not the 'eternal feminine' that leads us to the heights.
>
> I am thinking of the last chapter of Proverbs, of the woman who is there glorified: she makes possible the life of men, she is the home of men; but the husband has a life outside the home; he has a seat on the city Council. He has a public life, he is in the service of the universal. He does not limit himself to interiority, intimacy, the residence, yet without them he could do nothing.
>
> (*SS* 135, *NTR* 169)

Could it be that speaking in his own philosophical voice Levinas would say that the sphere of the political is precisely the interregnum, the 'interface' where universal legality is exposed to challenge on one front by illeity and on another front to seduction by elleity – but that the frank face of illeity and the less than frank face of elleity are, if not one in the Parmenidean senses of 'are' and *hen*, a hendyadic two-in-one and one-in-two illelleity? The nation that Abraham went on to found was also a people sprung from his and Sarah's loins, a natio-nality, a folk, a *Volk*, whose formal civic relationships are capable both of being reviewed as ties of blood and of being proto-ethically *reaktiviert*, to use Husserl's word in order to draw attention to the intersection of Levinas's thoughts on responsibility with the thoughts on responsibility and refounding expressed by Husserl, particularly in the *Crisis of European Sciences*, a text on which Levinas conducted seminars.[14]

If, rather as the poets provide non-probative clues to Heidegger's thinking, Levinas's midrashic elaborations may be taken as non-probative clues to his, then it is not impertinent to follow up these *Winke* in construing what he regards as his philosophical texts. Commenting on a Rabbinic commentary on the text of Genesis 5:2, 'Male and female created he them (at the same time)', Levinas adduces grounds for saying that equality is or ✓ should be grounded on hierarchy. The more than textual question raised by the assertion 'Man was made in the image of God' (Genesis 9:6) is whether 'He first had in mind to create two and in the end created only one' (*SS* 140, *NTR* 172). Does Levinas read in Rav Abbahu's answer to this question a clue to a certain diachrony in the synchronicity of the creation of female and male? That answer, in Levinas's paraphrase, runs as follows: In order to create a well-ordered world one of these principles had to be subordinated to the other.

> Humanity is not thinkable on the basis of two essentially different principles. There had to have been a *sameness* that these *others* had in common. Woman was prescinded from man but she came after him: *the very femininity of woman is in this initial 'after the event' [après coup]*. Society was not founded on purely divine principles: the world would not have lasted. Real humanity does not allow for an abstract equality, without some subordination of terms. What family scenes there would have been between the members of that first perfectly equal couple! Subordination was needed, and a wound was needed; suffering was and is needed to unite equals and unequals.
>
> (*SS* 142, *NTR* 173)

Setting aside the questions whether the family scenes provoked either by equal partnership or by an inversion of the hierarchy would have provided the suffering needed to unite the partners, the temporality of this 'after-cut' merits attention. The offcut of the rib from Adam is an initial event, perhaps an event anticipating or commemorating the initiational event of circumcision to which we shall shortly return. The word 'prescinded' employed here for *prélèvement* preserves the priority connoted by *pré-*. *Après coup* though she may be, Eve is not an afterthought. Maybe, Levinas wonders toward the end of the essay, man's priority was provisional, almost as though he was made with the making of woman in view, as though for her sake! Man may perform a role in universal public life some centuries before woman, but complete humanity is reached only when woman enters on the scene after languishing in the wings not because she is assigned a secondary role, but because her being reserved offstage is a way of keeping sexual relations offstage lest libidinal pleasure as analysed by Freud prevent the full blossoming of relations that are fully interhuman. Or as left unanalysed by Freud, Levinas would say, for:

> Freud himself says little more about the libido than that it searches for pleasure, taking pleasure as a simple content, starting with which one begins an analysis but which itself does not need to be analyzed. Freud does not search for the significance of this pleasure in the general economy of being. My thesis, which consists in affirming voluptuousness as the very event of the future, the future purified of all content, the very mystery of the future, seeks to account for its exceptional place.
>
> (*TA* 83, *TO* 89–90)

This association of femininity with voluptuousness does not prevent Levinas associating femininity also with the legal concept of right (*droit*), but his way of doing this in *Totality and Infinity* blocks the inference that the domain of the feminine is a domain of authority vested solely in law. When he speaks there of 'woman having to be treated as woman, in accordance with the imprescriptible rules of policed political society [*la société policée*]', that is, in accordance with rights that cannot be taken away, these words are meant to state one side of the equivocity that constitutes the epiphany of the feminine. The other side is a certain force. We are told that both this force and this right arise from the gentleness (*tendresse, attendrissement*) and vulnerable weakness (*fragilité, faiblesse*) of femininity that inspires compassion and yet can turn from discreteness and modesty into violence and immodesty.

Before investigating further the nature of this violence a comment on this gentleness is due. Femininity is tenderness both in the passive sense of vulnerability, like the sensitivity of skin, and in the active sense of responsive treatment of another, sensitivity of the heart. Femininity's tenderness toward the other is the counterpart of the pity her fragility calls forth from the other. In 'Damages Due to Fire', another of the five Talmudic readings published in *Du sacré au saint*, Levinas notes the possibility of an etymological connection between the Aramaic word for mercy, *Rakhmana*, and the Aramaic *Rekhem* ('womb'). In the text of the Guemara on which he is commenting the first of these words is used of the Eternal, God, and of the Torah, Law. Because, next to the tomb, there is no more secure home than the womb, not only do these assimilations connect femininity with the mercifulness of God, and therefore with Elohim, that is to say, with God as principle of justice; not only therefore do they stand for the intersection of maternity with divine paternity, like the exaltation of weakness by the circumcision of virility (*SS* 158, *NTR* 183); not only do they connect maternity with sensitivity, 'of which so much ill is said among the Nietzscheans' (ibid.); they connect too the law with the feminine presence in the home, so that Levinas's reference in *Totality and Infinity* to femininity's *droit* can mean the feminization of law itself as well as feminine rights.

Feminization of *droit*, but not without *force*. Feminine *force de droit*.[15] Feminine *droit de force*. From intimacy in the home, in the *for intérieur*, via the directness, *droiture*, of face-to-face presence in the economy of the market place – in the *marché*, *agora*, *forum* – the *for extérieur* is forced forth (*fors*), as the less-than-nothing beyond the face of an absence that is not simply the nonbeing of a being, but the neither-being-nor-nonbeing of the not yet, the *Schritt vorwärts*, the *pas encore*. In the eyes of the You I am met by the direct regard of the Him thanks to whom, *grâce à Dieu*, the You is distanced from the intimacy of the *tu* of voluptuous love that, unlike friendship, which goes toward the other, is a voluptuousness of voluptuousness, love of the other which is also love that returns to the self: egoism *à deux*. But from beyond the veil of modesty turned into the violence of immodesty's *dévoilement*, where words have less meaning than force, the wordless, the *infans*, comes on to the scene: dualism *à un*, transubstantiation.

> Here we are before a new category: before what is behind the gates of being, before the less than nothing that eros tears from its negativity and profanes. It is a question of a nothingness distinct from the nothingness of anxiety: the nothingness of the future buried in the secrecy of the less than nothing.
>
> (*TEI* 244, *TI* 266)

Distinct from the nothingness of anxiety, distinct from the anxiety of nothingness, distinct from extinction, sepultured in the less-than-nothing of the not yet, neither being nor nonbeing, life beyond death is both being and nonbeing because the father both is and is not the son. The son is the multiplication of the beings of two parents, therefore not the being of either alone. But neither is he only the being produced by their conjugation, since his being is also his own. Filiation falls under a new category: fecundity.

FECUNDITY AND FILIATION

The new category of fecundity is a category of newness. And although it is a category of a future *beyond being*, it must be granted the status, Levinas reminds us, of an *ontological* category (*TEI* 254, *TI* 277). It is not an existential, a structure of ecstatic projection. Nor is it just a category of *existenziell* or otherwise ontic behaviour, whether biological, psychological or sociological. Levinas's reminder is relevant at this stage because it may well seem that what we have been rereading under the heading 'Beyond the Face' is an empirical *De generatione et corruptione*, a natural history of birth, copulation and death. That ontogenetic story of production, seduction and reproduction is a *Leitfaden*, a storyline to give flesh to figurations and disfigurations that are ontological – and logical in a disfigured, deformalized and, it might be said, uglified sense of logic. For logic is about 'is', 'the little connecting word', the copula. And so too is the Levinasian meditation on the genealogic of copulation. It concretizes the most abstract conception of being by certifying that at least one of the manifold senses of being owes its parentage precisely to parentage. At least one scion of *Sein* is lineage, filiation, paternity. But its paternity is not attributable to Father Parmenides. Parricide is inflicted upon him once again. Because fecundity is a doubling and halving of identity. The father is and is not the son.

It is also relevant to take note here of Levinas's statement that the filiation that breaks with Eleatic philosophy is exemplified by the way philosophy itself, including both that which he himself is in the course of expounding and the Eleatic philosophy it would displace, is addressed to future readers. The future is constituted by such dissemination. And it, no less than biological begetting, comes under the philosophical category of juvenescence. Juvenescence is not simply renewal or change, however protean, under the philosophical category of possibility. Such renewal is not radical. The fulfilment of potentialities, the germination of the seed and the ecstatic being ahead of oneself as already having been are but ways in which a being continually and continuously grows old. It is substantial senescence. Trans-substantial juvenescence is the discontinuous creation accomplished when a subject encounters the feminine Other and engenders engendering. The goodness of the face to face engenders goodness beyond the face. This is the infinition of time. Not time as the meaning of being, given time, or time that gives, time that *es gibt*, but time as the time of giving 'above and beyond the sacrifice that imposes a gift, the gift of the power of giving, the conception of the child' (*TEI* 247, *TI* 269).

In the Postscript of 'What is Metaphysics?' Heidegger writes of the sacrifice (*Opfer*) of the calculative intelligence of beings to an essential thinking beyond 'logic' of what is 'other' than beings. Such sacrifice would appear to be other than a *quid pro quo*. It is outside the exchange of one thing for another. But is it beyond imposition? Heidegger says 'Sacrifice is rooted in the nature of the event through which being claims man for the truth of being.'[16] Is this claim an imposition, despite it's being a claim made by being rather than beings? Should we answer this question in the affirmative because Heidegger, in line with his reading of Parmenides, describes *Dasein*'s response as a response to being's need, *Not*, as though to a cry for help that being makes? (Heidegger's expression is *in den Anspruch nimmt*, but one of the editions of the Postscript says *braucht*, the very word Heidegger uses to translate the first word of Parmenides' fragment *chre to legein te noein t'eon emmenai* ('Needful: the saying also thinking too: being: to be').) For Levinas these questions are not urgent. There are at least three reasons why they are not. First, because, as we know well by now, more clamant for him than the call of being is the call of the Other who is more and otherwise 'other' than being. Second, because, as we shall learn from *Otherwise than Being*, if we have not learned already, the response to the call from the Other is given before that call is heard. Third, because, as Levinas is telling us in the words we have just cited, filiation breaks with the economy of being by breaking with the reciprocity of gift given and the giving of thanks. According to Heidegger, *Dasein*'s sacrifice of calculative thinking to the other thinking that thinks being is a thanking for the gift of being that *Dasein* receives. This confirms the Parmenidean belonging together of being and the human being's thinking. Utterly different from that belonging together is the proximity in separation of the face to face and filiation beyond the face, after Isaac. The ego does not echo that to which it is a response in the way that, as Heidegger says, original thinking is the response with which man echoes the word of the soundless voice of being.[17] Or if the response of the ego is an echo, it is a pre-echo. And if the primary response of responsibility before the obligations of my station and its duties is an expression of gratitude, it is an expression of proto-gratitude:

> Men have been able to be thankful for the very fact of finding themselves able to thank; the present gratitude is grafted onto itself as onto an already antecedent gratitude. In a prayer in which the believer asks that his prayer be heard, the prayer as it were precedes or follows itself.
>
> (*AE* 12, *OB* 10)

The antecedent gratitude could not be gratitude for the Other's gratitude without entering into system and symmetry. This is why, on pain of returning to return, the giving of thanks or the giving of oneself has to be a response to ingratitude. Antecedent gratitude makes the everyday giving and receiving of thanks possible by saving it from being only possibility or power. This is why sacrifice gives up the gift of the *power* of giving. And why in a subsection of *Totality and Infinity* entitled 'The Infinity of Time'

Levinas takes up again the subject of the giving of pardon.

In what Levinas describes as its immediate meaning it is a moral wrongdoing that gets pardoned. How then does the gift of forgiveness escape being a systematic relation between terms? By undoing the past. Like in a drama in which one act may be the *dénouement* of the one that precedes it, forgiveness gives another chance. The psychological phenomenon of the *felix culpa* points to the ontological truth of time: contrary to the doctrine of *Being and Time*. It is not the finitude of being that is the essence of time, not *Dasein*'s being toward death. The essence of time is the infinition of being across the dead time between the father and the son and the son's son, and so on. So the future of temporality is not the ecstatic projection of possibility. Nor is it merely the future as measured by clocks, the future of a time rendered timeless by being construed according to the analogy of physical space whose limitations are exposed by both Heidegger and Bergson. But the future is not continuous accretion like the snowball gathering more and more snow that Bergson offers as an analogy of continuous duration. The future is the good infinite. Not the bad infinite of replicative repetition, but the good infinite of resurrection. 'Death and resurrection constitute time' (*TEI* 261, *TI* 284). And death is malediction: *le mal*. Death is suffered, like the corruption of old age. But when Levinas asks 'Why – in order to go towards the good – must there be evil [*le mal*]?', must he not be asking why in order that there be this *il faut* there must be (*il faut*) a misdeed (*une faute*)? For he maintains that forgiveness is the renewing of the reality of a past misdeed and that it is this forgiveness, the son's forgiveness, that interrupts what would otherwise be a continuous accumulative duration. The fissure (*faute*) of infinite temporality going towards the good is the ethical infinition of goodness expressed in the forgiveness of fault (*faute*) beyond the face, across dead time, across the death of the person forgiven, therefore beyond the reciprocity of response. Not that absolute pardon is the pardon of a particular misdeed. It is a pardon in default of such fault, the pardon of the absolute responsibility entailed by my occupying a place in the sun. Bearing this in mind, it must be said that the infinition of time entails goodness and goodness entails suffering or evil. Dare it be said, across the fissure between French and German, that the *mal* of suffering or evil is entailed by the *Mal* of time?

Whether and how *das Mal* ('time'), could ever be protected against the revenge of *le mal* is a question raised by the thought, expressed in the final paragraph of the main part of *Totality and Infinity*, that although the infinity of time is accomplished in the manner that has just been described, and although with it is accomplished one condition of the possibility of judgement, which is in turn the condition of truth, another condition of truth, in addition to the infinity of time, is a time that is itself finished and fully accomplished, a time on which truth could stamp its seal. As from its very beginning *Totality and Infinity* has been aiming to show, that completion of truth could not be death, for it is by death that truth is endangered. A time of finished infinity could only be the messianic time in which eternity triumphs over perpetuity. 'Is this eternity a new structure of time, or an extreme vigilance of the messianic consciousness?' (*TEI* 261, *TI* 285) Like the infinity that overflows its idea, this question, Levinas comments, overflows the framework of *Totality and Infinity*. It is a question for another kind of book. Perhaps for a book like the one that has been that book's guiding star, too often present to be cited. Or for Levinas's own Talmudic readings and writings. Something has already been said about the relation of the Talmudic to the philosophical texts. Something more than has been said in passing must now be said about the second of his two philosophical *chefs d'oeuvre* and about the relationship between them. As relevant a topic as any with which to begin saying something about that relationship is a genealogical relationship that is treated in both books but about which we have so far said nothing.

Part III

11 Liberty, Equality, Fraternity

FRATERNITY

Although in *Otherwise than Being* parental descendence is not treated anything like as explicitly as it is in the section of *Totality and Infinity* entitled 'Beyond the Face', the later book continues to invoke the ideas of paternity, maternity and fraternity introduced in the earlier one. The third of these ideas brings with it the idea of filiation no less than do the other two. One of Levinas's reasons for introducing it is that it gives him the opportunity to appeal to the implied notion of shared fatherhood that he considers to be missing from the idea of belonging to the same biological race. The shared father is not to be understood biologically. Nor is it to be understood theologically. Levinas's 'monotheism' is to be understood ethically as human kinship deriving from the 'idea of a human race that refers back to the approach of the Other in the face, in a dimension of height, in responsibility for oneself and for the Other' (*TEI* 190, *TI* 214). To say that this monotheism is ethical is to say that the human kinship in question shared by human beings is not due to any shared genetic relation to a paternal being. It is precisely such a commonality of genus that the ethical kinship disrupts. The identity of one brother is not in internal relation to the identity of the other brother. Brothers are not terms defined by their relation. However, the identity of each is in part defined by a relation to a self-identical father. The ethical individuality of each brother is not that of genus and differentiating quality or relation in which each instantiates and participates in the concept of Ego. Ethical individuality prior to ontic individuality is due not to participation but to facing, in which each individual before individuality is a unique me facing and faced by a unique Other beyond conceptuality. Each me is therefore beyond the distributive plurality which would attempt to save the individual from absorption into the totality by stressing the particular ontological essence of each entity, its *haecceitas*.[1] A plurality of unique thises is still a plurality within a system. The compossibility of Leibnizian monads passes through the idea of the system of the world as thought by the mind of the Highest Monad. Its theological height is not the dimension of height of *illeitas* alluded to in Levinas's description of human fraternity.

If no straight answer can be given to the question *what* the individual before individuality is, it seems also that no straight answer can be given to the question *who*? Explaining the meaning the word 'monotheism' has for him in his philosophical thinking, Levinas remarks that the individual prior to individuality goes by the name of God (*AE* 69n., *OB* 190n.). This does not prevent his applying the same phrase to the unique me. It is 'an individual fleeing individuality' because its oneness beyond being is the oneness of being elected by the Thou or You whose non-phenomenality Levinas names illeity, and this is a proname for what goes by the name of God. Beyond the principle of intuition of Cartesian method and the intuitional principle of all principles from which Husserl says phenomenology draws its life and to which it owes its responsibility, anarchic and non-intuitional election is what gives life to ethics and to the universality of all principles (*DL* 45, *DF* 26). As Levinas takes the third Meditation of Descartes to show, the Infinite is in the finite in the form or non-form of infinite responsibility. That is how he interprets the idea that the finite human being is made in the image of God, as responsibility whose infinity is prior to the infinity of the freedom of the will.

In standard logic, if A is a brother of B then B is a brother of A. Brotherhood is symmetrical. Ethically speaking, however, brotherhood is asymmetrical. That is what we are told in *Totality and Infinity* long before we reach the section 'Beyond the Face' in which fraternity is connected with filiality. Fraternity has already been introduced before that section, for instance in the subsection on 'The Asymmetry of the Interpersonal' which begins by asserting that the presence of the face commits me to human fraternity. The preceding subsection on 'The Other and the Others', 'Autrui et les Autres', expressly anticipates the subsection of 'Beyond the Face' in which the connection between fraternity and filiality is to be more fully explained. As the title of the earlier subsection indicates, the question of fraternity arises once it is acknowledged that I am faced by more than one Other. For once the question of the plurality of Others has arisen the question of equality has been raised. Liberty, Equality, Fraternity. Just as fraternity on Levinas's interpretation is older than the exercitive freedom of the will, so too is it older than equality understood independently of fraternity as interpreted by him, that is to say, understood as a universal symmetrical and transitive relation cut off from the asymmetrical Relation of all relations in which the Other (*Autrui*) faces me. Strictly speaking, it cannot be said that the Other in the sense of *Autrui* is instantiated in the Others in the sense of *les Autres*. This is why Levinas considers that the name God is well fitted to mark not only the Illeity or Him-ness that modifies with pastness the presence of the You-ness of *Autrui*, but also *Autrui*'s uniqueness. And fraternity is his name for the respect in which the many others are Other, *Autrui*, without instantiating as cases instantiate a concept. And this is why he writes in the essay 'Language and Proximity' that starting from absolute singularities fraternity rediscovers universalization rather than universality (*EDE* 232, *CPP* 122). For the 'Language' to which the title of this essay refers is not what is said, the *dit*, but the saying, the *dire* of *langage*, where this saying is the non-indifferent proximity of fraternity (*AE* 104, *OB* 82). My proximity to the Other is not nearness based on resemblance, but approach or, better, approaching, a going up to the Other that keeps the distance and difference of height from which he approaches and commands me. So I and the Other are in this sense not equals. I am infinitely more responsible than the Other. This inequality of responsibility, however, does not exclude my being equal with the Other in so far as the Other and I are both brothers, both sons of one father. Freed from its limitation to biology, paternal filiation confers on the son an identity which is not that of the son's existing on his own account. For paternity as construed by Levinas is precisely what disrupts the identity of the logic of Father Parmenides. It admits an identity of the One that is an identity of both being and non-being, for the son's identity is both one with the father and is yet other than the father. The son's oneness in separation from his father is the oneness conferred by paternal love. Paternal love is the paradigm of all true love, Levinas maintains, in so doing once more warning against confusing human paternity ethically understood with its biological prototype and giving notice that the former is not a metaphor of the latter.

The son's oneness and separation from the father are not to be understood numerically. It is not the arithmetical but the prior ethical oneness and separation of the father–son relation that is being characterized here. So that when Levinas writes of the mastery of the father and of the 'strange conjuncture' of the family made possible because the father commands the son, it is not a power relationship that is being described (*TEI* 256, *TI* 279).

Although the inheritance–disinheritance of filiation is beyond the face, it is still an ethical relationship that is being described, but now an ethical relationship that reaches into the future and thanks to which the historical continuity of a family and a nation escapes destiny because it leaves room for discontinuity. Levinas at one point calls this relation of posterity to its past a 'dialectical conjuncture', thereby inviting his reader to note how this dialectic differs from other dialectics of history, for instance Hegelian, Marxist or Bergsonian.

Again, although the resumptive–disruptive, Odysseic–Abrahamic genealogy of father and son is beyond the face, it passes into faciality. The son is also a brother. Critical of Heidegger's idea of *Dasein*'s belonging with others to a dispensation (*Geschick*), and a *Generation* (*SZ* 384 and n. viii), Levinas's account of *Brüderschaft* aims to give an analysis of the we that leaves room for the symmetry of justice and for the asymmetry of the face to face. Indeed, on this account it is the asymmetrical face to face itself that demands the symmetry of justice.

JUSTICE

Although the uniqueness for the father of the chosen son is not numerical, it communicates with number. For if a son is chosen he is chosen from among other chosen ones. Still, he is not only one brother among others. Each brother privileged as chosen is placed before the face of the others. His privilege is also a subordination in that, as he is commanded by the father beyond the face, he is commanded by the Other facing him. But the other other is involved in the face to face. Each brother is commanded by the other not only not to kill him. He is also commanded not to kill any of the other brothers. While I cannot on my own behalf claim equality with my brothers, for I am immeasurably more culpable than any of them, each of them makes an equal claim as naked face, as uninvested *Autrui*, that is to say as Other destitute of particular properties and relations, as *absolutely* naked, orphaned or widowed.

Not only is there no incompatibility between the equality of others and my inequality with the Other who faces me. The inequality actually requires the equality. In *Otherwise than Being* this demand is variously expressed. It is expressed, for example, as a demand which saying makes upon the said: 'It will be possible to show that there is only a question of the Said [*Dit*] and of being because Saying or responsibility calls for [*réclament*] justice' (*AE* 58, *OB* 45). If both the other and the other other, the third party, call for responsibility, my responsibility calls for third personal justice, the institutionalized system within which competing claims are to be judged; and such judgements are made within an instituted linguistic system. What is said in these judgements, their *dit*, is addressed to a being with a face. That is to say, the said calls to be unsaid by being resaid as a to-say, a *dire*. Justice would be primary violence without this repeated reconversion of said into saying, without the tie to fraternity, without the manifold of claims and symmetrical counterclaims being folded back to the asymmetry of the face to face. The face to face is the Relation of the incomparable Other and the incomparable me. *The* incomparable me becomes *a* comparable me among other mes only thanks to the others or, as Levinas expresses this, between inverted commas, 'thanks to God' (*AE* 201, *OB* 158). So if the incomparable demands comparability, the converse also holds. 'Justice is impossible without the one that renders it finding himself in proximity' (*AE* 202, *OB* 159). His or her function is not restricted to the subsumption of cases under rules. It is not simply the 'function of judgement', Levinas writes in inverted commas, intending no doubt an allusion to B93ff. of the *Critique of Pure Reason* and hence a questioning of the fundamentality of the transcendental unity of apperception. That synthetic unity and the analytic unity of the judgements whose forms Kant takes as clues for his table of categories of knowledge are functions only of what is and what is said, not of my saying. And Levinas suggests that Kant himself glimpses that this is so when he says that the I is not the specification of the more general concept of the soul and, at A354 of the Transcendental Dialectic, that 'if I wish to represent to myself a thinking being, I must put myself in his place, and thus substitute, as it were, my own subject for the object I am seeking to consider (which does not occur in any other kind of investigation)'.

This last reference to Kant is made in a note to the first chapter of *Otherwise than Being* (*AE* 17n., *OB* 187n.). Kant's 'substitution', *an die Stelle jedes anderen intelligenten Wesens zu setzen*, translated by Levinas as *se mettre à la place de l'autre*, becomes the title of the fourth chapter, which Levinas considers to be the central chapter of the book. Although no one can substitute for me in my substitution for the other, substitution, that is to say, the pre-original Saying that says and signifies itself in the giving of the one for the other, 'demands [*requiert*] the signification of the thematizable, enunciates the idealized Said, weighs and judges in justice' (*AE* 205, *OB* 161). So must not the giving of myself in signifiance, a giving made possible only by the asymmetry of this signifiance – for in symmetry there would be only the appearance of giving, a giving which would be no sacrifice because equalled at least by gratitude given in exchange – include a giving of that very signifiance into the hands of semantic signification, a supreme sacrifice on the altar of conceptuality where, after all, and before all, the incomparable me becomes a case falling under a rule?

Not quite. For that sacrifice remains a sacrifice that is suffered by me in the most extreme passivity. It is one that calls to be made again and again because judgements call to be rejudged, pronouncements to be denounced, the said to be unsaid interminably. The categorial possibility and necessity of the modalities of theoretical knowledge to which Kant allows himself to be led by the logical forms of judgement are themselves otherwise necessitated by and can be deduced from the signifiance of the subject's one-for-the-other (*AE* 107n., *OB* 192n.).

It is only this disequilibrium that makes justice possible: 'justice remains justice only in a society where there is no distinction between those close and those far off but in which there also remains the impossibility of passing by the closest' (*AE* 203, *OB* 159).

ETHICS, POLITICS AND VIOLENCE

Is this impossibility of passing by the closest a logical or an ethical impossibility? If it were a logical impossibility would not totalitarian violence be impossible, logically and tautologically impossible if totalitarian violence is understood as the violence that would be imposed by totality unmitigated by infinity? For to understand violence in this way is to understand it as the posing of what is said independently of saying, and therefore to pass by the closest. Therefore, if totalitarian violence is possible, must not the impossibility of passing by the closest be an ethical impossibility? Yet some of Levinas's remarks suggest that he considers this to be a logical impossibility. For example, in *Totality and Infinity* he argues that one can pursue war – and commerce! – only against a being with a face, a being with whom asymmetrical interlocution can take place. War is not waged against an animal or an element. To think that it is is to confuse violence with hunting and work. So-called violence in nature is force exerted against beings that cannot form part of a totality. The violence of warfare is possible only with beings who are capable of forming part of a totality, a nation or community of nations, but who break away from such totalities, affirm their independence and thus expose themselves to risks that exceed the calculability and predictability preserved for the play of forces operating within a closed system. But there is a further condition of violence and war. Although those who participate in violence suspend their participation in a totality and in so doing deprive themselves of the ordered system of law by which each is protected against being seized by any other, any being thus exposed to seizure in war must still be safe from seizure through being a being with a face. 'Violence bears only upon a being both graspable and escaping every hold. Without this living contradiction in the being that undergoes violence the deployment of violent force would reduce itself to a labour' (*TEI* 198, *TI* 223). So the Hobbesian war of each against all presupposes the peace pronounced in the command 'Thou shalt not kill.' Both war and peace are possible only for beings 'structured otherwise than parts of a totality' (*TEI* 197, *TI* 222).

Does this mean that although violence outside the totality is possible, violence inside the totality is not? If totalitarian violence is not possible, what is the point of Levinas's criticism of Hegel? The point is that a being that appears in a face cannot be totally inside a totality. He can be outside the totality because he can take himself outside it in order to conduct commerce or war, but he can do that only because he is already outside it through being a being that speaks peace. In his very project of totalizing the history of philosophy and in his very pursuit of the science of the con-sciousness of experience Hegel contradicts himself, for in so doing he is addressing a reader, a possible interlocutor. The very discourse in which he would totalize being belies, *qua* discourse, its intention (*AE* 217, *OB* 170).

But is not contradiction a good thing according to Hegel? Is contradic-tion not the motor of his dialectic? Indeed it is. However, Hegelian con-tradictions are contradictions between dicta, between one *dit* and another, and they get superseded when the dialectic lifts itself to a higher level. This *relèvement* is not the *élèvement* to which Levinas would draw his reader's and Hegel's attention. *Elèvement* is the teaching that takes place as saying, not simply as said, and the contradiction to which Levinas would have us attend is one that cannot be reduced finally to a contradiction between saids. What Levinas calls 'reference' to an interlocutor is not to be confused with reference to something as that about which something is said. Reference to the interlocutor is address. And address is address to a face, hence the moment of address, its *Augenblick* or *clin d'oeil*, does not belong to the time in which a past moment is recuperable in the present. It does not belong to belonging or assembly. Its temporality is a different temporality from that of retention and synthesis. It is not of the same time, the time of the same, as that which conceptual contradiction assumes. It is a temporality which crosses that temporal continuum diachronically with a past that resists resumption and a future that could never arrive. As traces of this alternation interrupting the direct current of continuous time Levinas cites the recur-rence of scepticism despite the contradiction between what it claims and the fact of its being made the topic of a claim. He cites too Hegel's own recourse to prefaces in which the reader is addressed, notwithstanding that according to the theses of the Hegelian encyclopaedia the latter should leave behind nothing of importance to say. The encyclopaedia, Levinas comments, forgets that the saying cannot be remembered, cannot be in-teriorized (*erinnert*), cannot be digested. In its mouth there remains the word or the morsel of bread that it is impossible for me not to give to the closest, my neighbour, or to my neighbour's neighbour, however remote he or she may be.

To return to the question whether this is a logical or an ethical impossibility, one is tempted to answer that as regards the morsel of bread it is ethically but not logically impossible for me not to give it, to pass by on the other side, whereas it is logically impossible for me not to address my word to him or her. Is not even withholding my word, keeping silent, an acknowledgement of his or her appearing as a face? However, that acknowledgement does not circumvent violence. It is a condition of witting violence. Is there always violence therefore? If violence means falling short of my responsibility to the other, then the answer to this question must be 'Yes'. Not necessarily the violence of declared war, but the violence of declared peace, of saying to my neighbour 'Shalom' when by so doing the rights of a third party are infringed. But in such circumstances, and perhaps they are the inescapable circumstances of the human condition, violence is equivalent to wrongdoing, relative to particular needs, interests or claims. Is there only violence in this sense, only relative violence?

Levinas's answer to this question appears to be 'No'. But what on his account could absolute violence be? Since, as we have just seen, violence can be inflicted according to his account only upon a being with a face, would absolute violence be failure to regard the face of such a being, to treat a being that has a face as a being that is faceless? If so, one could be absolutely violent through ignorance or forgetfulness. Note that it was of witting violence that we were speaking in the immediately preceding paragraph. Note too that at the end of the paragraph immediately preceding that one, we spoke of the possibility of a philosophical forgetting. It is of a philosophical forgetting that Levinas is speaking when his topic is what we are calling absolute violence: the absolute violence of the rationality of absolute knowledge. Thus, toward the very end of *Otherwise than Being*, before the last brief chapter entitled 'Outside' or 'To the Outside', '*Au dehors*', in the course of reflections on reflection on discourse, he observes that the most extreme form of such reflection, philosophy, can get harnessed by medicine and the State. This linkage results in a violence that may be just or repressive. Yet reason or *logos* as saying resists absorption into reason or *logos* as said, even when the latter becomes ideology when co-opted and enforced by the machinery of the State.

In mentioning here medicine he is touching on a topic of Foucault's then still recently published *Birth of the Clinic*.[2] His mention of the State is also an allusion to a philosophical tradition stemming from Plato's *Republic* and passing via Spinoza to Hegel. Although that line begins with a dialogue, or at least the representation of a dialogue, the logical rationalism of this tradition bears witness to an alliance of logic with politics and state power, another Foucauldian theme. In the broadest sense of the word 'political' Levinas may be implying that this association holds for structuralism, the then most recent form of logical rationalism, which could be said to identify the primacy of the *polis* with the 'death of man'. Of course, if by this phrase is meant the end of the Enlightenment conception of the subject defined primarily by the freedom of the will persisting in its existence, then Levinas's own thinking is another nail in man's coffin. But that thinking is intended to point in the direction of an alternative both to structuralism or logical rationalism and to liberal humanism. It would point not to a humanism of the same man who remains egological no matter however capable he might be of 'humanity' understood in the manner of eighteenth-century philosophers like Adam Smith and Hume or twentieth-century philosophers like Scheler as the sentiment of sympathy, benevolent feeling *with* others.[3] Levinas would point to a humanism of the other man, of man whose selfhood is distinguished by his being addressed. Man can call himself man only because he is called by his neighbour. The human being is human and capable of sympathy only because his humanity is responsible being for the other, only because responsibility for the freedom of the Other is anterior to freedom in myself, only because no one is willingly good (*AE* 176, *OB* 138). Goodness beyond the opposition of good and evil is not an exercise of the will to power. In a parody of the Heideggerian formulation of the being of *Dasein* as being-ahead-of-itself-already-being-in-as-being-alongside and of authentic *Dasein* as the-potentiality-for-being-one's-Self (*SZ* 196, 322), Levinas, keeping the hyphens, describes the being of the human being as being-torn-from-oneself-for-another-in-giving-the-bread-from-one's-mouth and the-power-of-giving-up-one's-soul-for-another (*AE* 99, *OB* 79). Absolute violence is done to the human being so described therefore not just because the power of logical compulsion is reinforced by the addition of the power of the State, but because from the power of logical compulsion is subtracted the impower of absolute passivity. Because the woman in the man is sacrificed to phallologocentrism. Because man's maternity is passed by, and therefore the closest, the Other in the mother.

MATERNITY AND ENIGMA

Despite the difference between the *with* of the fellow-feeling as described by the eighteenth-century philosophers just named and the *for* of Levinas's description, the latter is still the description of a sensibility, albeit a sensibility deemed to be the condition of the highest rationality, a condition even of humanity as defined by Rousseau and Kant in terms of rationality as freedom and freedom as the capacity to universalize. And whereas the dialectic of Hegelian spirit is motivated toward absolute knowing by contradiction, the motivation toward justice, universalization and the intentionality of epistemological objectivity is located by Levinas in sensibility. 'The modification of sensibility into intentionality is motivated by the very signification of feeling as *for-the-other*' (*AE* 89, *OB* 71) and 'The dominant signification of sensibility which was already caught sight of in vulnerability and which will reveal itself in the responsibility of proximity, in its inquietude and in its insomnia, contains the motivation of its cognitive function' (*AE* 80, *OB* 63–4). But maternity is the paradigm of the sensibility of proximity, so it is no wonder that in discussing paternity and childhood in *Totality and Infinity* Levinas should remark that the notion of maternity must be introduced to describe the nature of care.

Rather more is said about this notion in *Otherwise than Being*, particularly in the chapters entitled 'Sensibility and Proximity' and 'Substitution', where, although in the verse of Numbers (11:12) cited by Levinas it is of a father carrying a suckling child that Moses speaks, maternity is carrying *par excellence*, the carrying of responsibility, vulnerability and suffering that is pre-natal not just in the biological sense, but in the philosophical sense in which the ethical is prior to the natural, to *phusis*, to being. For the very selfhood of the self even in its corporeal sensibility is psychism understood not as substantial monadic soul whose relation to a substantial body then becomes a problem, but as 'the flesh made word' (*AE* 120, *OB* 94) in dyadic substitution where the other is given a place already before conception, immaculately, so to speak, in the only way that the other could ever share my place in the sun. It is worth recalling here that when Princess Elizabeth asks Descartes to explain more clearly to her the union of the body and the soul, he begs her not to ask for a philosophical explanation of this and assures her that she will best understand the connection through taking part in conversation. Levinas is endorsing Descartes's advice when he writes:

> What seems incomprehensible in a humanity of flesh and blood to the Cartesian conception – the animation of a body by a thought, which is nonsense according to the intelligibility of a system in which animation is understood only in terms of union and jointing and requires a *deus ex machina* – outlines *signification* itself: the one-for-the-other. In the subject it is precisely not an assembling, but an incessant alienation of the ego (isolated as inwardness) by the guest entrusted to it – hospitality

– the-one-for-the-other in the ego, granted more passively than every passivity of links in a causal chain.

(*AE* 99, *OB* 79)

It is in a footnote to this paragraph that Levinas expresses the approval to which we earlier referred of Descartes's denial that the corporeal seat of sensibility has anything in common with knowledge of ideas. That earlier reference must now be amplified by noting that Levinas demurs at Descartes's doctrine that through sensibility nature teaches us how to save our own skin. Prior to such prudential lessons of nature is sensibility to the lesson taught by the Other who is under my skin, making the irritating demand that his safety be put first. None the less, Levinas's approval of Descartes's refusal to regard the union of body and soul as a topic presented simply to thought explains why Levinas's own philosophical thinking on the topic of the proximity of the father, the son, the brother and, it must be insisted, the sister, the daughter and the mother, cannot be simply what he several times describes as the virile philosophy of logical rationality that assumes that there is no more to philosophy than the concatenation of dicta. Philosophy may be called upon to show that philosophy is also something other than this. It follows that it cannot show this simply by further ratiocinative concatenation. The recessive maternal dimension which is complemented by the assertive paternal dimension in sensible rationality cannot itself be apodeicticly proved. The tracking backward through conditions of possibility and the tracking forward of synthetic dialectic supervised by the classical principle of ground or the law of identity of the logic of Father Parmenides may be required to alternate with the more enigmatic saying associated – by Nietzsche! – with a feminine logic and truth couched in phrases like 'one can ask whether . . .', 'it is not excluded that . . .' with which Levinas's writings abound. The 'paternal house' of philosophy is also home to the mother who gives birth to a legitimate child repeating again and again the cry of scepticism (*AE* 108n., *OB* 192n.).

This explains in turn why, especially in the chapter entitled 'Substitution', *Otherwise than Being* is so repetitive – and why this study of the work of its author is so repetitive too. An *ainigma* is indeed a dark saying, but the darkness of the enigmatic saying to which Levinas binds even the most clear and distinct propositions of philosophy is not the darkness of a mystery understood as an obscure or confused proposition that could at least in principle be made clear or distinct. It is the unsaidness of the saying that is a giving to understand, where the giving itself surpasses all comprehension. Its law is not the law of synchronic contradiction but the law of diachronic dediction. This is a law under which nothing can be subsumed or assumed, according to which every regressive tracking toward an *archê* or first cause and every progressive tracking toward an *eschaton* or *telos* is interpellated by the interminable methodological marking of time, a time of absolute diachrony, that effaces the traces of the philosopher's footsteps and incessantly effaces the traces of the effacing (*AE* 24–5, *OB* 20). Only by the way of this iteration and obliteration, as performed in Levinas's own critique of other philosophers, which calls for criticism in its turn, only by this critical oscillation across the cutting edge of executive decision, thematizing the difference and deference of the absolute one-for-the-other and then dethematizing it, can both the one and the other be set free. Only in this way, adopting this 'quasi-hagiographical style' to define the anthropological by the holiness that disturbs the holism of genus, can philosophy, not as the love of wisdom and ancilla of theology but as the wisdom of love in the service of love – philosophy therefore as the love of love, Levinas explains in his preface to the German translation of *Totality and Infinity* (*EN* 252) – justify the laws of Being and the State. The reign of being and the rule or reigning of the political state, their verbal *Wesen* or *essance*, owe their meaning to what Levinas compares to the biblical Kingdom of God, *le Règne de Dieu* (*AE* 67, *OB* 52).

In an epoch in which there is so much talk of the death of God, how can Levinas say that the Kingdom of God is not an epoch of the reign of being that has come to its end? How can he say that the Kingdom of God was no more ever an aeon of being than was the Good beyond Being of Plato's *Republic*, but that, on the contrary, the reigning of being and of the political State are emanations subordinate to the Kingdom of God where reigning is not the superordination of a principle or power, not an *arche*, but an-archy, that does not reign (*AE* 127n., 128 n., *OB* 194nn.)? Is it not an anachronistic abuse of language to say these things? And to say, as Levinas does, that the response to this last question must be 'Yes', indeed, Amen'?

12 Atheology

GOD IS DEAD

At the beginning of the first chapter of *Otherwise than Being* Levinas refers to 'strange rumours about the death of God or the emptiness of the heavens' (*AE* 5, *OB* 5). That his book purports to say 'Amen' to that rumour is evident from his making precise in the very next paragraph and in the very last paragraph of the book that the death here rumoured, the death rumoured by Nietzsche's Zarathustra, is the death of a certain God inhabiting a world behind the scenes. But what is it to say 'Amen'?

AMEN

In *The Star of Redemption*, the work of which Levinas says in the preface of *Totality and Infinity* that it is too often present in its text to be cited there, Rosenzweig writes that God is neither dead nor living. 'To say the one or the other of him, with the old [philosopher] that "God is life", or with the new one that "God is dead", reveals the same pagan bias. The only thing which does not resist verbal designation is that neither/nor of dead and alive.'[1] The resistance to designation of what is other than this neither-nor referred to in the last book of the *Star* mirrors a similar resistance to designation referred to in the first book of the *Star* where Rosenzweig writes of a word that is often considered to be the last word but is in fact the first, or rather is before the fact and before the law, before the distinction between the *de facto* and the *de jure*. This word is 'Amen', the first tremendous and unlimited Yes of a 'positive theology'. In the light of Levinas's acknowledgement of Rosenzweig as his guide let us consider a few paragraphs in which Rosenzweig treats of the words 'Yes' and 'God', in the hope that this may help to articulate together two allusions in Levinas's two main philosophical writings: first, his allusion in *Totality and Infinity* to the plane on which 'yes' is opposed to 'no', neither of these opposed words being that which institutes language (*TEI* 11–12, *TI* 41–2), and, second, his allusion in *Otherwise than Being* to an unconditioned and critical Yes (*AE* 156, *OB* 122). Because Rosenzweig's 'grammatical thinking' of the word 'yes' is at the same time a grammatical thinking of the word 'God', in pursuing this exegetical aim progress may be made also toward either allaying or deepening what for some of Levinas's readers may be more a disquietude than a question of exegesis.

After endorsing Nietzsche's proclamation of the death of the God of onto-theology, why is Levinas either unable or unwilling to eliminate the word 'God' from the lexicon in which he expounds what he himself describes as a humanism of the other man? Would the appropriateness of that description of Levinas's account of ethics not be increased if the description could be conducted without that word, at least after, like Dante bidding farewell to Virgil, it had, for the reasons Levinas gives in the first section of *Totality and Infinity*, said goodbye to the gods of paganism? In other words, although Levinas is seeking to show in *Otherwise than Being* that, as he writes there, 'The problem of transcendence and of God and the problem of subjectivity irreducible to essence – irreducible to essential immanence – go together' (*AE* 20, *OB* 17), could he show that the problem of transcendence and the problem of subjectivity go together without showing that these two problems go together with the problem of God? Is it possible that in this sentence of *Otherwise than Being* and in other sentences of that book the name of God is traced only with a view to its own effacement?

Bearing in mind these questions as well as their place within what, remembering Levinas's reference to the need to get away from the climate of Heidegger's philosophy (*DEE* 19, *EE* 19), might be called the wider question of philosophical meteorology as to whether it is possible to breathe freely both in the atmosphere of Levinas's thinking and in that of Nietzsche's, let us now read a few paragraphs of Rosenzweig's grammar of assent.

Having called 'Amen' the first word of a 'positive theology', Rosenzweig writes that the point of departure of negative theology is a Something from which by the negation of predicates it moves to a Nothing or a Nought, a *Nicht*, where, he says in the first paragraph of the first book of the first part of *The Star of Redemption*, mysticism and atheism shake hands. Rosenzweig's method is the reverse. Putting the Nothing behind it, even before the Yes and the No, it aims at a Something or at an Aught, as the English translation renders the *Icht* Rosenzweig prefers to *Etwas* in order to keep at arms length the Hegelian definition of the latter as a definitely qualified existing being whose moments are being in itself and being for another reflected into each other through the negation of negation. The *Nicht* which Rosenzweig here distinguishes from this *Icht*, although not defined, is yet not the uncircumscribed universal, *allgemein* Nothing of Nothing at all. It is the Nothing of God. That alone is presupposed, the Nothing of a fragmentary all, not the Nothing of the one and universal totality. Rosenzweig, who is readier to write of methodology than Levinas is, contrasts his method with the method of decomposition, destruction or deconstruction of essence (*Verwesung*), which is the method of atheism, and the method or way of *Entwesung* which is the mystic way and which takes essence away. The dissolution or deportation of the essence of something leads to a formless night of nothing, a *Nacht des Nichts*. This, notwithstanding Rosenzweig's concern to distance himself from Hegel, is a close relation of the night in which all cows are black of Hegel's innuendo about Schelling. The method of annihilation (*Vernichtung*), the method of Mephistopheles, the method in which atheism and mysticism shake hands, affirms the Nothing. As against these methods, Rosenzweig's method is to ask hypothetico-positively: if God exists, what can be truly affirmed of his Nothing? This is not an affirmation either of Nothing in general or of the Nothing of God. Nor is it a negation of Nothing. Distinguishing the beginning from the point of departure which is at most the beginning of our knowledge, as Descartes does in the Third Meditation and as Levinas will do in his meditation on that Meditation, Rosenzweig argues that No cannot be the beginning because it would have to be the negation of a presupposed positive Yes. But both Yes and No presuppose a Nothing which is no more than a positionless posit for the posing of a problem. 'It is no "dark ground" or anything else that can be named with the words of Eckhart, Boehme or Schelling. It does not exist in the beginning. *Es ist nicht im Anfang.*' In the beginning is the Yes. But, as already explained, this Yes is not the Yes opposed to the No, but the Yes that is presupposed by the No. Before the neither-nor, it is before the either-or, before the *enten . . . eller*: this *Ent-scheidung* before *Entscheidung is avant toute décision*, prior to *every* decision (*AE* 153, *OB* 120).

It might reasonably be objected that this archetypal Yes presupposes an archetypal No, the No of the presupposed Nothing. And Rosenzweig himself admits an archetypal and, as he describes it, tremendous (*gewaltiges*) No. He even says that the No is as original as the Yes and does not presuppose it. A derived No may presuppose the archetypal No, but the original archetypal No presupposes nothing but the Nothing. However, although it does not presuppose a Yes, a *Ja*, it does presuppose an affirmation, a *Bejahung*, which when taken together with what Levinas says about pre-original patience and culpability recalls Nietzsche's 'highest affirmation, a Yes-saying without reserve, to suffering itself, to guilt itself'.[2] For the Nothing it presupposes is, as we have seen, not the utter Nothing of Mephistophelian meontological annihilation, of the 'dark ground' or of the 'abyss of divinity', but the Nothing only of the cloud of unknowing as a problematic point of departure from which affirmation concerning the divine essence would come. On the basis of this fine distinction Rosenzweig asserts that the archetypal word 'No' is younger than the archetypal word 'Yes'.

God's essence is infinite yessence. Here Rosenzweig's notion of the infinite appears to be derived from the sense in which a judgement is defined as infinite, for example by Kant, when it affirms that S is non-P. So although following Rosenzweig's method only the Nothing of God is given, and since the Yes cannot refer to the Nothing because that would be to exceed the merely heuristic positing of the Nothing as a point of departure for knowledge, the Yes must relate to the non-Nothing: 'Therefore the affirmation of the non-Nothing circumscribes as inner limit the infinity of all that is not Nothing. An infinity is affirmed: God's infinite essence, his infinite actuality, his *phusis*'; 'so umschreibt die Bejahung des Nichtnichts als innere Grenze die Unendlichkeit alles dessen, was nicht Nichts ist. Es wird ein Unendliches bejaht: Gottes unendliches Wesen, seine unendliche Tatsächlichkeit, seine Physis'.[3]

That Rosenzweig is aware how difficult these sentences will be found by his reader is indicated by his warning that they state only purely formal preliminaries. An obvious source of difficulty for the reader following the *Star* as a guide to the interpretation of the words 'God' and 'Infinity' as understood by Levinas is Rosenzweig's reference to God's infinite essence. How can that be anything but a hindrance to interpreting the 'beyond essence' referred to in the title of Levinas's book? This would be one reason for agreeing with the statement made by Robert Gibbs in his admirable study *Correlations in Rosenzweig and Levinas* that in the sense intended in this title Levinas and Rosenzweig are not in correlation – to which statement it can be added that in Levinas's sense of that word no two human beings are ultimately in correlation. Rather, 'Levinas creates a *drash*', Gibbs says, and the verb here is carefully chosen; 'he makes an adaptation of Rosenzweig'.[4] However, it can be added also perhaps that Levinas creates a *drash* – a Hebrew/Greek chiasmic *drash*, perhaps one could say – of essence, as at least in *Totality and Infinity* he creates a *drash* of being. That is to say, he exalts, emphasizes, creatively exaggerates these words beyond their ontological sense, or discovers that they exaggerate and produce themselves, as with scores of others, not least the word 'ontological' and, to return to our immediate worry, the words 'Amen' or 'Yes' and 'God'.

'Yes', Rosenzweig writes,

> is the arche-word of language, one of those which first make possible, not sentences, but any kind of sentence-forming words at all, words as parts of a sentence. Yes is not a part of a sentence, but neither is it a shorthand symbol for a sentence, although it can be employed as such. Rather it is the silent accompaniment of all parts of a sentence, the confirmation, the 'sic!', the 'Amen' behind every word. It gives every word in the sentence its right to exist, it supplies the seat on which it may take its place, it 'posits'. The first Yes in God establishes the divine essence for all infinity. And this first Yes is 'in the beginning'.

Why does Yes make words but not sentences possible? Rosenzweig's answer to this question both anticipates and qualifies the Saussurian structuralist doctrine that the meaning of a word is more negative than positive. While recognizing the reason for saying this, Rosenzweig says almost the opposite. Having associated position with the position of a word, he goes on to grant that what is posited depends not only on the other words in a given sentence but on words in other sentences in which that word might figure. The meaning of a word is the class of its sentence-frames. But this relation of a word in one sentence to words in the same and other sentences is expressed by the arche-word No. This No expresses opposition rather than position. However, since the identity of what is posited is a function of the alterity of what is opposited and vice versa, a third original word has to be posited, the word 'And'. This primordial And expresses the systematicity of language as *langue* on which every speech act of language as *langage* or *parole* depends. The question of the relative priority between Yes and No thus raises the question of the relative priority between system and act of speech, and this question raises the question or pseudo-question of the relative priority between historical and logical priority.

Saussure says that while the linguistic system and some mastery of it are logically presupposed by the performance of acts of speech, the latter are historically prior.[5] There are problems with this claim that can only be mentioned here in passing. For example, can even locutary acts, let alone illocutary acts be performed without presupposing competence in finding one's way about a system of grammar? Are not *langue* and *parole* conditions of each other? Are they not equiprimordial? The same answer would seem to be called for when the analogous question is raised with regard to systematicity and sincerity as treated by Levinas. Yet Levinas sometimes says that the giving of my word to the Other is not equiprimordial with the grasp of a grammatical or conceptual system, but prior to it. In what sense can it be prior? In a sense of priority that is presumably prior both to the priority of formally logical system and to that of historical events. So the priority of neither, a priority that is constitutive and at the same time deconstitutive of the continuum of time and of the order of logical implication and presupposition: the priority of a certain primary 'position', of a *Setzen* before *Gesetz*.

In trying to sort out Rosenzweig's answer to these questions concerning the order of priority of Yes and No and of the historical and logical his distinction between originality and age must be recalled. When he says that the original *Non* is not *propter sic* but *post sic*, that is, not on account of but after the Thus affirmed by Yes, it sounds as though he is saying that although Yes and No, and we now conjoin And, are all original, Yes is in some sense historically older. But when he says that No is not on account of Yes, can he be denying that it is logically dependent on it? And has his quasi-Saussurian and quasi-Hegelian argument not shown that the reverse holds equally? It would seem that he is arguing both for systematicity and for its delimitation. If No is more immediately connected with the infinity of non-Ps affirmed of the Nothing of God from which Rosenzweig's argument departs, and if No is more directly connected, as he also maintains, with God's freedom, God's essence is, as we put it, his Yessence because No itself is a word that must be affirmed. We must distinguish on the one hand the rhetorical opposition between the Yes and No of affirmation and denial, as well as the non-parallel semantic opposition of True and False, from, on the other hand, the affirmation that appends a speaker's signature, *firma* or mark to what he says, whether what he says, the word that is marked by it, is positive or negative, and whether what he says is true or false.

We must distinguish truth from truthfulness or, as Levinas variously writes, veracity and sincerity, meaning not the veracity that is opposed to the deceit or insincerity with which I may address myself to another or to myself, but the veracity in the name of which even such deceitfulness must be practised. A No may masquerade as a Yes. One may be suspicious whether what appears to be a Yes is a No, but one's suspicion is always backed by a Yes. However far back one retreats, what one moves toward is not a No behind a Yes but a Yes behind a Yes or a No. Even the Hear-Hear of Nietzsche's ass is doubled by an Amen Amen posited in the beginning, however remotely the beginning is postponed, however immemorial its past, the past quasi-performative Thereby to which every Hereby owes its force.[6]

This difficult phrase 'past quasi-performative Thereby' marks the difficult time and place of the tacit contract that any explicit contract presupposes. Rosenzweig's primal Amen is also tacit. It is, we noted, the silent accompaniment or companion (*der stille Begleiter*) of all parts of a sentence. This absolute reticence is required also by Levinas when he says that the Saying of witness without words, but not with empty hands (*Dire sans paroles, mais non pas les mains vides*) precedes the Said (*DVI* 122, *CPP* 170). In saying this he runs the risk, fine or otherwise, of implying a primal speechless scene behind the scenes, a post-ontotheological version of the theological transcendentalism with which he and Nietzsche try to break. It is all too easy to slip into thinking of the unrememberable past on analogy with the myth of an age before the ages of the world. Perhaps this idea is fostered by reading Levinas through an oversimple reading of Rosenzweig and of a book that is too often present to be cited in the text of *The Star of Redemption*, Schelling's *Ages of the World*.[7] Such a reading of Levinas cannot be correct for it makes use of a naive continuist notion of time that would be at best appropriate only to the Said. Nor are matters much improved when Levinas's many references to the unrepresentable past are taken together with his less frequent references to the unrepresentable future and that future is pictured as a messianic promised land on which we have not yet set foot. The chances of interpreting in this way Levinas's assertion of the precedence of Saying to the Said are dashed and drashed by his apparently contradictory assertion that something must be said (*dit*) about how things are before purely and simply saying (*dire*) (*AE* 183–4n., *OB* 198n.). This appearance of contradiction is the pivot of Levinas's appeal to the return of scepticism despite scepticism's apparent self-refutation. Rather than repeat here what he says about that, let us take note of the apparent carelessness with which, in *Otherwise than Being* at least, Levinas employs the expressions 'on this side' (*en deçà*), and 'on the other side' (*au-delà*). There seems to be no consistent pattern in his uses of these expressions. To mention only a few of these uses: 'on this side of' is prefixed to references to nature and its states (*AE* 106, *OB* 83), to being, to the said, to the free and unfree (*AE* 94, *OB* 75), to ontology (*AE* 59, *OB* 46); the Self is said to be on this side of coincidence with itself (*AE* 143n., *OB* 195n.); responsibility is said to be on this side of memorable time. 'On the other side' or 'beyond' is prefixed to essence, but in one and the same paragraph, when writing of the reduction of the said to the saying, Levinas says that this is a reduction to what is on the other side of Logos, and when explaining that it is not to an entity that reduction of being leads he writes disjunctively of what is 'on this side or on that side of being' (*AE* 57, cp. 121, *OB* 45, cp. 95). It is as though his title could just as well have been *Autrement qu'être ou en deçà de l'essence* or *Autrement qu'être ou au-delà ou en deçà de l'essence.* Either prepositional phrase is correct, depending on your point of view, and there are two points of view. However, to speak of points of view is to speak representationally and so to misrepresent the saying as a said. One moment of discourse is translated, but the other moment of discourse is betrayed (*AE* 31, 88, *OB* 24, 70). Betrayed, however, in both senses of the word. The point is made early in *Otherwise than Being* when Levinas distinguishes verbally infinitive to-be from nominalized essence but notes that the verbality of the propositional to-be 'makes essence re-sound without entirely deadening the echo of the to-say that bears it and brings it to light' (*AE* 60, cp. IX, *OB* 47, cp. xli). Perhaps there is a re-echo of this echo in John Austin's discovery that his original attempt to distinguish constative from performative speech acts ends in defeat, because on the hither and thither side of what is stated there resounds the 'hereby', the 'hear! hear!' or Amen of ratification performing constation, perforating the message.[8] But the defeat of the moment of pure constation is not the triumph of the moment of the pure to-say. The to-say must suffer the defeat of the attempt to constate it. Only thus, through struggle and the pain of mourning (*lutte et douleur*) is confirmed the 'thus', the *sic* of the saying that confirms or ratifies; only by contestation does it receive attestation (*AE* 148n., *OB* 195–6n.). Only if the not entirely deadened echo of the to-say is an absolutely passive suffering in the activity of speech. Only if in this not entirely deadened echo resounds the death-knell of a certain God, as Levinas says.

That certain or uncertain God was a God of the *Jenseits*, the Beyond. But Levinas maintains that the transcendence of the beyond of the beyond-being transcends the beyond of that onto-theological transcendence. Its thither, unlike the *Jenseits* of the God whose death Nietzsche's Zarathustra proclaims, is not to be simply opposed to its hither. No wonder we could find no consistent pattern of opposition between Levinas's uses of *au-delà* and *en-deçà*.

LONG LIVE GOD

But, to return to our point of departure, why does his ethics within the bounds of ratification alone not also say Amen, Finis, End of History, to the word 'God'? Why does his critique of pure religion say only *À-Dieu*, Goodbye, God-be-with-you, notwithstanding that the extraordinary word 'God' will be a scandal to many potential readers of *Otherwise than Being*? One reason perhaps is that the God you don't know is better than the God you think you do. If 'God' is a word in the life of those to whom one is addressing in 'Greek' the claim that ethics is *protê-philosophia*, then it is a word from which it would be dangerous to avert one's eyes. Ignored, it could hardly fail to be a stumbling-block. This is a lesson Levinas teaches more insistently than do Heidegger and Derrida, the lesson that the old words cannot be simply abandoned in creating the new, that one cannot take leave without ceremony, the lesson, embalmed in the phrase *faire son deuil*, that to take one's leave may be to take on the difficulty of mourning. If, with some risk of oversimplification, it can be said that *Totality and Infinity* rises beyond being and fundamental ontology by demonstrating how being and ontology rise emphatically above their selves to what is 'more ontological than ontology' (*DVI* 143), it can perhaps be said that *Otherwise than Being* performs a similar feat for the word 'God'. 'I pronounce the word God', Levinas writes in that book, 'without suppressing the intermediaries that lead me to this word, and, if I may say so, the anarchy of its entry into discourse, just as phenomenology states concepts without ever destroying the scaffoldings that permit one to climb up to them' (*AE* 165, *OB* 128). Indeed, maybe this hyperbolization of the word 'God' leans on the hyperbolization of 'being' – and of another word whose power *Totality and Infinity* would interrupt: the word 'power' itself, or *pouvoir*, to be able. For the de- and re-construal without destruction of the word 'God' that *Otherwise than Being* would effect is modified by the adverb *peut-être* ('couldbe'). The essay entitled 'The Name of God according to certain Talmudic Texts' is collected in the volume entitled *L'au-delà du verset*. Although the subtitle of this volume is *Lectures et discours talmudiques*, that does not make them purely confessional texts. For when Levinas seeks to get beyond the verse it is in order to teach a philosophical lesson, and to do so in 'Greek' (*TRI* 47). The essay in question is grouped with other readings Levinas calls 'Theologies' in the plural, meaning by this not that any dogmatic theology is propounded in them, but that they seek to speak in a rational way about God. And it is in a subsection entitled 'Philosophy' of the essay on the name of God that he writes: 'But the language of thematisation that we are using at this very same moment has maybe been rendered only possible [*a peut-être été rendu seulement possible*] by this Relation and is only ancillary' (*ADV* 157, *BTV* 128). The Relation here referred to is that of the animating responsibility of which he has said a moment before that, 'before discourse bearing on the said', it is 'probably the essence of language'. Here, meeting the difficulty for our 'correlation' of Rosenzweig and Levinas presented by the fact that the latter wishes to pronounce the word 'God' without letting divinity be said (*AE* 206, *OB* 162), the word 'essence' should be heard with scare-quotes, the shudder- or *Schaudern*-quotes (as we shall shortly find reason to say) with which Rosenzweig might have invested the word in the sentence I cited earlier which declares that 'The first Yes in God establishes the divine essence for all infinity.' It could be that the same should be said about the 'could-be' or 'maybe' in the sentence just cited from Levinas, even though he says in it that at that very same moment he is using the language of thematization. Does not the very same word in the moment of its thematization resound with the diachronically re-, pro- but not in-tended moment of the echoing Amen? And must not the same be said of those other modal words here encountered, 'possible', 'probably', and of the 'maybe' as it is said once again in Levinas's statement that the word 'illeity' – a nominalized pronoun, marking the excluded third beyond being and non-being, beyond the modalities that are *Seinsweisen*, *manières d'être*, beyond scepticism and its self-refutation – marks maybe what is said also by the name or pronoun 'God'?

This 'maybe' must be distinguished from the 'maybe' that is opposed to epistemological certitude which, Levinas would say, is not the only 'maybe' of Descartes's *Meditations on First Philosophy*, but is one that is provoked by the repeated return of epistemological scepticism despite the vulnerability of scepticism to self-refutation (*AE* 210ff., *OB* 165ff.). This other enigmatic 'maybe' must be distinguished too from the 'maybe' of the temptation of temptation. The temptation of temptation is the distancing of philosophical dilettantism. It is the ego's distancing itself in knowledge that gives itself the illusion that it can remain free to flirt with the object of desire without the engagement of Desire (*QLT* 74–5, *NTR* 34). The moment, of which Kierkegaard learned that it could be no more than a moment. It is the temporary fancy that I can, with clean and empty hands, separate myself from the separation across which I am responsible for the Other. As though the philosopher were not called to reduce thematization. As though there were not another 'maybe', the 'maybe' of the Other whose saying exceeds what is said.

This latter 'maybe' is said, but still very unstraightforwardly, when Levinas refers to 'The Revelation of the beyond being which is certainly not maybe only a word [*sic: qui certes n'est peut-être qu'un mot* [!]],' adding 'but this "maybe" belongs to an ambiguity where the anarchy of the Infinite resists the univocity of an origin or principle; to an ambiguity or ambivalence and an inversion that is enunciated precisely in the word God' (*AE* 199, *OB* 156). This 'maybe' does not belong to Heideggerian belonging. It is not simply from the meaning of being that the meaning of maybeing is engendered. Nor does it belong to the epistemological range of certitude and doubt. It belongs to the enigmatic unplace of unbelonging between the epistemologico-ontological and the proto-ethical. This *peut-être* draws its breath, or finds itself out of breath, in a climate other than that of the capacity to know or of the enabling of being, *Seinkönnen*. However,

Levinas's claim that ethics is proto-philosophy is not a simple inversion of the claim Heidegger made at Zurich in 1951 that 'the experience of God and his revelation (so far as this comes man's way) takes place in the dimension of being'.[9] But we should have to try to speak of the shudder-producing things the 'experience' or experimental testing (*épreuve*) of God means for Levinas – *schauderhaft* things, we might say, following his citation from Goethe's *Faust* by way of epigraph to the final chapter of *Otherwise than Being* (this epigraph has a key line in common with the epigraph of Otto's *The Idea of the Holy*)[10] where the last thing that that citation invokes is sacramental fear and trembling – if we are to test the worry which has motivated this chapter and which will return like an itch beneath the skin in the last. That worry is a disquietude in the sense of the *Besorgnis* which Heidegger distinguishes from and subordinates to *Sorge*, existential care or concern, and its existential modes (*SZ* 192). It is the worry over what *more* might be said except 'illeity' and that anagram of 'name', 'Amen', by the exceptional name or pro-name 'God'. We should have to try to speak of the tests, trials or ordeals (*épreuves*) Levinas is remembering when he says that phenomenology must be concrete, among them the events that took place between 1933 and 1945 of which he says that they contributed to his break with the later phenomenology of Husserl (*EN* 142), events which overflowed any idea of concrete experience Rosenzweig and Schelling could have invoked to explain what they meant when they described their philosophy or theology as 'positive'.[11] If Levinas is not caricaturing his teaching when he writes in *Entre nous* that human being is not only being-in-the-world, hence not only being toward one's own death, but being toward the Book (*zum-Buch-sein*) (*EN* 127), it may well be that the lay reader of that Book will have to make an effort to learn the ancient languages in which it was written, for 'One cannot reject the Scriptures without knowing how to read them' (*DL* 77, *DF* 53). That is a responsibility and risk to which the reader may be called. However, if the *cri de coeur* of that reader after the death of God is to receive a response – and how, consistently with Levinas's doctrine, could the responsibility to give a response be denied? – it is important that that Book should be able to untie one's tongue from a shibboleth. It is important to see therefore that notwithstanding the oblique references on so many of Levinas's pages to the unpronounceable Name of God, notwithstanding his reference to the word 'God' as a *hapax legomenon* (*AE* 199, *OB* 156), he insists that the relation to God is presented non-metaphorically in the relation to the transcendence of the face of the other human being.

It so happens that the transcendence of the face is traced through the transcendence of a word in an exegesis recorded by Levinas of an incident commented upon in the Talmud (*Sôta* 53b). According to Numbers 5 a woman suspected by her husband of adultery must be taken to the Temple where the pontiff exclaims 'If a man had intercourse with you, may you be cursed by the Eternal (written as Tetragram)'. And the woman responds 'Amen, amen.'[12] The pontiff's words containing the Tetragram are then written in ink on a parchment from which they are effaced by being immersed in the bitter water. In this way, Levinas notes, the ancient prohibition against the effacement of the Name is superseded for the sake of the reconciliation of human beings (*ADV* 152–3, *BTV* 123–4).

Another, though inevitably still not unenigmatic clue to the way an entry into the Book may be an entry into a humanism that is neither specifically Jewish nor specifically Christian is provided by Levinas's citation of the New Testament in support of his claim that although the Other is not to be identified with God, the Word of God is heard in the Other's face (*visage*), that is to say in his or her looking to me (*EN* 128). According to Matthew 25, when those on the Lord's right hand and on his left protest that they have neither given nor refused food, drink or shelter to Him, they are told 'Inasmuch as ye have done it unto one of the least of my brethren ye have done it unto me.'

So in this humanism of the other human being in which atheism is defined as the restriction of thinking to intentional representation where the thinking and what is represented may in principle be mutually adequate (*EN* 145, 246), and, precisely by being so defined, allows of subversion by the non-intentionality of ethical 'experience' that accompanies every intentional experience (*EN* 146) as the pre-original *responsio* Amen accompanies (*begleitet*) every word, maybe that experience, although expressed by the word God, is not dependent on that word for its expression; maybe that word does not have to be said when one says Amen. '"Me voici, au nom de Dieu". . . . "Me voici" tout court!' (*AE* 190, *OB* 149).

Or, reminding ourselves that hidden stumbling-blocks are more dangerous than unhidden ones, lest the silent return of the God of a reality behind the scenes be facilitated by the obliteration of His name, should perhaps the iterated effacement of that name be effaced in turn by the eternal return of the name, forever coming and forever going, enigmatically on the hither side and on the thither side of the opposition between Yes and No, like the winking of a star? If so, although we may begin by reminding ourselves, as Léon Brunschvicg reminds us, of the danger of worshipping the shadow of concepts we believe we have slain (*DL* 71, *DF* 48), and that a concept cannot be redefined without keeping the concept's old name, readers of Levinas must keep on reminding themselves that he is seeking neither to reinstate an old concept nor to introduce a new one like an astronomer scanning the heavens until his telescope comes to rest on a heavenly body so far overlooked. His writing is disastrous, a patient *écriture du dés-astre*. The frequentative trace in it of Rosenzweig's *Stern* means precisely that the thinking beyond thinking that endures in it, its consideration beyond consideration, is not the tracking of a star, not *auf einen Stern zugehen*, even when that star is not a being but being, uniquely this, *nur dieses* (*DMT* 164).[13] On the hither and thither side of any star fixed in the firmament, susception before and after perception and conception, is the Amen, the pre-original Yes in which experience originates, affirmed by the Other in me (*TEI* 66, *TI* 93), thanks to whom this me is never a me and no more, never a me *tout court*. If You, *Autrui*, the pronoun of the pronoun Me, has as its pronoun He, and He is the pronoun of God, otherwise other than *Autrui*, then, Yes, Amen, like Jonah, I cannot escape from God. But if (hereby to repeat Levinas's constation of contestation), voicing, the *en gage* of *langage*, is the fact (*sic: fait*) that 'God' is the only word that always proffers itself as *Opfer* and is the very word that verily paroles transcendence, thereby suffering from an equivocity of which one moment is the contestation voiced by 'It is maybe only a word' (*AE* 199, *OB* 157, *NP* 137), then it is maybe the only word that voices the worry with that word from which I cannot escape. *De l'évasion*? *Plus d'évasion*!

I can no other, God help me!
Amen.

Thus spoke the wandering shadow of Zarathustra.[14]

13 Anthology

ULTRA- AND ALTER-HUMANISM

The wanderer who calls himself the shadow of Zarathustra is one of the higher men who despite being on the way to becoming free spirits disappoint Zarathustra by occasionally declaring, in the final part of Nietzsche's 'book for all and none', that in the case of gods death is always a mere prejudice, and that the old god lives again. However, it is Zarathustra himself who in the Prologue has said 'I love him whose soul is overfull, so that he forgets himself, and all things are in him: thus all things become his going down.' These words are cited by Levinas as an epigraph to his essay 'Humanism and An-archy'. How does humanism of the other man relate to the over-humanism of Nietzsche? The man Zarathustra loves is the man who is a bridge from the beast to the overman. This man willingly goes down in order to make a way for the overman. His self-sacrifice anticipates that of the overman and of Zarathustra his prophet. That this man's soul is overfull and that all things are in him is something that could be said of Levinas's human being who supports all, in the spirit of Rabbi Hayyim of Volozhyn's *The Soul of Life* and of Dostoevsky's Markel in *The Brothers Karamazov* who says 'Each of us is culpable before all for all and me more than others' (*AE* 186, *OB* 146).[1]

Despite these similarities, a significant difference remains. The man Zarathustra loves becomes a bridge by forgetting himself, yet this forgetting is active, not passive in Levinas's non-dynamic sense. And Levinas would say that Nietzschean man's happening to forget is possible only because of a past and passedness that is forgotten absolutely because it is absolutely incapable of being remembered; it cannot be brought to mind because it is outside all capacity and incapacity. Nietzschean will to power is in its early stages a will to will. Even when turned against oneself and one's egoism, even though the power it wills means one's own death, it remains a *conatus essendi*. It remains a power in the play of the difference of powers, and it remains in the sphere of being, even when being ceases to be remaining and confers the dignity of being upon becoming only because being becomes construed as pure affirmation free of all negativity. This active affirmation puts behind it the gravity that still invests the services performed by Zarathustra's donkey and camel. Ultimately it becomes lightness, childlike innocence and creative play. Levinas's frequent references to play, sometimes explicitly associated in his texts with references to Nietzsche, Jeanne Delhomme and Eugen Fink, 'thinkers . . . who require, among the conditions of the world, . . . a freedom of play' (*AE* 148, *OB* 116, *NP* 69–77)[2] make it clear that for him play is not an ultimate, and that creativity, which for Nietzsche is *par excellence* the creativity of art (but see the next chapter), is for Levinas *par excellence* the creativity of ethical excess. If the essence of the creativity of being as becoming is expressed most felicitously in the production of art, creativity will be the production of metaphors. And that is what it is for the philosopher as artist.

METAPHORS

In the posthumous fragment 'On Truth and Lie in an Extra-moral Sense' (1873) Nietzsche asks

> What then is truth? A mobile army of metaphors, metonyms, and an-thropomorphisms – in short, a sum of human relations, which have been enhanced, transposed, and embellished poetically and rhetorically, and which after long use seem firm, canonical, and obligatory to a people: truths are illusions about which one has forgotten that this is what they are; metaphors which have lost their pictures and now matter only as metal, no longer as coins.[3]

The task of the new philosopher-artist is one of recoinage, neologism, the reintoxication of sober truth through the creation of new metaphors. This is not the task of the new philosopher as Levinas sees him. Although on page after page of the texts in which he practises philosophy as both the love of wisdom and the wisdom of love Levinas seems to be offering new words or newly burnished words for old, those apparent semantic neologisms are more like pre-semantic paleologisms. And he denies explicitly again and again on those pages that these pseudo-neologisms are metaphors. In order to reach an explanation of these denials, and at the same time to locate this explanation in relation to other conceptions of philosophy and metaphysics more or less plainly in view throughout Levinas's articulation of his own conception in *Otherwise than Being*, let us pause at the point of chiasmic contact – and he never uses the word 'contact' lightly – at which Levinas says his path makes contact with Derrida's. By looking in the direction in which Derrida's path leads it will become clear whether Levinas's ethical conception of philosophy, like Zarathustra's shadow tempted to put his trust again in the metaphysical god he thought he had killed, reinstates truth in the extra-moral sense which Nietzsche's artistic conception of philosophy puts to rout. One thing is already clear from Levinas's redefinitive emphasis of philosophy from love of wisdom to wisdom of love, or the former inspired by the latter. It is clear that given this distinction – made in *Otherwise than Being* and underlined in the preface to the German edition of *Totality and Infinity* in 1987 where the wisdom of love is equated with philosophy as the love of love (*EN* 252) – there need be no conflict between Derrida and Levinas if the former says in 'Violence and Metaphysics' that not to philosophize is to philosophize still[4] and the latter says in 'God and Philosophy' that not to philosophize is not to philosophize still (*HLR* 166).

Further, by going some way along Derrida's path before returning to Levinas, it will be possible to learn how Levinas might respond to one of the questions of primordial importance, as he calls them in his essay on Derrida, which the latter poses in one of his essays on Levinas, namely why Levinas cannot acknowledge that the conditions of non-violent discourse that he seeks are already to be found in Husserlian phenomenology and the fundamental ontology of Heidegger. Lastly, we shall find placed in our hands a key to a reading of *Otherwise than Being* if we begin groping for it in certain texts of Derrida's that treat of metaphor, metonymy and rhetoric. Although that reading will be a reading that sees double, it will be stone-cold sober. But because we begin the trip toward it in the company of Nietzsche's tipsy terpsichorean Dionysus, swaying from right to left and left to right, seeking support now from one column of text then another, it should be borne in mind from the outset that what is in play throughout this Derridian interruption is, as we might say metaphorically, the relation between, in the one hand, a glass of clear water, and, in the other, a glass of heady red wine; that is to say, literally, what is in play is the connection between two little connecting words, the copulative 'is' and the 'as' or *qua* of the *qua*-lity predicated of a thing in a metaphor.

In the *Rhetoric* (Bk III, ch. 4, 1406b 20–4) Aristotle defines a metaphor as an abbreviated or implicit comparison, as an analogy from which the word 'as' or 'like' is omitted, as for example 'All the world's a stage'. For our and Derrida's purposes it suffices to define a metaphor as an expression employed with a transferred sense, the sense of this as that, where the transfer is motivated by resemblance. This definition of metaphor as the trope of resemblance allows allegory, fables, myths and even explicit comparisons like Hölderlin's 'words, like flowers' to count as metaphors, as they do in *The Garden of Epicurus*, Derrida's comments on which are about to become the topic of our concern.[5]

Given the breadth of this definition of metaphor, what we are about to find Derrida saying about it here should be kept in mind when our concern is what Levinas writes concerning myth and the place of metaphor in the philosophical text. This is the tropical topic that is announced in the subtitle of Derrida's essay 'La mythologie blanche'.[6] At the end of this essay on white or blank mythology ('White Mythology: Metaphor in the Text of Philosophy') stands a stone, a white, blank or black gravestone commemorating the death of philosophy. This degenerative genitive 'of' is double, both objective and subjective. The death of which it deals is dealt, says Derrida, by metaphor, which, he says, always carries its death within itself. When he says this is he not talking about death metaphorically? If he is, does this mean that metaphorical death will deal death to metaphorical death? Will that return metaphor to life and life to philosophy? What he means by the doubleness of the degenerative but also possibly regenerative 'of' of 'the death of philosophy', philosophy's coming to be and passing away, is amplified when he goes on to say that this death

> is sometimes . . . death of a genre belonging to philosophy which is thought and summarized within it, recognizing and accomplishing itself within philosophy; and sometimes the death of a philosophy which does not see itself die and is no longer to be found within philosophy.[7]

How are we to see the relation between this interiority and this exteriority, between these two deaths? From the assertion that one of these deaths is not seen we can already see that the relation between the two must remain invisible. In words unstitched from the end of Emily Dickinson's verses beginning 'I heard a fly buzz when I died', it will be something that we cannot see to see.

The stone marking the boundary between these two deaths at the end of 'White Mythology' relates to the corner-stones of an essay in the anthology *Dissemination* entitled 'The Double Session'.[8] These *pierres angulaires* are *pierres d'attente*, toothing stones, that is to say, 'stones that reach out from one space to another, at the extremity of a wall, to make a connection with the wall one plans to erect alongside', as the Littré dictionary explains, adding that the expression is also used, as by Voltaire in a letter to the King of Prussia, with the figurative sense of 'something that serves as a beginning, certain repetitions, certain loose and unstitched lines of verse that are used as *pierres d'attente*'. Derrida unstitches certain lines of Mallarmé's prose piece *Magie* so that they can be wrapped like a curtain-wall around the keep of the text.[9] Those lines are broken after 'philoso-' on page 196 of the French edition and before 'phale' on page 318 in Mallarmé's phrase 'The null stone, dreaming of gold, called philosophal' ('La pierre nulle, qui rêve l'or, dite philosophale'). Derrida's essay, itself bipartite, occupies the space opened up by his hyphenation of this last word. But, says Derrida in *Psyché* (posing as what he calls a *pierre d'attente* at the end of 'Moi – la psychanalyse' the question whether there is any crypt or phantom [any haunting *psychisme* or psyche Levinas might prefer to say] in the Ego of psychoanalysis), one does not want to assume knowledge of what is meant by the word *pierre*.[10] As for the stone called 'philosophal', the 'phal' alludes no doubt to the phallogocentrism of classical (glassical) meta-physics, to the symbol borne in Bacchic orgies, and to the colossal columns of India news of which passes to Greece through the pillars of Hercules and whose treatment by Hegel will be one of the passages to be remarked on in passing in the columns of *Glas*.[11]

The other section from the Hegelian corpus whose passing *Glas* will toll is that which treats of the religion of flowers. Without stopping to examine the way in which the passage from one to the other of these passages is effected in Hegel, we should nevertheless remind ourselves that a stone may be the stone of a fruit of a tree that might be a metaphor for a family genealogy or a tree of Porphyry, and that porphyry is also a stone. Note above all that the heliotrope, the sunflower, that grows in the garden of Epicurus – we revisit this garden below – is introduced in 'White Myth-ology' under the subtitle 'Exergue'. An exergue is an epigraph, so neither properly inside nor outside the main text. An exergue is also an inscription on a coin. The heliotrope, planted on the margin of the text, even before 'White Mythology' gets properly under way, is also, as is announced in the essay's very last words, a kind of oriental jasper, a stone, neither the black or anaemic white of mourning now, but 'a precious stone, greenish and streaked with red veins', the colours of wine, blood, life and (*j'espère*) hope. So the sunflower is the figure both of oriental figurativity and at the same time of the thing itself, of *la Chose*, which is etymologically con-nected with *la Cause*, which may be the first cause, for example, the first cause, through the Latin *causari* meaning 'to make out a case', of the French *causer*, meaning 'to chat'.

All this will sound like etymologism and metaphorologism gone mad. Let us now remind ourselves therefore that there is a method in this madness. Let us remind ourselves that we are guided by the thought that out of this diaphorous riot of images, symbols and icons, we are hoping to reach some sober conceptual truth. Let us remind ourselves that the sunflower is the emblem of what could not be more simple, the connection between those two little connecting words, the 'as' and the 'is', that is, the 'is' as such. Yes, *si*, it is as if dialectical negation is being put in reverse, as if *Sa*, signifying *Savoir absolu*, the absolute knowing of absolute being or the concept of the system of Hegelian idealism, is being spelt back to front, rewritten as 'as'. Or at least that is what would seem to have to be the case if what the philosopher's stone is expected to perform is not the magic of metamorphosing base metal or matter into the nobility of gold, the gold of the sunflower and the flowers of rhetoric, but the trick of returning to base, to dig down to where one's spade is turned in the ground in which grows Mallarmé's and Van Gogh's flower that is absent from all bouquets. If what philosophy wants to do is not to carouse with Columbine or get tipsy with Bacchus, but to turn wine into colourless, odourless water, into the neutrality or nullity of blank being, then the really and truly blank mythology will be the mythology of the bare existential quantifier or of pure predication, the relationality of sheer apposition, the transparent rationality of logical connection, the virginity of copulativity as such.

But blank mythology *is* a mythology, or rather it turns out to be white mythology and the whiteness turns out to be constituted by every colour of the spectrum refracted in the prism of colourless glass. On the one hand, to speak with Hegel up to a certain point, being as 'is' and 'is' as 'as' (or as 'has', as property or attribute) turn into each other as the sensible orient sun whose circling is followed by the flower that turns in every sense into the source of the light of sense and truth. On the other hand, what is a source, and what is the light of sense, what is truth, *alêtheia*, what is the what-is, what is its *qua*, what is the *ti esti* of 'as', and of the 'as as such'? We seem to be caught up in a circle, a circle that turns out to have been an ellipse with one focus as 'is' and of which the other focus is 'as'.

But, it will be objected, there remains the distinction between 'is' and 'as' even if we cannot say what something is without recourse to the 'as', without recourse to what something is like or to what it is to be like what one is, without recourse to the *analogy* of being. And even that we cannot do this has not yet been shown. For our wanton indulgence in explicit metaphors so far does not mean that one cannot say non-metaphorically what one wants to say. The question is whether we can do that in philosophy, in philosophy which must include a metaphysical theory of metaphor.

QUASI-METAPHORS

Can there be a metaphysical theory of metaphor? Not without difficulty if we hold what we might call the 'metymological' theory of metaphysics defended in Anatole France's *The Garden of Epicurus* by Polyphilos. His metymologism is a combination of five theses, at least one of which we have already been made familiar with by Nietzsche. It asserts:

1 The sense of an expression cannot be severed from its root sense.
2 The root sense of an expression is sensory.
3 The senses of metaphysical terms are taken by metaphysicians to be literal and non-sensory. This is because:
4 The memory of the derivation of the so-called literal senses of metaphysical terms from sensory meanings has been effaced like the figures on a coin worn blank by use.
5 Metaphysics must reveal its metaphorical credentials.

Metymologism thus defined presents a difficulty for the special version of white mythology known as metaphysics. The language of metaphysics purports to be both literal and abstract, though not necessarily abstracted – for it may not be quite coherent to say both that a term is literal and that it is abstracted. The images on the coins of metaphysical exchange, their exergues, have, in the image both Polyphilos and Nietzsche use, been used up, worn down. Their relief, as Derrida's Hegel says, has been relieved, *relevé, aufgehoben*. (As Levinas might say, the image is no longer *accusé*.) While not denying but indeed affirming the immediately sensory connotation of words in their earliest applications, Hegel is not a metymologist. *Glas* observes that Hegel 'did not entrust to etymology the right to regulate a concept's content. . . . That the same word or two words of analogous root can have two conceptually different, verily opposite significations proves that a word is never a concept'.[12] The prime example of such a word for Hegel is *Aufhebung*, whose verily opposite significations of negating and affirming at a more elevated level of synthesis Hegel delights in. They enable that word to perform the function allocated to it in the development of the Hegelian concept itself. That development is indeed one of abstraction from out of the supposedly pure sensory, but since the sensory is already an abstracted fragment of experience the development Hegel calls *Aufhebung* is the reverse of abstraction. By the criteria of the logic of spirit it is concrete reintegration. It is not impossible that it is for rationalism of the Hegelian variety that Polyphilos' interlocutor in Anatole France's dialogue stands. This would not be altogether inconsistent with his being called Aristos, a name that may be intended to suggest that his conception of metaphysics is aristocratic and Platonistic to the extent that it defends the dignity of ideas against the indignity of being reduced, as they are by Polyphilos, to a material, empirical base. It is anyway quite clear that Aristos does not agree with Polyphilos that metaphysicians are 'sad poets' or metataphysicians, students of what is *meta ta phusika*, beyond the physical – or beyond the *Physics* of Aristotle. However, it would be too hasty to infer Aristotelian sympathies from Aristos' name, especially if Aristotle is thought of as a founder of empiricism. We can only guess what Aristos' positive views are because after Polyphilos has produced an elaborate and, as he says, Vedic (he might have said Presocratic) reconcretization of the sentence 'The soul possesses God to the degree that it participates in the absolute', a sentence he has found in a manual of systems of philosophy from the Eleatics to Lachelier, Aristos bids his companion goodbye, remarking that he could easily have refuted the argument for the dependence of metaphysical *logos* on *mythos* if only in presenting it his companion had abided by the rules.[13]

However, it is not Derrida's intention in 'White Mythology' to take sides either with Polyphilos or with Aristos. That this is not his purpose is implied by his reference to the cause for which Aristos stands as a mythology (*mythologos*), and in his calling metaphysics a 'white mythology'. Derrida's 'thesis' or 'position', if one can use these words here, is not that the sensory sun and the Platonic sun are one and that one person's East is another person's West, so that the sun's way up is the same as the sun's way down. Closer to the mark is the idea mentioned by Aristotle (*Topics* V, 3, 131b, 20–30) that from a given point of view the source of light is out of sight, eclipsed, and ellipsed. Derrida mentions that there appear to follow from this two consequences that appear to be contradictory, 'but whose opposition in a way constructs the philosophical concept of metaphor, dividing it according to a law of ambiguity confirmed ceaselessly'.[14] As follows.

On the one hand: heliotropic metaphors are imperfect metaphors in that the occasional invisibility of the sensory sun means that its presence cannot be mastered. This makes the sensory sun a good metaphor of metaphor in the sense that a perfect metaphor would not be a metaphor. A metaphor must always to some degree be elliptical. In particular, the sensory sun is a good metaphor of the sensory in general in that the sensory is that which appears and disappears. However, this philosophico-rhetorical discourse on the nature of metaphor, as a discourse of the appearing and disappearing of the sensory sun and of the sensory as such of which the sun is a metaphor, presupposes the sun – the sun that rises naturally, physically, *phusis*-ally, in the abstract 'artificial' discourse of metaphysics.

On the other hand: if, as Aristotle says, the vanishing of the sun means that we can no longer be sure what is proper to it, the sun is not completely natural. It is in part an artificial construct or invention. So, as the metaphor *par excellence* of the natural, it:

bears within itself the means to emerge from itself; it accommodates itself to 'artificial' light, eclipses itself, ellipses itself, always has been other, itself: father, seed, fire, eye, egg, etc., that is, so many other things, providing moreover the measure of good and bad metaphors, clear and obscure metaphors; and then, at the limit, the measure of that which is worse or better than metaphor.[15]

To emerge from itself is *phuein*, to do what comes naturally. So if 'what is most natural in nature' is at the same time artificial, one cannot be content with Polyphilos' programme of requiring that the abstract artificiality of the language of metaphysics be 'cashed' in or converted into natural terms or natural gold. The very idea of a demetaphorization by which the transferred metaphysical concept is returned to the physical, sensory sense where it was originally at home itself trades on the ideas of idea, *eidos*, *Idee* and home that define the space of metaphysics and of the philosophico-rhetorical *theôria* of metaphor. 'Metaphor is less in the philosophical text (and in the rhetorical text coordinated with it) than the philosophical text is within metaphor' – though we must be careful with this 'less', for it is not a less that is straightforwardly opposed to a 'more', any less or more than *relève*, Derrida's translation (so in a sense metaphor) of Hegel's *Aufhebung*, is addition without subtraction or the reverse, for example, in Derrida's sentence or appositional phrase 'La métaphysique – relève da la métaphore.'[16] *Plus de métaphore* says that there is both more metaphor and less. When one attempts

> to conceive and to class all the metaphorical possibilities of philosophy, one metaphor, at least, always would remain excluded, outside the system: the metaphor, at the very least, without which the concept of metaphor could not be constructed, or, to syncopate an entire chain of reasoning, the metaphor of metaphor. This extra metaphor, remaining outside the field that it allows to be circumscribed, extracts or abstracts itself from this field, thus subtracting itself as a metaphor less.[17]

What unease is expressed by the words 'is not exactly a metaphor' when in his paraphrase of Polyphilos' view Derrida writes that 'The primitive meaning, the original, and always sensory and material figure . . . is not exactly a metaphor'?[18] Why would anyone be inclined to think that it is, given that it is primitive and original? Must not a metaphor be at least one remove from the original? But we must remember that metaphysical metaphors so-called have forgotten their metaphoricity. They are a kind of blind or dead metaphor, an 'as' masquerading as an 'is', a concept oblivious of its origin in a sensory image so that to the possessor of such a concept it will seem that the original sensory image is the metaphorical sense. He will be doubly blind, blind to the derivativeness of the metaphysical term and blind to his blindness. The very effacement of the metaphor's traces will be effaced in its turn. A live metaphor for Polyphilos would be one that was primitive and original in the sense that it makes recourse to primitively or derivatively sensory and material terms in order to represent other primitively or derivatively sensory terms in a way that spotlights a hitherto unremarked or under-remarked resemblance. If there is a derivativeness of this sort in the case of the operative term, the 'vehicle' or 'frame' of the metaphorical statement, for example, 'stage' in the statement 'All the world's a stage', then there will be a double transference corresponding to the double blindness or double forgetting involved in the blank mythology of metaphysics.

The most live and most eye-opening metaphors are typically those of literary or in the broad sense of both words, poetic texts: creative *poiêsis*, *Dichtung*. One might suppose that they belonged therefore to the right column of *Glas*, the one that is nearer the East if a page of *Glas* is read as a map. The so-called dead metaphors would belong to the onto-encyclopaedic left and western side of the page. One might suppose that one of the issues raised by *Glas* is one already raised by the Hegelian encyclopaedia, namely whether the sensory and material life represented by the column on the right is more than a transitional albeit necessary stage through which consciousness passes toward an absolutely spiritual life. And if that spiritual life is conceived as that of the word spoken by the living breath, one might suppose Derrida to be announcing the victory of death. Is that not the message conveyed by the spatial layout of *Glas*? Is it not the living word that is betrayed by its judases? Surely, that this is Derrida's thesis in *Glas*, his anti-synthesis to Hegel's synthesis of thesis and antithesis, is what we have been led to expect by Derrida's reduction of speaking to script, to epigraphs on the graves of departed spirits? This at least is one of the messages of 'White Mythology', according to *La métaphore vive*, the book in which Ricoeur proclaims, allegedly against Derrida, 'The metaphor is dead. Long live the metaphor.'[19] However, as Derrida writes in 'Le retrait de la métaphore', it is the simple opposition between life and death that he wishes to question.[20] We must distinguish the death that is ordinarily opposed to life from the death that is in life, the life-death that makes the ordinary opposition possible, along with a whole host of other oppositions, many of them ones that provide metaphysics with its focus and frame. For example, the simple metaphysical opposition between the visible and the invisible assumed by the doctrine that the abstract sense of metaphysical terms is a metaphorical derivative from the sensory meanings of original literal and sometimes literary expression. Whether or not this doctrine of metaphor and the simple opposition of the visible to the invisible on which it is based are endorsed by Heidegger and Levinas remains to be seen. They are not endorsed or re-endorsed by Derrida, as Ricoeur seems to maintain that they are, any more than is the simple opposition of literal life to literal death, or of the literally literal (e.g. the letter 'I'?) to the literally figurative (e.g. the physical shape, form, figure of something, e.g. of the letter 'I'?), or of the figuratively literal (e.g. the letter of the law?) to the figuratively figurative (e.g. the figure of speech, e.g. metaphor?). The simple is less simple than that. It is complicated by the fact that although these simple oppositions serve their purpose in what we are pleased to describe as ordinary life, the so-called metaphysical poles they mark or assume are no more separated by an equable equatorial line than so-called metaphysics is enclosed within a delimitable frontier. The delimitation of metaphysics de-limits itself. As Derrida writes in the words of 'La Différance' cited in 'Le retrait de la métaphore', the 'text of metaphysics' is 'not surrounded but traversed by its limit'. It is 'marked in its inside by the multiple furrow of its margin', by a 'trace that is simultaneously traced and effaced, simultaneously living and dead'.[21] These sentences attempt if not to capture or encapsulate, at least to head, *mettre le cap*, toward what Derrida is not unwilling to call the structure of the predicament we earlier described from which it appears that no metaphysics or rhetoric can capture the structure of metaphor because, as we said, this philosophico-rhetorical discourse on the nature of metaphor, as a discourse of the appearing and disappearing of the sensory sun and of the sensory as such of which the sun is a metaphor, presupposes the sun – the sun that is natural, physical, in the abstract 'artificial' discourse of metaphysics. There is an over- and underlap between metaphysics and metaphor. The columns of *Glas* are not in parallel, but in chiasmus, like the extraordinary columns in the transept of the cathedral at Wells. One model Derrida employs for this geometry is the lip of a vase. We might think of the intersection of the convex and concave surfaces at the cusp of a bell, like the bell that tolls the knell between the two columns of *Glas* or the bell held in one of the left hands of a Bodhisattva. A Bodhisattva is a being (and *sat* is the Sanskrit for being) that holds out a hand to help others toward enlightenment, holding Buddhahood for itself self-sacrificially in reserve. The bell which it holds is a metaphor of the flower of the lotus and of the vagina deflowered by the diamond-shaped thunderbolt held in one of the Bodhisattva's right hands. The bolt is hollow, like the bell, and in some representations the handle of the bell replicates the bolt. There is a double invagination, a chiasmic crossing such as is figured too in the ambiguity of

Shiva, who is at once creative or constructive and destructive: decon-structive.

Invagination then is a metaphor in the light of which can be carried out a deconstrual, a re- and de-reading, a de-scription and reinscription (*délire, dédire, dé-crire, déc-rire*) of the relation of the exteriorizing and interioriz-ing of the Hegelian dialectic that is already a reconstrual of the under-standing's understanding of an inside cut off from an outside by a simple line, a cutting off consequent upon the Kantian cutting off of the under-standing from reason that Hegel rejects, comparing it to what he considers to be the circumcised abstractness of the mentality of the Jew. The Derridian schema's difference from the Hegelian schema is that the step it makes beyond synthesis is not the step of determinate negation. It is not the *pas* of a *pas*. It is a *pas sans pas*.

There is more than one way of rejecting a proposition. One can deny it. But one can also deny both it and its denial, as one would do in order to move away from what might be considered the categorial nonsense of affirming or denying that the wind is green. But the divisions between categories are still relatively clean cuts, even if a certain indeterminacy or vagueness – or metaphoricity – may make it difficult to decide on which side of a line a predicate falls. Undecidability or indecidability of that kind is not the indecidability for which Derrida co-opts Heidegger's, Gödel's and at one remove Kierkegaard's word *Ent-scheidung*, written with a hyphen. Well-known attempts have been made to resolve Gödelian un-decidability and Frege's contradiction by ruling that an expression of a given level (say, 'is green') may have as its argument only an expression of the type-level immediately below (say, 'this apple').[22] However, such would-be solutions assume the validity of a hierarchic account of the world. They take for granted the ontological applicability of the notion of a line between something above and something below. They leave in place the difficulty of the non-place of the meta- of metaphor and metaphysics. They skate over the difficulty that each of these metas cuts across the other. There is no clear and distinct cut. There is no sharp-edged scission (*Riss*) or simple *Scheide* (*Scheide* can mean 'vagina'). So there is no decision pro-cedure that puts everything in its place. The very idea of putting a thing, *la chose, la cause*, in its place assumes that placing, what Heidegger calls *Erörterung*, faces no *aporia*. If that assumption does not pass the tests to which it is exposed in *Glas*, 'White Mythology', 'Le retrait de la méta-phore', and other writings by Derrida, we may have to take seriously the possibility that the possibility of *Entscheidung*, the kind of decision one can take, is conditioned and de-conditioned by *Ent-scheidung*, the cut that is not a cut, the de-cision that takes itself and takes itself away.

BEYOND METAPHORICS?

In what has since taken on the aura of an aphorism Heidegger asserts in *Der Satz vom Grund*, 'The metaphorical obtains only within metaphysics.'[23] He makes this assertion because the metaphorical calls for the distinction between what is more and what is less present or near, what is here and what is absent but representable. That is to say, metaphoricity has to do with beings in the widest sense of an entity, process, event, state or state of affairs, whether sensory, abstract or transcendental. Presence or the being-ness of beings, *parousia*, is what marks metaphysics off from what he calls the other thinking or thinking otherwise beyond metaphysics. So beyond Hegel on Heidegger's reading of him, for according to that reading even Hegelian ontology is one more epoch of metaphysics in which the ontological difference between being and beings gets forgotten and being as such finds itself being treated as a being, as, for example, *eidos*, *energeia*, subjectivity, will, or now with Hegel the Concept writ large. It follows that the thinking of being as such cannot be metaphorical, even if that *Denken* is *dichtend*, that is, poietic and productive. It follows too that Hölderlin cannot be speaking metaphorically when he utters 'words, like flowers' and that Heidegger cannot be speaking metaphorically when he says at the beginning of the 'Letter on Humanism' that language is being's house. So in *On the Way to Language* he writes that 'To want to take as a metaphor Hölderlin's trope [*Wendung*] "words, like flowers" would be to remain stuck in metaphysics.'[24] Yet – and this is Derrida's supplementary turn – the movement by which being as such is concealed by being conceived as a being would seem to be quasi-metaphorical, a metaphor of metaphor as such. Metaphor withdraws quasi-metaphorically where what disappears is being, not a what, not a being of any type, not even a process or predicate. As Derrida all but says, a typographical error or type fallacy could have printed the *re-trait de la métaphore* as a *re-trait de la métaphiore*, as the withdrawal of the flowers of rhetoric and the redrafting of the rhetoric of metaphors such as those for which the right-hand column stands in *Glas*. The re-trait is a drawing away in the many senses of withdrawing, re-drawing and drawing upon, as drawing upon a bank account or drawing milk from the breast (*sein*). But whereas according to the classical conven-tion the metaphorical expression is the one which, because it is better known or closer to one's understanding, casts light on or brings closer the expression that is less understood, the *re-trait* of the *re-trait de la métaphore* draws its force from the less understood difference between what is (the *Seiendes*) and being (*Sein*). Unless we have an understanding of this ontological difference we cannot understand why metaphor disappears from the thinking of being. When being as such is thought meta-phor disappears because beings disappear, and with them the direct literal and indirect metaphorical presence to beings. This is why the absenting itself from all anthologies and herbaria of Hölderlin's words as flowers, of Heidegger's *Entziehung* or *Sich-entziehung* and of Derrida's *retrait* is at best a quasi-metaphor, the quasi-condition of metaphorical discourse about entities, the quasi-condition of metaphors of being understood as a being.

Understanding being as a being is perhaps not a misunderstanding, nor is anyone, Hölderlin, Heidegger, Ricoeur, Derrida or Greisch,[25] denying that there are metaphors. There are only beings, understanding beings as including processes, states, events: anything one can properly say some-thing about. Heidegger says that about being as such we cannot properly say that it is (*ist*), or exists. Rather, being gives, obtains, holds sway, holds way, gives way. *Es gibt.* Heidegger also says that we must be careful not to be misled by this *Es* from the thinking of being as such back to the thinking of being as a being. As for the *gibt*, Derrida would probably say that this is another quasi-metaphor. The genitive of the giving of being is a subjective genitive, like that of being's withdrawal. There is no other way for being to give itself than for being to give itself away, to sacrifice itself to beings. But metaphors are beings, complex entities implicitly or explicitly likening one thing to another. And metaphors, like other entities, are in good supply. But metaphoricity as such, like being as such, gets carried away with itself. Metaphorics, the metaphysics of metaphoricity, beats its own retreat. For although there are plenty of metaphors, there are none whose structure can be conceived. Both *logos* and *mythos*, *Denken* and *Dichtung*, perform a *pas de deux*. Each dances around the other maintaining a certain distance, *Ent-fernung*, *Ent-ziehung*, *Ent-scheidung*, *chôrismos*. Like the *chôra* of Plato's *Timaeus*, the space in which this terpsichorean dis-*tanz* takes place, like the ballroom of the film *Last Year in Marienbad* surrounded by distorting glassical mirrors, distances classical space from itself. And the time which gives this mytho-logical *pas de deux* of literal *logos* and literary *mythos* its beat is immeasurable according to the metric of the continuum of Standard Western Time, Standard Eastern Time or any other standard chronology. It is as though there were an uncertainty principle delimiting the relativity of the partners to each other in this space-time such that their location and velocity cannot be jointly ascertained.

BEYOND QUESTION?

Does the metaphorical obtain only within metaphysics? The philosopher who answers this philosophical question in the affirmative must first be able to answer the question, 'Where are the limits of this metaphysical within?' We have been considering Derrida's questioning whether this second question can be answered by Heidegger or anyone else. Derrida's questioning is a calling into question of the assumption that philosophy can maintain control over a meta-language in which questions are asked about the relation between metaphysics and metaphor. In the wake of Gödel, Frege, Russell and Zermelo he is questioning the possibility of the completeness and consistency of a meta-language in which there can be philosophical questioning as such. Not the first or last to do that, in his essay 'Violence and Metaphysics' he is questioning Levinas's way of questioning that possibility. Not without irony, not without Derrida being conscious of this irony and conscious that Levinas is too, his questioning of Levinas in one section of this essay appeals to a Heideggerian motif. And so in turn does Levinas's response. Levinas, we have seen, challenges the philosophical tradition of holism exemplified by Spinoza, Hobbes, Hegel and modern structuralism. He thinks holism on its own, if valid, would do a violence to the singularity of human beings because they would be at best interacting nodes of a totality according to the doctrines associated with philosophies of system. Levinas argues that the violence of systematic and symmetrical holism can be prevented only by what we might call dissymmetrical holy-ism, understanding the word 'holy' in the etymological sense of 'apart'. Paradoxically, it is only the holy, the *heilig* or the *saint* in this sense of separation *à sens unique*, that allows violence at all. In no way can there be violence without the one way of the face to face.

Derrida wonders why such violence is not already prevented by the phenomenological ontology of Heidegger where letting beings be, as already Husserlian phenomenology's requirement that philosophy go back to the things themselves, would seem to guarantee for the individual the fullest possible care and respect. Is not Levinas failing to see that the ontological thinking of being as such, even if it is taken, dubiously, to inherit the totalizing propensity of Hegelian Spirit, allows and may even demand respect at the ontic level of relations among individual human beings? Is he not also failing to remember the ontological difference? Is he not thinking of being as a being if he believes that being can be in any way repressive? Only a being can repress another being, not being as such.

Now Levinas frequently criticizes the doctrine that would ground morality upon respect. What he has in mind when he does so may not always be the Kantian tenet that one thing alone is unconditionally good, namely will motivated by respect for the moral law. Respect for the moral law may be the foundation of justice, but justice itself is a violence unless it retains what might be provisionally called respect for the face. However, where respect is understood as no more than an attitude based on sympathy, it is, so to speak, too lacking in a certain good violence to forestall the bad violence threatened by the earlier mentioned holistic philosophical doctrines, all of which are ultimately philosophies of war. Peace is the traumatic violence of my being hostage to the Other, called to stand bail and to expiate for him or her. It is because Levinas can find no hint of this peaceful violence in Heidegger's thinking of being and letting be that he judges it to be a letting be of totalitarian violence and war.

Yet, just as Heidegger remonstrates with those interpreters of his own poietic thinking (*dichtendes Denken*) and of Hölderlin's thinking *poiêsis* (*denkendes Dichten*) who would describe their language as metaphorical, so Levinas warns his interpreters incessantly against mistaking as metaphorical the use he makes of certain key terms. For to suppose that those terms are being used metaphorically is to suppose that their crucial function derives solely from their belonging to a semantic field. The reason for his taking exception to this may be compared to Heidegger's reason for demurring at the supposition that his and Hölderlin's *etyma*, their original words for being, are metaphors for being.[26] That would turn being into something signified or represented by the metaphor, hence to conceal precisely what the metaphor would purport to reveal more articulately. The most one might say is that being is itself metaphorization.

This difficulty over articulation might seem to be the same difficulty as the one to which negative theology was a response. But it is not the same difficulty if negative theology is a theology about a being, albeit the highest. A nearer antecedent in the genealogy of Heidegger's, Derrida's and Levinas's difficulties with metaphor is identified in a remark made in *Otherwise than Being* about something Husserl says in §36 of *The Phenomenology of Internal Time Consciousness* (cited above in the third section of chapter 4). In *Transcendence and Intelligibility* Levinas says that when Husserl writes of the flow of time he has not reached 'the ultimate or living metaphor'. This is time as pro-phecy, inspiration or *à-Dieu* (*TRI* 36). In *Otherwise than Being* Levinas says that Husserl is not speaking metaphorically at all at that point, notwithstanding his statement there that he is; he is not drawing an analogy between time and a river. 'To speak of time in terms of flowing is to speak of time in terms of time, not in terms of temporal events. . . . Temporal modification is not an event nor an action nor the effect of a cause. It is the verb to be' (*AE* 43–4, *OB* 34–5). A verb is a 'time-word', a *Zeitwort* in German; and its modes include tenses, modes of time. So for being and its verbality and for time and its adverbiality 'we lack names', Husserl says, followed by Heidegger. Once nominalized, being and time are killed. As is God, when He is named. So when Levinas follows Nietzsche's Zarathustra in proclaiming the death of God yet appears to be unable to get by without the word 'God', this word is no more being employed by him as a metaphor than a metaphor is being given for a word in Hölderlin's phrase 'words, like flowers'. To use the word 'God' as a name for a transcendent being is to do Him a mortal violence. It is also to do mortal violence to man. The paradoxical reason for this is that only the extraordinary proname 'God', with pro-pronames for it like 'Infinity', is sufficiently violent to utter my being an unsubstitutable substitute in responsibility for the Other. This 'for the Other' could at some risk be said to be metaphoricity itself or quasi-metaphoricity.[27] But not only would this metaphoricity itself be non-semantic; it would not only exceed the field of the semantic standing of one thing for another, the representation of things present and absent. It would exceed also the field of presencing, of being and its truth, *alêtheia*, and of being's permanence through ecstatic temporality or the homogeneous chronological continuum. When the signification of one thing standing for another is interrupted by my standing for the other human being, both the humanism of the ego persisting in its being and the ultra-humanism of Nietzsche find their selves overtaken by the alter-humanism of my self expiating for the Other. Then, and now, 'at this very moment in this text', there erupts a diachrony that resists synchronization. There explodes in my face an ethical diaphorization bearing no implicit or explicit resemblance to metaphor as defined by Aristotle and a succession of other rhetoricians through the ages. Incomparable with classical metaphor, other than the flower that is absent from all anthologies, it is an utterly other trope.

There are many other such tropes alleged by Levinas not to be metaphors. Our next chapter will list them at length. Anticipating that roll call, let us note here two or three of the cautions he issues against mixing with metaphors what only seem to be metaphors. He warns, for example, that the expression 'in one's skin' is not a metaphor of the in-itself, adding, in a phrase similar to one cited earlier from Derrida, that it is 'better than metaphors'.[28] He also observes that the diachrony of the subject is not a metaphor but is the subject itself (*AE* 73, *OB* 57). This holds not only for the phenomenological and ontological diachrony of the ego's ecstatic persistence through a recollectable past toward a projected future. It holds too for the ethical diachrony of the self's unrecollectable past and unsynthesizable future forever to come. So there are two levels or two space-times of non-metaphoricity. Heidegger draws attention to the ontological non-metaphoricity. While applauding and retaining that insight, Levinas thinks that there is an ethical non-metaphoricity underlying the ontological non-metaphoricity. But how can he think this? Is there not a problem here?

Derrida writes of what he calls etymological empiricism, which, he says, transporting a well-known metaphor from Kant via Heidegger, is the hidden root of all empiricism.[29] Etymological empiricism is the empiricism of Polyphilos, as well perhaps of Nietzsche. At its most extreme it will say that even the metaphysical or meta-metaphysical notion of being has an etymological root in concrete notions like, for example, respiration. Indeed, both Nietzsche and Levinas say this. We learned already in our discussion of concreteness in the second chapter that Levinas is no less preoccupied than Heidegger with the problem, to solve which Kant invoked his doctrine of schematism, the problem that at B177 of the first *Critique* is referred to as that of the application of concepts *in concreto*. Levinas's agenda at least from *Totality and Infinity* onward is to rethink ontology *in concreto* by emphasizing Greek *pneuma* as Hebrew *ruah*, revealing how one breath is intermingled with the other.[30] Now Nietzsche will say also that this etymological connection is a movement of metaphor. But in thinking of being as metaphor he is forgetting, as Derrida reminds us Hegel reminds us, that, like empiricism in general, he is using the verb to be, thinking by metaphor without thinking the metaphor as such. Empiricism forgets what Husserl calls 'categorial intuition'. So that to think of metaphoricity as such is to think of being again, a metaphor more or less. And when Levinas, instead of affirming metaphoricity, again and again denies it, is not he embarrassed by the same predicament? Since he has to think metaphoricity if he has to deny it, he has to think being. He seems to be unable to evade the Parmenidean–Heideggerian thesis that being and thinking are one. He can put this problem behind him only by substituting for it a difficulty, the difficulty of substitution, the difficulty that if ethical substitution and diachrony are to be otherwise than being they will have to be what as such cannot be thought.

14 Tropes

AMPHIBOLOGIES

The ontological non-metaphoricity, that to which we have been alerted by Heidegger, is referred to again by Levinas when he writes that we should be on guard against the danger implicit in the widely held idea that in a predicative statement, a statement of the form 'S is P', the verb signifies an event, action, process or change of state.This idea is plausible and correct for such statements as 'The boy is running.' But to analyse such a statement into a nominal component signifying an entity and a verbal component signifying an event, action, process or change of state is to reveal less than the truth. It is to obliterate the force of the verb 'to be'. That force persists even in so-called tautologies, statements of the form 'A is A'. The force of the 'is' in 'Red is red' is more faithfully preserved if this statement is construed not simply as the appending of an adjective to a nominalized adjective, but as 'Red reds', except that the force of the verb 'to be' is concealed also here if the verb is taken to do no more than signify metaphorically an action analogous to what is understood as dynamic action in a literal sense. In the verb 'reds' resounds the temporalizing of being and the tensing of the verb 'to be'. The verb is more than a signifier standing for a signified that could stand on its own independently of and external to signification. It is the way of being's essencing. This is what Heidegger means when he says that language is the house of being, and this is why in saying that he was not speaking metaphorically.[1]

But 'being' is ambiguous. With an ear to the non-metaphor of being's house in language, being may be said to be amphibological. We can expect an amphibology of *logos* corresponding to the amphibology of being, to the ontic-ontological difference that Heidegger traces back to the ambiguity in Aristotle's Greek of *to on* meaning both a being and the being of beings. This ambiguity, Heidegger surmises, is inherited from that of the archaic *eon* found in Parmenides, Heraclitus and Homer. One might go as far as to say, he adds, that the fate of the West hangs on the translation of this word, assuming that translation (*Übersetzung*) depends on the carrying over (*Übersetzung*) into the unconcealment of truth what comes to language in it. This participle and its derivative *on* is the singular of *eonta*, meaning 'beings', hence it announces in the history of metaphysics the totality of beings or the highest being, God. But it names also 'the simply singular, the singular in its numerical unity that is singularly and unifyingly one before all number' ('das schlechthin Singuläre, das in seiner Einzahl einzig das einzig einende Eine vor aller Zahl ist').[2] Being before all number is that which the verb of a proposition endeavours to express, the 'is' expressed in 'reds'. In 'Red reds' and in 'The apple reds', the verb is an *éon*, Levinas writes, cultivating the ambiguity between the already ambiguous *eon* and *aeon*, sometimes spelled *eon*, a hypostatic emanation of the One in Neo-Platonism. Levinas speaks of hypostasis in this sense here (*AE* 56, *OB* 44). This new ambiguity throws into relief the choice between interpreting the One before all number as being as such, or as the Good or God, a choice Levinas resolves by reserving pre-originality for the Good and God beyond being, while allowing to being the originality it has in the thinking of Heidegger.

POETICS

In both Levinas and Heidegger this originality of being is an originality of language itself as *poiêsis*, dighting, *Dichten*: production in the sense of the definition given in the preface of *Totality and Infinity* as bringing into being and bringing to light, exhibition, exposition. Levinas cites Paul Valéry's remark that poetry is a prolonged hesitation between sound and sense.[3] He suggests that in saying this Valéry may have in mind the play between the materiality of the word and the etymological senses which the word's shape or sound may evoke. He wonders whether another implication of Valéry's remark is that there is an analogous hesitation in all arts between meaning and materiality, be it that of paint, musical notes, syllables, stone, and so on (*AE* 52, *OB* 40). At all events, the word 'hesitant' is used again a few pages later of the unstable moment between the exposure of poetry to the eventuality of becoming reduced to the common denomination of the world's prose, for example in art criticism and exegesis, and the chance of poetic reanimation even of the most banal and prosaic proposition, because the nominalized being of beings is always exposed to the resounding, echoing essence, essance or essencing through the verb.

Double exposure. On the one hand is the exposition of the properly propositionally said that may be written down and transferred and remembered from one generation to another. This is the inscribability of which the necessity is welcomed by Hegel in the section on sense-certainty at the beginning of the *Phenomenology of Spirit* and acknowledged somewhat begrudgingly by Husserl in *The Crisis of European Sciences* as the condition of scientific objectivity and historiography.[4] On the other hand is the exposition that is the exposing in Saying or to-say (*Dire*) of the proto-impressional temporal flow of being which is the poietic source of scientific life. The exposition of exposition. The ostension of ostension. These are both pairs of correlatives. And the *Dire* of which we have been treating so far in this chapter is a correlative of its *Dit*. It is vital that the properly, propositionally, prosely said not be supposed to be utterly dead in comparison with its living correlative to-say. It is to be noted that while Levinas is scornful of the idea that there is no more to language than names, he insists here more on the opposite error of overlooking the call that the predominantly verbal productive expression of the work of art makes for exegesis in predicative statements in which essencing veers toward nominalization. Not only in the predicative propositions of art criticism, manifestos and prefaces does this exposition take place. Such 'ineliminable meta-language' only confirms that the verbal being whose adverbiality is beautifully said in the sounding of the cello's wood and strings calls to be properly said in the apophantic exegesis of predicative propositions. Prior to such exegesis there is no world. Strictly speaking there is no pure poetry of the world. There is world only where there is prose. And there is world and prose of what is properly said (*proprement dit*), said according to the rules and structures of normality (*AE* 53, *OB* 41), only where there is saying properly speaking, *Dire-à-proprement-parler* (*AE* 61, *OB* 58). Without both there is only secrecy. So that the soul heard sighing or exulting in Xenakis's 'Nomos alpha for solo violoncello' is deceitful anthropomorphism or animism. As art calls for conceptual exegesis, so animism calls for substitution by the humanism of the other, substitution for the other. These calls are calls not of being, but away from being and its difference from beings, from *logos* as correlation of saying and said, to a saying that is without correlation where language as house is opened beyond monadological closure and disclosure. A second hypostasis, or another face of hypostasis. Already in *Time and the Other* a distinction is made between these two senses: on the one hand monist hypostasis or substantiation as the overcoming of anonymous existence by an existent who is master of his existence and capable of receiving a name; on the other hand plural hypostasis as the named existent being called to substitution by and for the other human being or, better, the human other, the Other

(*Autrui*) whose monotheistic proname is 'God' (*TA* 34, *TO* 54). Position (*Setzung*), is translated into *Übersetzung*. Ontological metaphysics as the presence of beings, and the other thinking of presencing as such, turn toward ethical metaphysics as presentation of myself, my self's approach, to the Other. The *Ursprung* of metaphysical metaphorization and of the phenomeno-ontological quasi-metaphorization of the *Es gibt Sein* turns out to have an anarchic presource and resource in a quasi-metaphorization of my giving myself and my word. Ever wary of the mystification liable to be wrought by metaphor (*HS* 49, *OS* 33), Levinas proposes pregnancy as a non-metaphor, a 'beyond all metaphor' for such giving (*EN* 230): the other in the one, under my skin, labour, and the giving of the breast (*sein*).

It would therefore seem that in turn the call to exegesis in art cannot be a call that emanates ultimately from the being of a being or from the existing *Dasein* calling on behalf of itself or of being. Exegesis is the leading out, education, of the self from the ego, the turning of the named subject's will to mastery over itself and others into the other's educative mastery over the subject: the subjection of subjectivity to teaching, its de-struction by instruction.

The verbal activeness and the adverbial modalities of the categorial and qualitative *façons d'être* are exposed to the risk of turning into the passivity of a named being. But both this activity and this correlated passivity are exposed to the more than passive possibility of the other's face, a proto-passivity prior to any such pre-predicative proto-activity as that to which Husserl refers in §13 of *Experience and Judgement* when, in words cited by Levinas, he writes that 'Simple perceptual contemplation of a pre-given substrate reveals itself to be already an achievement, an act and not simply a suffering of impressions' (*AE* 45n., *OB* 189n.).[5] It would have to be an exaggeration to say that this face is the *facies* which according to some dictionaries is mistakenly associated in the etymological genealogy of *façon* with *factionem*, from *faire* ('to make or to do'). For this to be an exaggeration in Levinas's sense *facies* would have to turn away from meaning that which I regard to meaning that which regards me, and in looking at me speaks. The eye in the face is the 'listening eye'. In the Heideggerian thinking of art to much of which Levinas subscribes, it is the silent resonance of being that is heard because of the invisibility of the light of being by which beings are seen. The eye in Levinas's philosophy of the face listens beyond being to the Good, to the incessant call of the other (*AE* 38, 48, 49, *OB* 30, 37, 38). In the paragraph following the one in which he states that only within metaphysics does the metaphorical obtain, and explaining why what might be taken to be a metaphor is not one, Heidegger writes: 'If our human–mortal hearing and looking are not authentically themselves in mere sensory impressions, and if thinking looks hearingly and hears lookingly, then it is not entirely unheard of that the audible might be at the same time looked at.'[6] And Levinas agrees. There is neither metaphor here nor monstrosity (*AE* 38, *OB* 30). But this is because in Levinas's ethics of transcendental aesthetics, in his demantling of space and time as *forms* of sensibility, Heidegger's *bloss sinnliche Empfinden* turns into the sensibility of bad conscience and the irritation of the other who gets under my skin, the last layer of clothing behind which I protect myself from the other's exposure to the cold.

Hearing and listening (*écouter, entendre, audire*) turn into, turn out to, turn out to have been always already turned out to obedience (*écouter, entendre, obaudire*). Since this trope by which the inner ear turns to *Autrui*, is the turning of my skin inside out, it is the turning of the ego into its self, a self whose responding to the other is its obedience, an obedience prior to the knowledge of what is commanded. What Levinas is saying goes beyond what is said when R. G. Collingwood asserts that every predicative proposition is an answer to a question.[7] The response and obedience of which Levinas speaks is prior to the communication of information. It is not the response of reciprocal *Mitteilung* and *inter-esse*. If one can speak of *com*munication here at all, and Levinas does (e.g. at *AE* 62n., *OB* 190n.), it is the one-way communication of myself to the other where the saying is not the *dire* of a said message, of a *dit*, nor a *se dire* in which the reflexive pronoun refers to language speaking itself – *die Sprache spricht*; the *se* is the undeclinable accusative of the accused me whose saying is a signifying only of its giving of its self to the other in saying. This giving is not an action that the self may or may not perform or a passion that it may or may not suffer. Its being disquieted by the other is the de-struction, the opening up, of the self-reflection and self-reference of its egoity, but a desituating de-struction that is constitutive of its more-than-egological self. Constitutive or 'constitutive' of its deconstitution. A displacement into substitution for the other of its identity as substance. It could be said therefore that there is an initial trope which is that of the ego being turned away from its egologism toward heterology, the for-itself deposed by the for-the-other. There is also a trope of this trope which is the return of heterology or heteronomy to the autonomy of the more-than-egological self. Levinas names this double trope 'recurrence' and 'prophetism'.

PROPHETICS

Recurrence is difference intruding upon the same as non-indifference. It is the re-identification of identity. Double identity, a doubling of the countable one with which one starts counting by the one understood as the incommensurably unique prior to understanding, unless understanding (*entendre*) is pre-original obedience (*entendre*), obedience before one starts, hypostasis before hypostasis. The challenge Levinas gives to the reader of *Otherwise than Being* is to understand philosophically, 'Greekly', why according to Exodus 24:7 and Shabbat 88a Israel declared at Sinai 'all that the Lord has spoken, we shall do and we shall hear' in that order, thereby promising to obey the Commandments before knowing what they will be, against everything that seems reasonable – for example, to Dorothea in *Middlemarch* when required by her husband Casaubon to do precisely the same. Or to Hegel, though when he says in the *Encyclopaedia* (§529) that human beings can truly obey only a law that they know, he is speaking of a law of civil society and therefore of an obedience secondary to the anarchic obedience of which Levinas speaks.

The appearance of unreasonableness will not be entirely dispelled. Levinas will argue that it is only on account of this appearance that rationality can ultimately prevail. For rationality is ultimately not justice as fairness defined by contract. The rationality and justice of universal reciprocity are required by my singular unrequited responsibility for the Other, *Autrui*. To repeat a warning already delivered, the syntax of this proposition must not be misconstrued. *Autrui* does not denote simply another empirical or ontic human being who enters a posteriori into my ken as a case falling under the formal concept of alterity. Nor does it simply name an a priori categorial or existential structure of my mind. It stands for an a priori aposteriority that precisely prevents another man or woman being simply a case, and its apriority destructures the mind, if by mind is meant something like the transcendental unity of self-consciousness. Recurrence is the anarchic condition of more-and-less than possibility, the quasi-transcendental condition of the transcendental condition of the possibility of experience. Responsibility for the other and responding to the other's command before responding to any question. Answerability prior to answer. Minding the other before having him or her in my mind.

Yet this minding is not simply outside my mind. It is both inside and outside my mind in so far as outsideness, ethical exteriority, is sensibility to the other human being prior to and requiring the spatial exteriority that according to the transcendental aesthetic of Kant is a form of all sensibility. Ethical exteriority, the exteriority of Levinas's quasi-transcendental aesthetic of ethics, is the deformation of forms of sensibility.

Prophetism is defined by Levinas as the 'turnaround in which the perception of the *order* coincides with the signifying of this order performed [*faite*] by the one who obeys it' (*AE* 190, *OB* 149). According to this it is the signifying that is done or performed, and this performance or deed is the obeying – the (*ob*)*audire* in the *audire*: the heedful response. This deed of heed is yet not an action in contradistinction to a passion. It is a Passion whose genealogy in Levinas's extra-phenomenology is crossed with that of what in Husserl's phenomenology is entitled passive genesis. Husserl gives the title 'passive genesis' to the temporality of the flux of representable proto-impressions which in Levinas's philosophy are prefaced by the non-origin of a past and postfaced by the non-*telos* of a future that never were or will be present and representable. The order of the time of my life is suspended between an unheard *order* indistinguishable from my response and a responsibility that is never enough. My responsibility and not that of anyone else. So I am its author. It defines my authenticity, my *Eigentlichkeit*. But it also de-fines it as *Uneigentlichkeit, Ent-eigentlichkeit*. Because my response is the obeying of an order that comes from no definable where. Both speaking for myself and speaking on behalf, the self for which I speak is not half-and-half. To think that it is is to represent it. To represent it is to misrepresent it, raising in Descartes's wake the problem of how the two halves can make one. The oneness of the identity of my self is the uniqueness of my having been chosen to respond. Ethically accountable prior to arithmetic, my identity is the uniqueness of my being called. The breath of that call coming from I know not where is my animation. The sameness of my soul is its inspiration by the other human being, not by the Spirit of History or the History of Spirit. Passion of that narrative of passion, my suffering is the inexhaustible patience of the exegete of the book of history.

Or of the exegete of the Book. One metaphor whose metaphoricity Levinas does not deny is that of the inscription of the law on the tablet of consciousness – where *conscience* can also mean 'conscience' (*AE* 189, *OB* 148). This Platonic metaphor of 'the true way of writing' (*Phaedrus* 278) is also a metaphor of the Torah and of the Talmudic texts. And the latter are metaphors of it, according to the interactive theory of metaphor which from his agreement with Bruno Snell it seems that Levinas is ready to endorse (*HAH* 23, *CPP* 78).[8] Unheard, inscribed upon tablets of stone, the Commandments add up to ten. According to a Jewish tradition the commandments written elsewhere total more than six hundred. According to a Jewish – and not only Jewish – tradition belief in God is not commanded but rather is presupposed. Both unwritten and unheard, this law of the law corresponds to my responsibility before the Other. Before specific laws, the responsibility that is mine nevertheless gets formulated as one of the ten, 'Thou shalt not kill'. What this brings out is that the priority of what is before the law is not that of a metalaw governing legality from above. In company with Heidegger, Merleau-Ponty, Wittgenstein, Husserl, Kant and a line of thinkers stretching back even to Parmenides, Levinas reckons that idealism and realism are one. The spontaneity and legislative activity of the a priori on the one hand and the inertness and passivity of the a posteriori on the other join hands in the phenomenon. So when the transcendental ego says: 'The world is my mine', the pluperfectly passive quasi-transcendental self responds: 'I and my world are thine.' Older than the opposition of the a priori and the a posteriori, unassumable into the phenomenon, the responsible self exacts its egohood, its worldhood and its history, giving them meaning in giving them to the Other. It implicates them, and not according to rules of logical inference, but as one may be implicated in a crime. The principles that give phenomenality its form, enabling the identity of the ego and the object to persist in their being and to be named in being's house, are shot through and shattered by my anarchic giving of my self and my word. This is a giving of an oral word that was never aural for me. Unheard, the written word calls to be spoken.

As well as a written Talmud there is an oral one contemporary with it, not appended to it as an afterthought (*DL* 158, 185, *DF* 117, 138, *ADV* 165ff., *BTV* 135–9). As a running commentary on the written text it runs back and forth in a hermeneutic zig-zag interpreting each sentence in the spirit of the whole (*ADV* 95, *BTV* 75). My primary responsibility, my pre-original secondness, is my responsibility as exegete. But the obligation of prophetic exegesis calls for more than the spelling out of words, be they words of devotion and love. The obligation of critical exegesis demands more even than the love of God, than which a greater love is the love of the Torah. But the latter love is not merely love of the letter. Prophetic exegesis demands a certain excess where my spelling out of the letter of the law may be the spilling out of my blood.

THE EXCESS OF IDENTITY

My merely consoling the stranger in his or her hunger or grief falls as short of my obligation as the doubly genitive love of God. Consolation is consolation, the submersion of solitude in being with. But neither the relation to the God of the religion of the Torah nor the relation to the illeity which expresses the pronominality of the extraordinary word 'God' is a mode of being-with in the religion of the other man. The other who commands me is no more *Mit-da-sein*, being together, than my selfhood is *Dasein*, being-here.

Hence Levinas's reservations regarding what he sees as the interpersonalism of Rosenzweig's collaborator in Bible translation Martin Buber.

Levinas applauds Buber's insistence that it is an evasion of responsibility to turn the I-Thou relation into a conscious experience of sociality.[9] They agree that Spinoza, the one-time grinder of lenses, errs in conceiving that relation optically. That relation, Buber holds, is dialogue, where dialogue is not to be conceived metaphorically. It is itself the concrete accomplishment of interrelation (*HS* 39, *OS* 24).[10] Perhaps because his conception of this dialogical relation is that of relation in the sense of the narration of a story or history, and because he shares Bergson's mistrust of the propensity of language to lateralize and objectify, Gabriel Marcel makes language and relation secondary to the concrete living of an I in corporeal co-presence in love with a divine Thou.[11] Marcel and Buber agree with each other that the I-Thou is prior to the I-It. While agreeing with them on this Levinas underlines the importance of retaining a different third-personal pro-nominality in the primary intrigue. In the space marked by the hyphen between the I and the Thou intrudes not It, but He. In the trace of the never having been here – the never Daseinly *Da* – of illeity stands the Thou whom I approach, lest even the asymmetrical proximity of response that conditions responsibility fuse into being-with (*HAH* 61–3, *CPP* 105–7).

Hence also Levinas's admiration for a certain fictional text, 'true as only fiction can be', that, as he writes with emphasis, '*presents itself as or pretends to be a document*' ('*se donne pour un document*') composed during the final hours of the Resistance in the Warsaw Ghetto (*DL* 190, *DF* 142). It is a script concerning a scripture; hence concerning the absence of an author; hence exposed to the risks of irresponsible interpretation with which that other script on scripture, Plato's *Phaedrus*, is concerned. For

> every discourse, once written, is tossed about from hand to hand, equally among those who understand it and those for whom it is altogether unsuited. And it does not know to whom it should be addressed and to whom it should not. And when misunderstood or unjustly criticized, it always needs help from its father.[12]

But father is *fort*. Dad is not *da*. God to all appearances is dead. And that hidden face, Levinas writes, is the face of Judaism. It is Judaism's moment of atheism when, deprived of an incarnate God with whom man may share communion or risk the madness of mystical trance, he is thrown back upon his own reason as the only mediator of the meaning of the Teaching inscribed in the Torah. Yet it is one Yossel ben Yossel, like Buber a Hasid, so one less fearful than Levinas of emotional enthusiasm, who says of God 'I love him, but I love even more his Torah.' 'Is this blasphemy?', Levinas asks. Blasphemy or not, the truth he sees in this fiction of or concerning the disappearance of God ('true as only a fiction can be') is that truly divine greatness consists 'in hiding one's face so as to demand of man everything – the superhuman; in having created a man who can approach God as creditor and not always as debtor'. The point here is that the creditor pursues the debtor through thick and thin until the debt is paid. Does this not bring out how dangerous it is to attempt to apply to Levinas's philosophical essays lessons learned from his essays on Judaism? For is it not argued in the former that my obligations to the other human being multiply in geometrical progression and that the more they are met the deeper grows my debt? But this is precisely the point of Levinas's reference to the creditor, and it is one made as often in the 'Hebrew' essays as it is made in the 'Greek'. The point is not merely that the amount owed is or is not ultimately paid back. It is that the debtor pursues the creditor through thick and thin. Even if God remains hidden, even if he presents himself as only a fiction, as unpresentable, I do not resign myself to this. Although the blood of Israel, where Israel is understood as a religious category of humanity, 'has been spilled for well nigh two thousand years', if Israel none the less obeys the 'Thou shalt not kill' of the Torah, it has 'access to a personal God against whom one may rebel – that is to say, for whom one may die' (*DL* 193, *DF* 145). Instead of what Nietzsche characterizes as the Christian 'pathological excess of feeling' that by the grace of divine mercy 'he bore all heaven within him',[13] every Israelite, as characterized in Levinas's exegesis of the story of Yossel ben Yossel and the cosmology of Hayyim of Volozhyn, in persistently studying the Torah and putting its precepts into practice bears all the world in responsibility upon his stiff neck. The rational sobriety of that study pursued not in fear and trembling is, Levinas remarks, 'to his credit', an education, an *élèvement*, in virtue of which it may not be entirely blasphemous to say that he is God's creditor, an elevation of man in humanism of the other man without which he would be all too unhuman.

Levinas says that Israel is shorthand for humanity (*HS* 59, OS 163), to be understood as standing for a 'particularist universality' that disturbs the general universality of Hegel, however concrete that may become (*DL* 74–5, 112–13, 229–31, *DF* 50–1, 82–3, 175–7). The identity of the Jew, unrecorded in his passport, performs at the level of the non-ethnic people and non-nationalist nation the same task within Levinas's genealogy of ethics as that for which he traces the genealogy of the family relations of father, mother, son, and so on. He also says that Israel is to be understood as a religious category (*DL* 191, *DF* 144), and in one of his uses of the term, 'religion' means the humanistic ethics of the other man, an ethical suspension and reduction of the theological. Israel is a moral category (*DL* 39, *DF* 22). '"God is merciful" means "Be merciful like him". God's attributes are given not in the indicative, but in the imperative' (*DL* 34, *DF* 17). So that when toward the end of 'Loving the Torah more than God' Levinas writes that what Yossel ben Yossel's fiction reveals is 'a complete and austere humanism, linked [*lié*] to a difficult adoration' (*DL* 193, *DF* 145), that tie must be the tie of religion to the ethical sense that completes human identity by turning it in the direction of the other human being.

This tropology of human identity is articulated by the already en-countered non-metaphorical image of giving another the bread that has passed one's lips, those same lips that kiss and utter words of love. To speak with exaggeration, it is as though the bread that I bite bites back. It is almost as though to eat it would be to eat my hungry neighbour, can-nibalism, *manger l'autre*.[14] For each bite that I take there is an agenbyte of inwyt, a re-morse of which the 're-' marks an anteriority. The anteriority of this remorse is that of a pre-face which is both absolute exteriority and absolute interiority. 'Remorse is the "literal sense" of sensibility; in its passivity the distinction between "being accused" and "accusing oneself" effaces itself' – or is effaced (*AE* 161, *OB* 125). A priori and a posteriori, diachronic, the tropology of the identity of the self is also diatopic. Ectopic, one could say, remembering that Levinas's paradigm of passivity and patience is the mother. Utopic is what Levinas says, because my self's identity is the interruption of *idem* by an *ipse*, the de-situation of site, the displacement of my place in the sun. It is even the displacement of the sun as source of light by the sun as the Good beyond being and light, the pre-original resource of the source of light. Most controversially, in *Totality and Infinity* my self's identity was seen as filiation, the sun as father giving rise to the son, the parricide of Father Parmenides (*TEI* 245–7, 255–7, *TI* 268–9, 278–9). And that seems to mean the parricide of any phallogocentric idea of the father and the substitution for it of the idea of the mother, of substitution or bearing *par excellence*. This inference of a notion of substitution in which the genealogy of paternity and maternity is unhierarchical but not a neutral androgyny is not unambiguously supported by Levinas's texts. As noted earlier, they leave the reader with only scat-tered remarks from which to infer how in Levinas's ethical interpretation of the family sorority and matrilineal filliation, as distinguished from patri-lineal filiation, fit in. Not to mention the variations permitted by the very notion of family. Even so, the inference to a de-positioning of any simple opposition of paternity and maternity does perhaps get some support from his statement that 'the feminine does not derive from the masculine; rather, the division into feminine and masculine – the dichotomy – derives from what is human' (*SS* 132, *NTR* 167–8).[15] This does not mean that the human cannot still depend upon and in a sense derive from the division into feminine and masculine. A chiasmic, non-neutralizing double derivation is what one would expect of a project that would de-neutralize and de-naturalize genus, as conceptualized, for example, in the idea of humankind, by concretizing it quasi-metaphorically in the categories of sexuality understood ethically or 'ontologically', as Levinas still says in *Totality and Infinity* (*TEI* 253, *TI* 276). Perhaps this is the force of the sentence immediately following the one reproduced a moment ago: 'Complementarity has no concrete significance, is only a lazy turn of phrase, if one has not previously grasped, in the idea of the *whole*, the necessity and the sense of the division.' He wonders whether it is such a concretized significance of complementarity that Vladimir Jankélévitch wishes to indicate when he speaks of *emboîtement* ('interlocking').

If interlocking is to indicate the manner in which the 'literal sense' of sensibility and passivity is related to the ethical sensibility and passivity in which my being accused by the other is at the same time my accusing myself, the interlocking cannot be compared to the binding of one link in a chain to another. The image of the *vinculum* between two substances employed by Descartes leads to the double bind of fetteredness either in the prison of impersonal ilyaity or in that of the self-contained ego. It is binding as the ligation of obligation to another that makes the difference between my self as me in the accusative, my *soi* as the singular accused *moi*, and the universal Ego or *Moi* of transcendental self-consciousness or its particular empirical case. It is from the anarchic priority of my having been obligated to substitute for the other that derives the meaning of transcendental or empirical freedom and of the power to persist as a substantial egological self, as what, adapting the title of Ricoeur's Gifford Lectures, might be entitled *Soi-même comme un Moi*.[16] To say again: the best clue that Descartes provides for unlocking the problems not resolved but indeed manufactured by the metaphors of substantialist metaphysics is the advice given in his correspondence with Elizabeth of Bohemia that 'it is the ordinary course of life and conversation, and abstention from the study of things which exercise the imagination, that teaches us how to conceive the union of soul and body'.[17]

The ordinary course of life and conversation admits a 'quotidian extraordinariness' (*AE* 179, *OB* 141). This is the ordinary extraordinariness of the disorder introduced into everyday life when the finite horizon of images shown and ideas conveyed is, to combine images from Descartes and Kierkegaard, broken by the perpendicular of infinite responsibility that no idea can contain. Yet this may be expressed in a simple greeting like 'Good-day' where the utterance of this is not merely a conventional tic, but is exponential exposition of myself, that is to say, exposition not only of my visible body, but exposition of my self as one whose corporeality is produced not just phenomenologically and ontologically in the manner of the definition of production given in the preface of *Totality and Infinity*, but produced further as the way by which to serve another without being his or her serf. Already one of the aims of *Time and the Other* was to consider how I can be in relation with another without my self-identity being crushed (*TA* 65, *TO* 77). The continuity of corporeal identity is a requirement for this service without servitude, as too, in so far as it is different from the ontological and phenomenological continuity of the lived body, is the continuity of the liaison of experience, memory and imagination through synthesizable time.[18] This further production is indeed anterior to and productive of the spatial and temporal continuity. Not of course anterior in the temporal order of those synthesizable and synchronizable continuities. Its productivity is not that of the transcendental imagination-cum-understanding or indeed of the mooded understanding (*befindliches* or *bestimmtes Verstehen* and *verständliche Befindlichkeit* or *Stimmung*) of the fifth chapter of the first division of *Being and Time*. This pro-duction is the offspring of sensible reason and rational sensibility, analogous to Kant's feeling of respect. It is their re-pro-duction, where the 're-', like the 're-' of 'remorse', has the reference backward to an immemorial, un-synchronizable, dia-chronically passed past and the 'pro-' is my being for a singular other through which it is respect for the universal moral law.

THE PROPHETIC PRODUCTION OF ART

If the production proper to being is already produced further for the other human being, then prophecy is not opposed to poetry. Poetry is prophetic. But when this is said poetry is being understood as *poiêsis*, in the broad sense given to it earlier in this chapter, as a translation of Heidegger's word *Dichtung*. That is the meaning Levinas's word *poésie* has when he says it is not used to name 'a species of which the word art would designate the genus'. In that broad sense poetry is inseparable from the word. 'It overflows with prophetic meanings' (*SMB* 79). It overflows infinitely, because poetry is the origin of language, language as origin. And because poetry calls to be interpreted again and again, language as origin is also language as pre-original address (*DL* 177, *DF* 132). The resonance of the word's production of being admits of being heard against the background of the pre-echo of speaking for the other, as though the Poetical Books, including the Book of Psalms and the Song of Solomon, achieve their meaning only by being read in the context of the Books of the Law that precede them and Books of the Prophets that follow. The song and the lyric as avowals of intimate love, are expressions of adolescence. Love comes of age, attains its bar mitzva, only when not opposed to justice. So poetry as *belles-lettres* reaches its majority only when it discovers that it has already taken the *beau risque*. It could be said that this word *beau*, 'a word to which there has never been given enough thought' (*AE* 154, *OB* 120), gives the meaning of that word *belles*, for 'language is already scepticism' (*AE* 216, *OB* 170).

It needs to be said again that his 'already' does not hark back to a linearly earlier moment of historio-biographical time. Nor is it the 'already' dialectically immanent in the 'not yet' in which the universal spirit of History results. It is the 'already' of a pre-conscious response to command hearkening to which is a readiness on the axis of my veracity regarding the singular other human being which cuts across the axis of any verity pronounced as the content of a proposition and of any truth as the unconcealing of being. A blank obedience, one could say, an *obéissance blanche* perpendicular to blank mythology of being, interrupting *logos* and *mythos* as story told, as fable, as fiction or as art.

In 'Reality and its Shadow' first published in 1948,[19] Levinas argues against the idea of art as social commitment, the idea that for the literary work had been defended by Sartre. The account Levinas gives of art as such in that essay is much like that which Levinas gives of Dionysian art. All art, he says, is ultimately musical. It depends on rhythm to produce a state of intoxication in which the distinctions between subject and object and subject and subject dissolve into impersonality and anonymity. Its time is not the time of the real world, but the time of the dream: a between-time, but one in which any future is replaced by fatality. So that although every work of art is in essence musical, and therefore, one might have thought, the very essencing of time, every work of art, not least what Nietzsche would count as Apollonian art, is an arrest of time, a statue. Such a statue, the shadow of reality, as for Socrates are sculpture and scripture left to stand on their own (*Phaedrus* 276), becomes engaged with reality only through criticism, for instance art criticism which in raising questions about technique and influence begins to awaken art from its dream, and the criticism of the philosopher who, like Pygmalion, requires that idol to speak, or at least to reach out a hand to shake the hand of another, to teach, as can the chiselled words of the poet, according to what Levinas learns from, among others, Proust and Celan (*NP* 59–66, 155–6).

One should therefore not be misled by Levinas's willingness to borrow for his own account of art the term 'intellectualist' with which he says modern literature is charged. If art must go beyond itself if it is to engage with reality, and if that means that it must expose itself to critical exegesis, this does not mean that it must give way to the promotion of a cause or the defence of a social or political thesis. If it means that the artist must interpret his myths to himself, it also means that the artist must be in a position to explain them to others. So although philosophical criticism will negotiate with semantic significance, philosophy, on Levinas's understanding of it as the love of wisdom moved by the wisdom of love, will be as much concerned to bring out how that significance is interrupted by one person's signifying of him- or herself to another. Exactly forty years after the publication of 'Reality and its Shadow', in an interview entitled 'The Other, Utopia and Justice',[20] he says that this assignation in unique responsibility for another is something that can be told by the nakedness of an arm in a sculpture by Rodin (*EN* 262). This is the nearest Levinas ever comes to appearing to deny that it is ultimately only a human being that has a face in his ethical use of that word. That the arm of Rodin's sculpture is not after all an exception is confirmed by Levinas's reference in his next sentence to the nakedness of the napes of the necks of the flesh-and-blood political prisoners in the mail queue at Lubyanka described by Vasily Grossman in *Life and Fate*.[21] On them the person behind can read the feelings and hopes of the wretchedness of the persons in front. Levinas cites the verses of Exodus 33:11, 23 which speak of God's face to face with Moses who sees only the back of God's neck – and the depression made in it by the knot of the phylactery straps (*ADV* 162, 174, *BTV* 213, 144). These and other verses (e.g. Deuteronomy 5:4 and Amos 3:8) are taken by the rabbis to say that all the Israelites present at Sinai and the whole of humanity at large have the gift of prophecy understood not as the power to see in advance, but the impower to listen and obey. Contrast the purely aesthetic visual appeal of those statues of Rodin which heave themselves out of the unworked marble as though to underline their 'exotic nudity of reality without world'. Without world because without exegetical word, as too in the 'talky' that might just as well be a silent film in so far as the technique of close-up is employed to project a hallucinatory quality upon the naked nape of the neck isolating it from the real world in which it is the bearer of that world's burdens (*DEE* 88, *EE* 55).

Although Grossman's book is an artefact, it is not from an artefact that the life and destiny of a person are read, as in Heidegger's allusion in 'The Origin of the Work of Art' to the peasant's shoes painted by Van Gogh which speak 'the uncomplaining worry as to the certainty of bread, the wordless joy of having once more withstood want, the trembling before the impending childbed and shivering at the surrounding menace of death'.[22] If the ethical face is to be a prophylactic against fetishism and idolatry, it may extend to other parts of the human body, but not, it would seem, beyond.[23] Even so, within this limit Levinas acknowledges the amphibology in which regard as ethical concern is a trope of regard as perceptual look – or is troped by it, he would prefer to say, in order to mark the non-logical and non-chronological anteriority to the logos of metaphysical and fundamental phenomenological ontology of ethics as proto-philosophy. Regard–regard, another doublet. Another twin in a very large family of twins. Not a twinning like that of the twofold of real object and aesthetic image. The twinning of representational art as conceived by Husserl among others would distinguish the original as posited from an image as resembling representation where engagement effected by positing is neutralized. On Levinas's account of the aesthetic object this notion of an image re-presenting an original thanks to mimesis or participation in a shared idea is already undermined by the infinite regress and circularity to which it is shown to be exposed by the argument of the 'third man' in Plato's *Parmenides* (131e–132b). To think of the image as a mental reality on which the inner eye comes to a stop and discovers by comparison a resemblance with the entity it images is to require a multiplication of comparisons of images of images without stop. If, on the other hand, imagination is said not to require any intermediate reality, but to be no more than the suspension of the reality of the world it imagines, what is to be understood by this suspension by which reality is modified as irreality?

Levinas proposes that instead of construing the image with Husserl as the real object imaged minus its being posited as really present anywhere, consciousness of the absence of the object be construed as an alteration of the being of the object itself. Beginning with the phenomenology of the picture in order to clarify the phenomenology of the image rather than proceeding in the opposite direction allows us to recognize explicitly something that has a density and destiny of its own in virtue of which it stands instead of the real thing. It presents itself in its own right not as merely a medium through which something else may be reached. Unlike a symbol or sign whose existence is essentially tied to something that is signified through it, the image and representations in general are signs or symbols in reverse, shadows that reality casts before it. They are allegories. Like the animals of Nietzsche's *Zarathustra*, they are not just semi-opaque screens or transparent lenses with the aid of which an abstract account of human psychology may be rendered more understandable by being made more concrete. They are fables, 'true as only fictions can be', in which men are seen as these animals. The world of the artistic imagination and of imagination in general is not merely a reflection or re-presentation of reality, but a double of reality presenting its sensible truth. Abstract math-ematical, scientific and philosophical theories are rational doublets of the reality of everyday life. Semblance and resemblance are thus productions of being, the way the truth of being is accomplished: phenomenology bi-genitively *of* ontology, being's perspective or regard (*CPP* 7, *HLR* 136).

But the regard of metaphysical being, produced in fundamental ontology and Heidegger's thinking of being as regard for being, is produced in Levinas's teaching as regard for the other human being. Ontological amphibology is doubled by an ethical amphibology. Sensibility of sensibility, rationality of rationality, intellectual non-intuition, metaphysics as ethics reproduces itself as a prodigious family of identical twins stemming from the excess of the identity of the self. Several members of that family have been named in this and earlier chapters. They and other members of this extended family could be collected in a glossary in which each of the interrelated words marks an amphibological crossing of a phenomenologico-ontological sense with an ethical or, more strictly speaking, proto-ethical sense in which the former is overdetermined and accomplished (*AE* 146, *OB* 115). The word 'accomplished' might be the first double-entry in it. The minimal references to Levinas's texts, mainly *Otherwise than Being*, given against some of the items in the following draft of such an alephbet of tropes should be supplemented by references given in the index of this study of his work.

AN ALEPHBET OF TROPES

accomplished (*AE* 62, *OB* 48, *HS* 30, 36, *OS* 16, 22), accusation (*AE* 140, 157n., *OB* 110, 197n.), address (*DL* 21, *DF* 7), affection (*HS* 68, *OS* 47), alteration, alternation, amen, antinomy, apprehension (*AE* 95, *OB* 75), approach, assumption (*AE* 111n., *OB* 192n.), autonomy (*AE* 189, *OB* 148), beholden/beheld, communication (*TEI* 75, *TI* 101, *AE* 62, 152, 203, *OB* 48, 119, 160), *conscience* ('conscience' and 'consciousness', *AE* 189, *OB* 148, *DL* 23, 33, *DF* 9, 17, *EN* 19), corporeity (*AE* 97, 139, *OB* 77, 109), creation (*TEI* 269–70, *TI* 293–4, *AE* 133, 144–5, *OB* 105, 113–14), critique (*AE* 25, 116–17, *OB* 20, 91–2), deduction (*AE* 107n., *OB* 192n.), Desire/desire (*TEI* 3, *TI* 33, *AE* 195ff., *OB* 153ff.), diachrony (*AE* 54, *OB* 42), *douleur* (*AE* 70–1, *OB* 54–5), emphasis, exegesis, experience (*TEI* 81, 170, *TI* 109, 196, *EDE* 177, *CPP* 59), exposition (*AE* 139, *OB* 109), expression (*EN* 20), exteriority (*TEI* 78, 266, 270, *TI* 105, 290, 294, *AE* 187, *OB* 147), face (*TEI* 22–3, 52–3, *TI* 51–2, 79–81, *AE* 112ff., *OB* 88ff.), genealogy (*AE* 108n., 223, *OB* 177, 192n.), God (*EN* 34), hearing, history (*TEI* 219–21, *TI* 242, *AE* 22, 113, *OB* 18, 89, *ADV* 20, 37, *BTV* 6, 21), humanity, hypostasis (*AE* 56, *OB* 44), implication (*AE* 173, *OB* 136), intelligibility (*AE* 87, *OB* 69), investiture (*AE* 63, 73, 127, 139, *OB* 49, 57, 100, 109), justice (*AE* 84n., 90, *OB* 71, 191n.), kerygma, kinship (*HS* 12, 23, 61, *OS* 3, 10, 40–1), liturgy

(*TEI* 23, 177, 272, *TI* 52, 202, 295), master, maybe, metaphysics (*TEI* 12ff., *TI*, 42ff.,, *AE* 131, *OB* 103), moi/Moi (*AE* 152, *OB* 119), nonsense (*AE* 208–9, *OB* 163), optics (*TEI* XVII, XXI, 51,149, *TI* 23, 29, 78, 174, *DL* 33, 352, *DF* 17, 275, *QLT* 104, *NTR* 47), ostension (*AE* 54, *OB* 42), passion (*AE* 64, *OB* 50), passive (*AE* 146, *OB* 115), persecution (*AE* 95, 130, 142–3, *OB* 75, 102, 111–12), philosophy (*EN* 252), position, possession (*DL* 23, *DF* 9), production, prophecy (*EN* 124, *CPP* 171, *TRI* 63), psychosis (*AE* 180, *OB* 142), rationality (*AE* 203, 211, *OB* 160, 166), recurrence (*AE* 130ff., *OB* 102ff.), reduction (*AE* 56, *OB* 45), regard (*AE* 91, 94, 116, 118, 147, 151, *OB* 72, 75, 92, 93, 116, 118, *DL* 24, *DF* 10, *EN* 172), relation (*TEI* 155, 271, *TI* 180, 295), responsibility (*AE* 61, *OB* 47, *ADV* 87), revelation (*HS* 30, *OS* 16), secret (*AE* 187, *OB* 147, *EEI* 89, *EI* 80–1), senescence (*AE* 66–7, *OB* 51–2), sense, sensibility (*AE* 89, 161, *OB* 71, 125), sign (*AE* 194, *OB* 152), silence, surprise, thematization (*TEI* 184, *TI* 209, *DL* 43), unconscious (*AE* 158n., *OB* 197n.), undergo (*AE* 71, *OB* 55), value (*AE* 158–9n., *OB* 197–8n.), vigilance, violence (*TEI* IX, 16ff., *TI* 21, 46–7, *AE* 56, 64, 158n., *OB* 43–4, 50, 197n.), welcome (*AE* 109n., 158, *OB* 192n., 123).

In order to mark the difference between the ontologico-phenomenological meanings and their anarchaic tropes the latter might have been rewritten in 'square letters', for example ReGaRD. Levinas insists that his aim is to speak of the prophetic in 'Greek'. Although this is not incompatible with also troping the 'Greekly' said into prophetical 'Hebrew' saying, this scriptic device could not be employed throughout the entirety of the above list, for example for *moi*, where it, not *Moi*, marks the ethical force. Heidegger differentiates beingness from being as essencing or presencing as such by erasing the word Being with a superimposed diagonal cross. Levinas could mark the difference between that ontic–ontological difference and the ontological–ethical difference by effacing Heidegger's mark, remarking it. It must be confessed that this remarking seems to make no difference. It seems only to stress, to emphasize, the mark it would efface. What one needs is a memento of an effacement that takes place not merely by doubling being with another perspectival aspect, but by turning it toward the face of the other. What one needs is a *memento mori* that turns toward the death of the other preoccupation with one's own. A mark in Hebrew is a *Taw*. This is the last letter of the alephbet, written mostly as a diagonal cross, though over a certain period of the history of the use of the letter the cross could be an upright one, like the mark on the back of Zarathustra's spider. It is the mark that the scribe is commanded to write in ink upon the foreheads of the faithful in the verses of Ezekiel cited as epigraphs of *Otherwise than Being*. If it is not to remain indistinguishable from the mark of being, vanishing into it without trace, it must be remarked again and again. Only in the marking and remarking can it be a memorial of the immemoriality of the pluperfect prehistorical past of responsibility. Once inscribed, it becomes indistinguishable from the marked mark of the historical narrative of events whose forgotten past is always in principle recoverable in future recollection. The amphibology of ethical allegory demands infinite alternation.

15 Ethical agoraphobia

PERSECUTION

The 'for' of the for-itself, the *pour-soi*, turns into, veers (*vire*) towards the 'for' of the for-the-other, *pour l'autre*. I approach the other. But my approach to the other is approach in the separateness or sanctity of proximity in ethical space, space that exspatiates the already non-geometrical space of being-in-the-world whose topography is described in the third chapter of the first division of *Being and Time*. And there is a further twist. This turn, precisely because it is the turn of ethics, of my approach to the other in responsibility, is the way of the other's approach to me. The trope of the for-myself turned into *for*-the-other turns into a *by*-the-other or *through*-the-other; the *pour* veers into a *par*. And this is another trope of Heidegger's trope of the ontic metaphor into the ontological quasi-metaphor. It is a going over of Heidegger's reflection in the 'Letter on Humanism': 'Thinking is *l'engagement par l'Etre pour l'Etre*. I do not know if it is linguistically possible to say both of these (*par* and *pour*) at once, in this way: *penser, c'est l'engagement de l'Etre.*'[1] If the 'of' of the engagement of being is both subjective and objective, speculative or, as one might also say, middle voiced, it might express conjointly the for and the by. Levinas's response to this, one might say, is that the care or concern of being thus construed is a derivation from my still middle voiced being both responsible for the other and suffering by or through or from the other. 'The *for-the-other* (or sense) goes as far as the *from-the-other*, as far as suffering from a splinter that burns the flesh, but for *nothing*. Only thus is the *for-the-other* – passivity more passive than all passivity, emphasis of sense – saved from the *for-oneself*' (*AE* 64–5, *OB* 50).

I could say of myself, though not on behalf of any other self, *je suis, donc l'autre me poursuit*, or *je vis, donc je suis poursuivi*: I am or I live, therefore the other persecutes me right up to my death. Readers unwilling to follow Levinas right up to this violent extreme should consider whether he sees the violence of this doctrine as the only way by which greater or worse violence can be forestalled. If one says that the good violence of peace is the price to be paid for the avoidance of the bad violence of war, one must go on to say that the good violence of peace is precisely the refusal to be content with merely paying the price. I am saved from the for-myself only because this excess is saved, only because no bargain is struck. A bargain makes too much sense, and sense of the wrong kind. There must be a surplus of senselessness if the giving of myself to the other is not to be balanced by a return, albeit a return of no more than gratitude. The passion of suffering for another is always in danger of recompensing me with an *apologia pro vita mea*. My suffering can be pointless suffering,[2] suffering for nothing, only if it is in spite of my ego, *mal-gré moi*; only if it is a suffering of *la douleur d'autrui*.[3] It is on account of my responsibility for this that I am infinitely persecuted by the other, sacrificed for the other, my flesh burned by contact with the splinter that kindles a holocaust from the ashes of which no meaningful historical genealogy can be finally made.

Therefore although the persecution by the other may be understood in part in the sense of prosecution in law, which is one sense of the French *poursuivre*, the persecution must be a manic persecution. Although it is not a persecution mania in the psychoanalytic sense, not a sickness unto death of the psyche, it is necessarily vulnerable to such diagnosis (*AE* 194, *OB* 152). Ethical psychosis, what Levinas calls 'this madness [*folie*] at the co fines of reason' (*AE* 64, *OB* 50), this malady of proto-ethical responsibility prior to consciousness, is a holiness, a healthiness and indeed a haleness or wholeness in the sense of the German *Heiligkeit*, but a wholeness that defies the normal logic of part and whole. The identity of the wholeness of the self is inseparable from separateness, from the pre-original split (*Vor-ur-teil*), signified by the French *saint* and the Semitic *qadosh*, that predates any psychiatric schizothymia. 'There is' (!) an illeitic 'unconscious' beyond the superego of the psychoanalytic unconscious, obsession obsessed. The complication of the self divided into *pour-soi*, *pour-l'autre* and *par-l'autre*, makes possible and, because it interrupts them, makes impossible the complexes of psychoanalysis and its categories of *ego*, *superego* and *id*. Likewise the narratives derived from Greek mythology to which the Freudian analyst has recourse, and language that structures the house of the being of the unconscious according to the Lacanian, are destructured by pre-psychoanalytic trauma.[4] But when the narrative of Oedipus is interrupted by the speaking of another father, be he Abraham or Moses or another 'exceptional teacher' (*DL* 156n., *DF* 298n.), there is nothing to prevent that speaking from becoming written into another sociological, political or psychoanalytic narrative. Such biographies of Abraham and Moses are not unknown. And such psycho-biographies of the author of *Otherwise than Being* are inevitable, reductive genealogies citing information about where he comes from (*Phaedrus* 275), his race, his religion, which books he read and with what teachers he studied, in order to explain away the face to face of teaching without which there can be no information, no form and nothing taught (*EN* 37, *CPP* 35).[5] This means that such reductive genealogies must submit to such reductions themselves, as universal scepticism must apply to itself, and as Nietzsche's perspectivism must avow that it is itself but another perspective. It does not mean that the reductions of such reductions that Levinas maintains it is the responsibility of philosophy to produce must exclude as irrelevant to philosophy the singular events of the philosopher's life such as Levinas recounts of his own life in the final essay in *Difficult Freedom* called 'Signature'. However, without begging the question and what is before the question it cannot be assumed that there is nothing more to these events and avowals than lived experience or accusative theme. It is as traces of accusation that Levinas writes the dedication and the exergues of *Otherwise than Being*. Not as *j'accuse* directed at their readers, but as *je m'accuse* in indistinction from *être accusé*. Whatever the historically causal genealogy of the fate of the members of his own family named in 'square letters' in his dedication, of the six million murdered by National Socialism, and of the 'millions upon millions of human beings of all confessions and all nations, victims of the same hatred of the other man, of the same antisemitism', Levinas's teaching in *Otherwise than Being* can be reduced to his saying that for what was and is suffered by each of those victims *je m'accuse*. It is for each one of his readers to say after reading to the end of that book, whether he or she has learned to say the same.

After reading to its end we can see better how to read the exergues placed at or before its beginning. From time to time throughout this exegesis of that book there have been moments when one of the epigraphs from Pascal's *Pensées* may have seemed to threaten to betray the lesson I have drawn from the pages to which it is prefixed. Pascal writes that the statement 'This is my place in sun' is 'the beginning and the image of the usurpation of the entire earth'.[6] Although that place is not one that has been chosen by me, although I did not choose to have any place in the sun at all, although I did not choose to be born, is there not at least the trace of a risk that my occupation of my place will be the beginning of a justification for my being accused? But we have taken Levinas to say that *in extremis* there can be no suspicion of a rational ground upon which my responsibility to the other can be required as the correlative of a debt. The responsibility in question, beyond any question, is not a relative one. This is what the second of the epigraphs from Pascal makes clear: 'We have used concupiscence as far as was in our power to promote the general good; but it is no more than a sham and a false image of love; for at bottom it is nothing but hate.' Socially pluralized greed, enlightened self-interest, the power of bargaining in the market-place in the shade or in the light of the sun, does not begin to plumb the depths of the senselessness of responsibility in the absolute sense. The response to the market-place, the *agora*, of that absolute responsibility is absolute ethical agoraphobia, a phobia of the 'unconscious' beyond therapy, what Philippe Nemo calls the 'other "other" scene' beyond the psychoanalytic unconscious, the unconscious of a night foreshadowed by the night of the *il y a* and impenetrable by the light projected from the torch of any human science.[7]

There is still more than a glimmer of the idea of justification as the payment of accounts in the first of the two citations from Ezekiel which serve as epigraphs of *Otherwise than Being*:

Again, when a righteous man doth turn from his righteousness, and commit an iniquity, and I lay a stumbling block before him, he shall die: because thou hast not given him warning, he shall die in his sin, and his righteousness which he hath done shall not be remembered; but his blood will I require at thine hand.

(Ezekiel 3:20)

Levinas's French version ends 'je te demanderai compte'. As if this were not scandal enough, he goes on to cite Ezekiel 9:4–6:

And the Lord said unto him, go through the midst of the city, through the midst of Jerusalem, and set a mark upon the foreheads of the men that sigh and that cry for all the abominations that be done in the midst thereof.

And to the others he said in mine hearing, Go ye after him through the city, and smite: let not your eye spare, neither have ye pity:

Slay utterly old and young, both maids and little children, and women: but come not near any man upon whom is the mark; and begin at my sanctuary.

He adds the gloss on this last clause made by the medieval commentator on the Talmud, Rashi:

The sages have said, Do not read 'begin at my sanctuary', but 'begin with those that sanctify me', . . . as teaches the Talmudic Treatise *Sabbath*, 55a.

In what way can *Otherwise than Being* be read as an exegesis of this? As an exegesis of excess and as an excess of exegesis. Taken together the quotations from Pascal, from Ezekiel and from Rashi seem to yield no more than the concupiscent ego plus the justice of an eye for an eye understood strictly according to the letter of the law. It is as though the exergues allow a silence to reign over the question how a connection is to be made between the two extremes represented by the ego and the system of justice. But it is this silence that is interrupted and it is to this question that a response is made by what is written on the pages which follow these exergues – and by the dedication written on the page that precedes. The gap between the exergues from Ezekiel and Pascal is the exergue of these exergues them-selves, outside the energy and allergy of activity, waiting for what the book is about to say: that the space between the extremes is not one that is bound to be closed by a principle of enlightened self-interest; that nothing speaks against the possibility of its being passed over by the anarchy of my responsibility for all others before all responsibility grounded in causality or free will. An extremity of a quite different order from those of the ego and the logic of universal justice under which every ego including my own is a case, the multiplying excess of my responsibility demands a justice that is more and less than the justice based on resemblance within a genus. More and less because the demand is inseparable from the Other's 'Thou shalt not kill.' This commandment is not a simple rule of conduct, but the condition of social justice through being the condition of discourse (*DL* 22, *DF* 9). It is dis-course before discourse (*DL* 364, *DF* 284). And it pursues me with the fact of my murderousness and indifference, the fact that I am the keeper of my brother Abel.

I am therefore unconsciously anxious in face of the Other who pursues and persecutes me under my skin. I do not look forward to the encounter. There is a cool passion amounting to horror, even hatred, but a pre-original ethical hatred that makes possible the hatred of the Other that remains undiminished when concupiscence is harnessed for the general good; an absolute hatred that makes possible Cain's. But the hatefulness of this absolute hatred is what makes possible also a love of the stranger as oneself where compassionate solidarity does not revert to the pathos of intimacy (*AE* 130, 212, *OB* 102, 166). It is a hatefulness that emphatically ex-aggerates into ethical repulsiveness the awe that Kant discerns in the moral law's sublimity. Yet Schiller's unfair verse comment to the effect that Kant's categorical imperative could not be obeyed joyfully would be no less unfair when transferred to responsibility in the teaching of Levinas.[8] The Talmud is such a *gaya scienza* that one may have to take precautions not to be carried away by its quality of joy (*SS* 176, *NTR* 174). Although it is not something to be taken lightly, the yoke of the Law can be borne with joy and a light heart (*DL* 45, *DF* 26). Under it some Hasidim found that they could even dance with light feet into the place where they were to breathe their last toxic breath. Crushing though its charge may be, responsi- bility is elevation, exaltation and glory (*AE* 119, 120n., *OB* 93, 193n.). It is the wonder, before the wonder before being, in which the genesis of philosophy may be traced (*AE* 206, 228, *OB* 161–2, 181). Not a noematic object, but adverbial of feeling, including the feeling of respect, the painful, bad and evil of this absolute hatred precedes the distinction between physical pain, mental pain and bad or evil defined by the standards of a moral custom or code. Ethical agoraphobia could be a name for this absolutely hateful ethical horror of this non-thing and non-nothing of which, as of feared YHWH, no name can be pronounced. Of this e-normous yet intangible malignity in which Descartes's evil genius shares Levinas might have written 'Il n'y a pas *du* mal', 'Il n'y a pas d'il y a.' When heteronomy turns back into the autonomy of responsibility prior to the autonomy of free will, the anonymous absurdity of the there-is turns out to be a *modality* adverbial of the-one-for-the-other (*AE* 208–9, *OB* 164): ad-verbial, a *contretemps* against the time of verbal activity, the active voice modulated into the passive, the intentionality of the subject's advance reversed under the *contresens* of the Other's regard (*DVI* 206, *CPP* 185). Anonymous Ilyaity recurs in pro-nominal illeity to the point at which the former may be mistaken for the latter (*DVI* 115, *CPP* 166, *HLR* 179). Between the one and the other there is a recurring alternation. Under the weight of responsibility of expiation for the Other elevation is liable to lapse into lassitude. Indeed elevation requires lassitude, for without it responsibility for everyone and for everything would not be, in the words of the accuser in Job, responsibility undertaken 'for nought' (Job 1:9). If in his earlier writings Levinas speaks of the *il y a* in itself and substantively of *le mal*, these come more and more to be thought of as moments or modali- ties, as the adverbial shadow of nonsense necessary for the ex-perience of *dés-inter-essement* (*EEI* 51, *EI* 52, *EN* 133).

Ethical agoraphobia is not an anxiety provoked by just any open space. It is an emphasis of the dread Pascal felt before the eternal silence of infinite space. Ethical agoraphobia is a response not to an open space, but to a space where words and money are exchanged, a *forum* or a 'crowded *agora*' I may go into 'with a dagger under my arm' (Plato, *Gorgias* 469). This is a response not so much to the contingency of my finding myself thrown into the outer space of the world. For the space of the world, incessantly expanding though it may be, remains a place in which I am incessantly immured (*AE* 229, *OB* 182). The open space before which I suffer ethical agoraphobia is a space without walls and without place, a u-topic exteriority in which I feel the pressure of responsibility for the others to whom I find that I have already responded, though always too late. A pressure that makes an unmeetable demand on the lungs from the first intake of breath to the last. A hyperventilation, as of the cry with which one comes naked into the world or the last choke of Nietzschean laughter that sticks in the throat at the approach of the other (*DVI* 115, *CPP* 166, *HLR* 179) – 'tragic and grave and on the verge of madness' (*HAH* 95, *CPP* 148). But in agoraphobic response there can be no refusal to say (*AE* 10, *OB* 8). The saying that cannot be refused is the to-say. In an article entitled 'Without Identity', first published in 1970, in one of his frequent references to contemporary youth, Levinas remarks that what it refuses is the said of solemn moralization and of the ideological set-piece. That elderly language requires to be broken up by the youthful language of the simple appeal – 'Please give me a glass of water', or of laughter, the prophetic word of the poet-philosopher, *parole nietzschéenne, parole prophétique* (*HAH* 100, 111, *CPP* 151).

The refusal of this word would be all the more explicitly named if the Greek word *agora* for market-place and the Latin word *ager* for field happened to share a common etymological root which there is no reason to believe that they do. For in being a response to the burden of difficult freedom ethical agoraphobia is a refusal of the audible silence of the *pays*, the enclosed space where pagan gods haunt the interstices of being. It is a response to the *bourdonnement* of Eleatic ilyaity that re-echoes anonymously in the inner chambers of the ear like those noises reverberating from the walls of Plato's cave (*Republic* 515) and the *tohu wa-bohu* of Genesis 1:2, a tinnitus from which the only escape is not through the freedom of a heroically persistent egological will, but through a speaking in which I am bound by the other who teaches me more than I can learn from the country which, although outside the city wall, is more hermetically enclosed than the *agora* (*Phaedrus* 230). The time of ill omen (*malheur*) of claustrophobia is broken by a countertime in the time between involuntary inspiration and expiration, the *contre-temps* of agoraphobia that is vertiginously exhilarating but not without a malice of its own. For my place in the sun is threatened with usurpation by the other who, as other, excludes me, evicts me from my dwelling, turns me out. Yet for this very outrage the only one responsible is me (*AE* 212, *OB* 166). This is because the identity of my selfhood is split by my already having responded to the other's call. For every responsibility undertaken by the other I have already responded. The other's responsibility hounds me, multiplying mine, as though in an accelerating potlatch; or as though I were a bidder at an auction who will never be outbidden. I am always one bid ahead of the other. But I am bidding on his behalf, and what is on offer is myself.

My responsibility for the other's every responsibility, including his to other others, is the transcending of the impersonality of *das Man*, the declaustration of the *Da* of *Dasein* and the de-mythologizing of place, of *Lebensraum*. It is accomplishable not by freedom but by 'the enlargement of a closure which the abstract notions of freedom and non-freedom do not exhaust', by the 'Behold me at your service' of exposition. 'Exposition to the openness of the face that is the "still further" of the de-claustration of the "self-same" ["*soi-même*"], of the de-claustration that is not being- in-the-world. A still further – a deep respiration as far as the breath cut by the wind of alterity' (*AE* 226–7, *OB* 180); exposition to infinitely accusative pursuit, absolute cata-agorization.

BLASPHEMY

From time to time Ezekiel is commanded to 'set his face' toward those against whom he prophesies, as though they are not to be permitted to avoid contact with what they will regard as the evil eye.⁹ His role appears to be very much that of the executor of the *lex talionis*. In his exegesis of that law Levinas recommends vigilance concerning things said in the text that, to use his word, 'humanize' the strict arithmetical interpretation in a manner that admits the asymmetry he likewise insists on preserving, for 'Everyone in Israel stands surety for everyone' (Shebuot 39a, Sanhedrin 27b). This is not to be heard in a manner incompatible with the meaning that I am responsible for the responsibility others have for me (*ADV* 106, *BTV* 85, *HLR* 226). We must be watchful of the fact that Ezekiel is a watchman. This is what we are reminded of by the statement in the verse that Levinas adapts as his first epigraph: 'he shall die; because thou hast not given him warning'. Not even the scales of justice can take from me the balance of responsibility that cannot be taken lightly, the weight (*kabod*) that is also glory and image. The computability of innocence and guilt with a view to judgement does not take the onus of final judgement from me. Is this blasphemy?

Again, after the tribes of Israel rebelled against their God and Ezekiel refused to obey God's command to say to the tribes 'Thus saith the Lord', is it blasphemy to say that for God to be someone against whom one may rebel is for him to be someone for whom one may suffer to die (*DL* 193, *DF* 145)? Was the death of the more than six million also the death of a God against whom one may rebel? Or the death of 'God' or his *kabod*, his image? 'Is rebellion', asks Jabès, 'one of the paroxystic forms of obedience?'¹⁰ – obedience exasperated or exaggerated, as Levinas would say (*DVI* 142)? 'What if the divine prohibition strikes the very Idea of God?',¹¹ asks again Jabès, who is reported to have written also that 'God was, or was *no more than* the only word for grief sufficiently vast, sufficiently empty that all griefs may be contained within it'.[12] One question for the reader of Nietzsche experimentally reading also Levinas is the question that was asked above in chapter 12. Do we learn from Levinas that the emptiness of the word 'God' is sufficiently vast to contain God's death? Is its vastness sufficiently generous to contain its continuing to be God's empty tomb? Is Levinas's approach to the ethical, if not describable simply as secular – for the approach to the other interrupts worldhood – nevertheless humanistic in a way that subverts or at least subordinates the humanism of the Revolution and the Enlightenment without insinuating a new humanism that is also a new theism? One is tempted to say that Levinas's humanism of the other human being insinuates not a new but an exceedingly old theism, a theism in which all -ism is subverted by enigma in its Ancient Greek sense of pro-verbial saying. So that, to cite Jabès one final time, 'God' would be 'a word before or after the word, a wordless word, in the past and in the future; a word therefore of no utility, by the use of which the mind is shocked'.[13] The ancient past and always promised future of this word would contain no moment of choice, no Kierkegaardian moment of mortal leaping toward one's salvation or Heideggerian movement of running toward one's death.

The moment of enigma is the moment of a maybe which is not the maybe of incertitude, but that of a 'principle of uncertainty' that is the anarchic 'principle' of all principles. Anarchic because the call of this so-called principle will have been always already obeyed, whether one opts for humanism as opposed to theism, for theism as opposed to humanism, or for a neutral in-between. The enigma of scepticism before scepticism regarding knowledge, the enigma of discourse before discourse, is exposed to being accused of responding with yet another paradox to the paradox of the origin of language that every contract presupposes a more original tacit or explicit one. The enigma of the naked face runs the risk of being ridiculed as but one more case of the emperor's clothes (*AE* 194, *OB* 152).

Cutting *across* principiality and power, *dia*-lectically interrupting the dialectic of Yes opposed to No and the dynamics of Hegelian or Nietzschean force, this fabulous enigma would be the moved mover of metaphor and myth, the motor both of the motor of the phenomenology of the experience of consciousness and of the genealogy of origins. But this mover would not be a power, and its affectivity and sensibility would be moved beyond the affectivity and sensibility of Nietzschean will to power.

Otherwise than Being and earlier versions of its chapters were published at the height of a period of intense attention to Nietzsche especially in France, occasioned in part by the launching of the Colli–Montinari edition of his works, but already underway in the influential study of Nietzsche by

Gilles Deleuze and culminating in Pierre Klossowski's translation of Heidegger's Nietzsche lectures and in the ten days of discussion of Nietzsche's work at Cerisy in 1972 at which many of the contributors were authors of important books or essays on Nietzsche.[14] We have seen that *Otherwise than Being*, published two years later, engages with a Nietzschean theme right from its beginning and earlier, right from its prophetic exergue, when it says:

> the ill-kept commitment to recompense virtue and chastise vice notwithstanding the assurances of those who claim that it was made for a term more distant than the distance that separates the heavens from the earth, will accredit strange rumours about the death of God or the emptiness of the heavens. No one will believe in their silence.

(AE 5, OB 5)

The later chapters of that book, and the books that precede it, are dramatizations of an intrication of immanence and transcendence, of interiority and exteriority, the denouement of which is not a final reconciliation but an infinite alternation in which the breath of Hegelian Spirit is taken away. This untying is at the same moment my being tied by an obligation to the Good that is beyond the being, the essence and the concept of the Hegelian phenomenology of spirit and beyond the oppositions of good and evil and of good and bad distinguished in the Nietzschean genealogy of morals. Levinas revalues 'Good' and 'God' and 'Good God' in a way that leads him to wonder whether 'The death of God signifies maybe only the possibility of reducing every value arousing a force [*pulsion*] to a force arousing a value' (*AE* 158, OB *123*); in such a way that death is survived by the good that calls not least the survivor of catastrophe to responsibility, if not in his or her prayer, appellation (*EN* 20), then in his or her blaspheming, calling God names, or perhaps in a pre-original cry in which prayer and blasphemy are not yet distinguished; an asphyxiated cry expulsed like a first or last breath in the very vanity without which it would not be possible even to take God's name in vain.

Blasphemy, Levinas remarks in the last pages of *Otherwise than Being*, is what some would call the attempt made in that book to contemplate an infidelity to Nietzsche, even to a Nietzsche dissociated from the slur of National Socialism. In those last pages of *Otherwise than Being* Nietzsche is associated instead with a kind of Epicureanism, while Spinoza and Hegel are deemed to be of the same Stoic lineage as Zeno of Elea. Both schools champion being and essence. For both virtue is the nobility of heroic, virile *virtù*. Another genealogy, another *parenté* for man requires to be found. Although in this other genealogy theism is identified with what it is difficult to refrain from calling the He-ism of illeity, it must be emphasized that the trace of the other passes also through the She-ism and elleity of maternity, so through a non-neutral illelleity.[15]

GENEALOGY AS HISTORY CATASTROPHIZED

Two years after the appearance of the first edition of *Otherwise than Being* Levinas read a paper entitled 'The Model of the West' in which the requirement of another genealogy is again formulated as an alternative to contemporary Nietzscheanism.[16]

> The West professes the historical relativity of values and their con-testation. But perhaps it takes every moment too seriously, too quickly calling them historical, leaving to this history the right both to judge values and to sink into relativity. Whence the incessant revaluation of values, an incessant collapse of values, an incessant genealogy of morals. A history without permanence or a history without sanctity.
>
> (*ADV* 37, *BTV* 21)

Otherwise said, moments of history are not all moments of narratable history. For instance, the moments when in writing the penultimate chapter of *Otherwise than Being* Levinas interrupts the flow of what he is saying with references to the very moment of his saying it. A historical context for these moments of history outside history is adumbrated when at that moment at the end of the penultimate subsection of *Totality and Infinity* to which we have already referred, he speaks of a messianic time in which the perpetuity of death is converted into eternity. Having asked 'Is this eternity a new structure of time, or an extreme vigilance of messianic consciousness?' he goes on to comment only 'This problem exceeds the bounds of this book.' No doubt this problem exceeds the bounds of any book, but in the Talmudic reading from which we have just cited his remark that moments in history are not all moments of history he explains why he names them moments of monotheism in spite and because of Zarathustra's proclamation that the old gods laughed themselves to death when one of them pronounced 'the most godless word . . . "There is one god"', provoking the others to rock in their seats and to cry 'Is not just this godlike that there are gods but no God?'[17] One has to say 'in spite of and because of' since, it will be recalled, Levinas more than once hails Nietzschean laughter as a disruption of history under-stood as a totality of events connected causally or logically according to the laws of, for instance, Hegelian or Marxian dialectic. So that to laugh God off the stage comes close to laughing on to it the holy and the eternal. There is an equivocation of theatre and temple (*DVI* 115, *CPP* 166, *HLR* 179).

When the eternal moments of holy separation from history are given a 'historical place' in Israel, one has to remember that in Levinas's thinking Israel stands for what is not the historical time of events narrated in history books, nor the geographical place of Eretz Israel, nor a particular genealogical race. It stands for the concrete accomplishing of transcendence in immanence, the effectuation of an infinite to-transcend, as the concrete accomplishing of what is said in the face to face to-say. It stands for facing. It stands for standing for the other. 'Jewish' sanctity is not sanctimonious spirituality. 'Jewishness' stands for giving the other the bread from one's lips, bread that some non-Jews would describe as a wafer. It stands for a certain universality that transcends Judaism. 'Don't be shocked! The authentically human is everyone's Jewishness and its echo in the singular and the particular' (*AHN* 192, *ITN* 8). So while standing for a not merely generic but genealogical universality Jewishness stands at the same time for a certain particularity, the particularity of a historical exemplar that reminds others of what in them exceeds and judges the judgement of universal history.

Levinas dares say that the Passion of Israel, from its captivity in Egypt up to its puberty at Auschwitz in Poland,[18] is constitutive of God's existence, as though God was the history of Israel and the history of Israel was the 'divine ontology'. Not that this Passion is a proof of the existence of God. Rather, this 'emphasis' of secular history as the holy history of separation is the unfolding of that existence itself, its drama, its *divina comedia* (*ADV* 20–1, *BTV* 164). So in speaking of the experience or experimental testing of God, God's *épreuve* (see above, third section of chapter 12), the genitive would be not only objective but subjective too, as in God's testing (*nissah*) of Israel and of Abraham when Isaac asks 'But where is the lamb?' More precisely, this genitive would be beyond the opposition of the subjective and objective, and outside simultaneity and synchrony. It would therefore escape the oppositions of history as narrated *Historie* and history either as ecstatically existed *Geschichte* or as the genealogy of Absolute Spirit. In the dramatic enigma of the excluded third of diachronic history divine ontology cannot be distinguished from divine meontology. Consistent with his warning that the enigmatic in his meaning has nothing to do with knowledge or certitude, Levinas's identification of the 'being' of God with the history of the sufferings of the innocent means that 'the semiotics of the word God' is such that it would be irrelevant to make the formal objection that, far from entailing his non-existence, the absence of God entails that God exists. Irrelevant also would be the objection that a similar logical entailment holds for the declaration of God's death. The semiotics of the word 'God' does not offer a choice between acceptance and refusal. Is not 'God' the name for what is accepted even in being refused? Although Levinas puts this question in a comment on a Rabbinic text (*DL* 104, *DF* 76), it soon becomes clear that the question is rhetorical and that what is accepted in being refused is the Other as both You and the third-personal He of illeity. Levinas is especially concerned in this text with messianism and the politics of Israel. Hence, immediately after putting this question he asks 'Does not freedom in general suppose an engagement prior to the very refusal of this engagement?' In the political sphere, 'Has not he who rejects the state been formed for this rejection by the very state he rejects?' Levinas's answer to this question is again 'Yes', like Hegel's. However, in giving it he appeals not to any Hegelian concrete universality, but to a universal particularism which, while recognizing the historical and political concreteness of the subject, does not subtract from subjectivity my being sub-ject in substitution for the Other. In Levinas's Talmudic readings the words 'in the name of the Father' obviously have a particular Jewish resonance. But in the commentaries included in *Difficult Freedom* under the title 'Messianic Texts' he reminds his reader of the rule of method of cabbalistic hermeneutics to proceed beyond the obvious or literal sense (*peshat*) through the allegorical or allusive (*remez*) and the homiletic or symbolic (*drash*) to the esoteric or mysterious (*sod*). If it is permissible to apply this exegetical method here – remembering that Levinas draws on Volozhyn and that Volozhyn draws on the cabbalah – it may be said that once 'Israel' is given the allegorical meaning of the one that is chosen for responsibility, then 'in the name of the Father' may be interpreted in the sense of our chapter on Generations, that is to say, in the sense of Genesis 10 in which all peoples are said to be brothers in that they descend genealogically from the three sons of Noah; and in the sense of the gloss (*midrash*) telling that these peoples were made when God took from the four corners of the world some yellow dust, some red dust, some black dust and some white, and mixed them in water taken from all the world's seas.

Therefore 'Israel' refers both to the particularity of a people and the particularity of a person, no matter to what people that person does or does not belong. 'I will say to them which were not my people, Thou art my people' (Hosea 2:23, *AHN* 11, *ITN* 4). And the same must be said of Israel's 'Messianic' role. Messianism is the role both of a historic people and my role as bearer of the suffering of all. Not one who arrives at the end of history, the Messiah is everyone who says 'me', 'send me' here and now (*DL* 120, *DF* 89).

Is there however a time when one is not sent, not chosen? One is certainly always late on the scene. Levinas finds it incredible that in 1936 Paul Claudel should sign a document denouncing German antisemitism yet refuse permission for his signature to be published; and that in the summer of 1940 he can write 'After sixty years France has been delivered from the yoke of the radical and anti-Catholic party (teachers, lawyers, Jews, freemasons)' after writing merely twelve months earlier that the scribes call Israel a witness and that the Greek term for 'witness' is *martyr*. Only very late in the day does Claudel proclaim the uniqueness of the martyrdom of Auschwitz. But if Auschwitz, if 'the suffering at the limit of all suffering', if 'the suffering that suffers all sufferings' that goes by the name of Holocaust is unique, is there not a particularity even more particular within the particularity of Israel? Are there not some who from among the chosen are chosen above all: the 'selected', the victims, or they and the 'survivors'? One may think that this is so if one does not think through the difference between responsibility for something, for a state of affairs or a free choice, and responsibility for someone. It is with the latter that Levinas is first of all concerned, for it is by the latter that the former is conditioned. One may well believe that only those who experienced the Holocaust have a right to decide whether Auschwitz was the scene of theocidy – 'My God, my God, why hast thou forsaken me?' (Psalm 22) – or of theodicy – 'My God, my God, why hast thou not forsaken me?' – or whether, as Levinas holds, it exceeded both of these alternatives (*EN* 114–18).[19] But this 'privilege' – which might even be the subject of 'a fearful envy'[20] – is not to be confused with the responsibility entailed by the fact that 'every survivor of the Hitlerian massacres – whether a Jew or not – is Other in relation to the martyrs' (*DL* 176, *DF* 132); every survivor in the sense of everyone who is alive and so able to say 'me', 'send me'. He and she is always sent. Sent at the very least to obey the commandment Emil Fackenheim adds to the 614 of the Torah: remember the victims of Auschwitz.[21] The messages those victims deposited in tins and bottles they buried beneath the floors there forbid us to remain silent.

'The coming of the Messiah is accompanied by catastrophes' Levinas writes in 'Messianic Texts', commenting on a Sanhedrin 88b (*DL* 106, *DF* 78). And the exergues of *Otherwise than Being* should have reminded us that Ezekiel refers to the catastrophe of the destruction of Jerusalem and the promise of its restoration. Without in the least reducing the confessional significance of these catastrophes Levinas elicits an ethical interpretation of catastrophe that holds good independently of confessional faith, unless by faith is meant what one does. Levinas reports a story Hannah Arendt told on French radio shortly before her death. When a child in her native Königsberg she announced to the rabbi from whom she was receiving religious instruction that she had lost her faith. To which the rabbi's reaction was to ask 'But who says that you have to have that?' What matters is not faith but good deeds (*AHN* 192, *ITN* 164), liturgy in the etymological sense of service without compensation (*HAH* 43, 53, *CPP* 92–3, 100).

A *katastrophê* is a violent turn of events, a cataclastic turning round or trope. Such an event is what is troped catachretically by the words Holocaust, Shoah, Genocide, Ethnic Cleansing, Chelmno, Dachau, Sobibor, Theresienstadt, Treblinka, Mauthausen, Majdanek, Gunskirchen, Rumbuli, Ponar, Kovno Buchenwald, Belzec, Belsen, Babi Yar, Birkenau and (a name that says it names a place where life is sweated out till death) Auschwitz. But the list contains more than six million extraordinary names, the proper names of millions upon millions of human beings of all confessions and all nations, or of none. When the bearers of these names are actively remembered catastrophe names the auto-accusation in suffering that is the turning of the ego into a self, the expropriative event or *Enteignis* that Levinas calls recurrence.[22] Recurrence is the overcoming of the I by the me, accomplishment that is not fulfilling but emptying, the *kenosis* of messianic *metanoia*.

'Messianism is nothing other than the apogee in being which is the centralization, concentration or twisting back upon itself of my Self' (*DL* 120, *DF* 90). Concentration that may be concentration upon *l'univers concentrationnaire*, recursion that may be the infinite resonance of 'never again', the *ewige Wiederkehr* of *nie wieder*, messianic remembrance of the Other is prayer in the root sense of *tephillah*, from *hitpalel* which is judging oneself even in judging history. In this responsion the ontological claustrophobia of being bound in the existent ego's exclusive concern with its own survival or in the unpeopled indifference of the existence of the *il y a* gives way to the ethically agoraphobic *dénouement* that binds souls in the bundle of the living referred to in 1 Samuel 25:29 and acronymically when *Otherwise than Being* is dedicated to the memory of the author's parents, parents-in-law and brothers. Their pointless suffering and that of all other victims of hate remains without explanation and without theodicy. As when asked 'Do you discern a meaning in Auschwitz?' a witness at the trial of Eichmann responded 'I hope I never do. To understand Auschwitz would be even worse than not to understand it.' Yet that pointless, absurd and obscene suffering calls for suffering that is not without point when philosophy as the love of theoretical wisdom calls for philosophy as the practical wisdom of compassionate love, and when the genealogy of being, becoming and morals, even from before the time of the gestation of being and becoming and from beyond the power of good and bad will to power, is disturbed by Emmanuel Levinas's genealogy of ethics traced back through phenomenology, thought and question to the Other's indeclinable request.

Notes

INTRODUCTION

1 Plato, *Republic* VII, 509b6–b10; *Phaedrus* 276a5–a9.
2 *De Generatione animalium* II, 3, 736b28. See also *De Anima* III, 5, 430a10.

1 ONTOLOGICAL CLAUSTROPHOBIA

1 M. Heidegger, *Sein und Zeit*, 7th edn, Tübingen, Niemeyer, 1953; trans. J. Macquarrie and E. Robinson, *Being and Time*, Oxford, Blackwell, 1967.
2 R. Kearney (ed.), *Dialogues with Contemporary Thinkers: The Phenomenological Heritage*, Manchester, Manchester University Press, 1984, p. 49; R. Cohen (ed.), *Face to Face with Levinas*, Albany, NY, State University of New York Press, 1986, p. 13.
3 *MT* 62, *DMT* 66–7. H. Bergson, *L'évolution créatrice* (1st edn, 1907), Paris, Alcan, 1934, pp. 293–4; trans. A. Mitchell, *Creative Evolution* (1st edn, 1911), London, Macmillan, 1919, pp. 285–6.
4 Ibid., p. 307; p. 299.
5 H. Bergson, *Les deux sources de la morale et de la religion*, Paris, Alcan, 1932; trans. R. Audra and C. Brereton, *The Two Sources of Morality and Religion*, London, Macmillan, 1935.
6 C. Baudelaire, 'Spleen', 'J'ai plus de souvenirs . . .', *Oeuvres complètes* (Pléiade), Paris, Gallimard, 1961, p. 69.
7 'Nur noch ein Gott kann uns retten', interview with Heidegger in *Der Spiegel*, 31 May 1976, pp. 193–219; trans. W. Richardson, 'Only a God can Save Us', in T. Sheehan (ed.), *Heidegger: The Man and the Thinker*, Chicago, Precedent Publishing Inc., 1981, pp. 45–67.
8 Plato, *Gorgias* 494a–b.
9 J.-P. Sartre, *La nausée*, Paris, Gallimard, 1938.
10 E. Husserl, *Cartesianische Meditationen und Pariser Vorträge*, The Hague, Nijhoff, 1973; trans. D. Cairns, *Cartesian Meditations*, The Hague, Nijhoff, 1960.

2 ONTIC ACCOMPLISHMENT

1 M. Heidegger, *Sein und Zeit*, Tübingen, Niemeyer, 1953, p. 1; trans. J. Macquarrie and E. Robinson, *Being and Time*, Oxford, Blackwell, 1967, p. 1. *SZ* references in my text are references to *Sein und Zeit* given in the margins of the published English translation.
2 E. Husserl, *Logische Untersuchungen*, 2 vols, Halle, Niemeyer, 1900 (rev. edn, 1913), 1901 (rev. edn, 1922); trans. J. N. Findlay, *Logical Investigations*, 2 vols, London, Routledge and Kegan Paul, 1970.
3 *Ideas*, vol. 1, §§3, 19. E. Husserl, *Ideen zu einer reinen Phänomenologie und phänomenologischen Philosophie*, Book I, The Hague, Nijhoff, 1950; trans. W. R. Boyce Gibson, *Ideas*, London, Allen and Unwin, 1931.
4 E. Husserl, *Cartesianische Meditationen und Pariser Vorträge*, The Hague, Nijhoff, 1973; trans. D. Cairns, *Cartesian Meditations*, The Hague, Nijhoff, 1960.
5 St Augustine, *Confessions*, Bk 10, ch. 35.
6 M. Heidegger, 'Der Spruch des Anaximander', *Holzwege*, Frankfurt am Main, Klostermann, 1972, pp. 330, 335; trans. D. F. Krell and F. A. Capuzzi, 'The Anaximander Fragment', in *Early Greek Thinking*, New York, Harper and Row, 1975, pp. 44, 50.
7 Wo aber Gefahr ist, wächst / Das Rettende auch. ('But where danger is, grows / The saving power also.')
  F. Hölderlin, 'Patmos', cited frequently by Heidegger, for example in 'Die Frage nach der Technik', in *Vorträge und Aufsätze*, Pfullingen, Neske, 1954, vol. 1, pp. 28, 35, and in *Die Technik und die Kehre*, Pfullingen, Neske, 1962, p. 41; trans. W. Lovitt, 'The Question Concerning Technology', in *The Question Concerning Technology and Other Essays*, New York, Harper and Row, 1977, pp. 28, 35, 42.
8 S. Weil, *La pesanteur et la grâce*, Paris, Plon, 1947; trans. E. Craufurd, *Gravity and Grace*, London, Routledge and Kegan Paul, 1952.
9 F. Rosenzweig, *Der Stern der Erlösung*, 2nd edn, Frankfurt am Main, Kauffmann, 1930; trans. W. W. Hallo, *The Star of Redemption*, Notre Dame, Ind., Notre Dame Press, 1985.
10 Rabbi Hayyim de Volozhyn, *L'âme de la vie (Nefesh Hahayyim)*, trans. B. Gross, Paris, Verdier, 1986. The original Hebrew edition was published in 1824.
11 F. W. J. Schelling, *Die Weltalter*, ed. M. Schröter, Munich, Biederstein, 1946; trans. F. de W. Bolman, *The Ages of the World*, New York, Columbia University Press, 1967.
12 M. Heidegger, 'Nachwort' to 'Was ist Metaphysik?', pp. 99–108 in *Wegmarken*, Frankfurt am Main, Klostermann, 1967, p. 102; pp. 303–12 in *Gesamtausgabe*, vol. 9, ed. F.-W. von Herrmann, Frankfurt am Main, Klostermann, 1976, p. 306; trans. R. F. C. Hull and A. Crick, Postscript to 'What is Metaphysics?', pp. 380–92 in *Existence and Being*, London, Vision, 1949, p. 385.

3 BEFORE TIME

1 *TEI* XIV, *TI* 26. Production is analysed further in chapters 6, 14 and elsewhere.
2 M. Heidegger, *Questions III*, Paris, Gallimard, 1966, p. 73. A. de Waelhens, *La*

philosophie de Martin Heidegger, Louvain, Publications Universitaires de Louvain, 1942, and *Phénoménologie et vérité*, Louvain, Nauwelaerts, 1969.

3 I thank Nelly Demé for her helping hand in providing me with a remarkable photograph of this sculpture.

4 *SZ* 205n. refers to W. Dilthey, 'Beiträge zur Lösung der Frage vom Ursprung unseres Glaubens an die Realität der Aussenwelt und seinen Recht', *Gesammelte Schriften*, Bern, Francke, 1954f., vol. V, pt I, pp. 90ff. *SZ* 210n. refers to M. Scheler, *Die Formen des Wissens und die Bildung*, Bonn, Cohen, 1925. This is reprinted in Max Scheler, *Gesammelte Werke*, vol. 9, ed. M. Frings, Bern, Francke, 1976, pp. 85–119. Compare *Der Formalismus in der Ethik und die materiale Wertethik*, *Gesammelte Werke*, vol. 2, Bern, Francke, 1980, pp. 127–72; trans. M. S. Frings and R. L. Funk, *Formalism in Ethics and Non-Formal Ethics of Values*, Evanston, Ill., Northwestern University Press, 1973, pp. 111–59.

5 J. G. Fichte, *Science of Knowledge (Wissenschaftslehre)*, trans. P. Heath and J. Lachs, New York, Appleton-Century-Crofts, 1970.

6 For *distentio* as 'distraction' and 'decontraction' see St Augustine, *Confessions*, bk 12, ch. 29.

7 G. W. F. Hegel, *Encyclopaedia of Philosophical Sciences*, part 2, *Philosophy of Nature*, trans. A. V. Miller, Oxford, Clarendon Press, 1970, §259, addendum.

4 ANNOUNCING TIME

1 M. Heidegger, *Die Grundbegriffe der Metaphysik*, *Gesamtausgabe* vol. 29–30, ed. F.-W. von Herrmann, Frankfurt am Main, Klostermann, 1983. Ontological responsibility is a main theme also of J. Llewelyn, *The Middle Voice of Ecological Conscience: A Chiasmic Reading of Responsibility in the Neighbourhood of Levinas, Heidegger and Others*, London, Macmillan, 1991.

2 M. Heidegger, *Kant und das Problem der Metaphysik*, Frankfurt am Main, Klostermann, 1973; trans. R. Taft, *Kant and the Problem of Metaphysics*, Bloomington, Ind., Indiana University Press, 1990, §§26–32.

3 E. Husserl, *Vorlesungen zur Phänomenologie des inneren Zeitbewusstseins*, Halle, Niemeyer, 1928; repr. The Hague, Nijhoff, 1966 (*Husserliana*, vol. X, ed. R. Boehm); trans. J. S. Churchill, *The Phenomenology of Internal Time Consciousness*, The Hague, Nijhoff, 1964.

4 Ibid., §39 and appendix VIII.

5 ANNOUNCING THE OTHER

1 I thank Elsebet Jegstrup for her comments on Kierkegaard's notion of *Øieblikker*.

2 See C. Bailey, *The Greek Atomists and Epicurus*, Oxford, Clarendon Press, 1928, p. 467.

3 See S. Petrosino and J. Rolland, *La vérité nomade*, Paris, La Découverte, 1984, pp. 22–3.

4 *EN* 104, *CWC* 214. E. Husserl, *Cartesianische Meditationen*, The Hague, Nijhoff, 1950 (*Husserliana*, vol. I, ed. S. Strasser); trans. D. Cairns, *Cartesian Meditations*, The Hague, Nijhoff, 1960. *Phänomenologische Psychologie*, The Hague, Nijhoff, 1962 (*Husserliana*, vol. IX, ed. W. Biemel); trans. J. Scanlon, *Phenomenological Psychology*, The Hague, Nijhoff, 1977. *Analysen zur*

passiven Synthesis, The Hague, Nijhoff, 1966 (*Husserliana*, vol. XI, ed. M. Fleischer).

5 E. Fink, 'Die phänomenologische Philosophie Edmund Husserls in der gegenwartigen Kritik', *Kantstudien*, 1933, vol. 38, pp. 319–83; 'The Phenomenological Philosophy of Edmund Husserl and Contemporary Criticism', in R. O. Elveton (ed. and trans.), *The Philosophy of Husserl*, Chicago, Quadrangle, 1970, pp. 73–147.

6 M. Heidegger, 'Nachwort' to 'Das Ding', *Vorträge und Aufsätze*, Pfullingen, Neske, 1967, vol. III, p. 57; trans. A. Hofstadter, 'Epilogue' to 'The Thing', in *Poetry, Language, Thought*, New York, Harper and Row, 1971, p. 184.

7 See J. Greisch '"Serviteurs et otages de la nature"? La nature comme objet de responsabilité', pp. 319–59 in *De la nature: de la physique classique au souci écologique*, Paris, Beauchesne, 1992, especially pp. 325–8.

8 *DVI* 189–207, *CPP* 175–86. See J.-L. Marion, 'Le mal en personne', in *Prolégomènes à la charité*, Paris, La Différence, 1986.

9 P. Nemo, *Job et l'excès du mal*, Paris, Grasset, 1978.

6 BEING FACED

1 F. W. J. Schelling, *Philosophische Untersuchungen über das Wesen der menschlichen Freiheit* (1809), *Sämtliche Werke*, ed. K. F. A. Schelling, Stuttgart, Cotta, 1860, vol. 7; trans. J. Guttmann, *Philosophical Inquiries into the Nature of Human Freedom*, La Salle, Open Court, 1936; M. Heidegger, *Schellings Abhandlung über das Wesen der menschlichen Freiheit*, ed. H. Feick, Tübingen, Niemeyer, 1971; trans. J. Stambaugh, *Schelling's Treatise on the Essence of Human Freedom*, Athens, Oh., The Ohio University Press, 1985.

2 For example, J. Llewelyn in *Beyond Metaphysics? The Hermeneutic Circle in Contemporary Continental Philosophy*, Atlantic Highlands, Humanities Press, 1985, ch. 10; repr. 'Levinas, Derrida and Others Vis-à-Vis', in R. Bernasconi and D. Wood (eds), *The Provocation of Levinas: Rethinking the Other*, London, Routledge, 1988, pp. 136–55.

3 Aristotle, *Metaphysics* 1005b19-20.

4 I. Kant, *Critique of Pure Reason*, B192.

5 F. Nietzsche, *Der Fall Wagner*, in *Werke*, ed. K. Schlechta, Munich, Hanser, 1954–6, vol. 2, p. 921; trans. A. M. Ludovici, *The Case of Wagner, The Complete Works of Friedrich Nietzsche*, vol. 8, Edinburgh, Foulis, 1911, p. 26.

6 M. Heidegger, *Gelassenheit*, Pfullingen, Neske, 1959, p. 33; trans. J. M. Anderson and E. H. Freund, *Discourse on Thinking*, New York, Harper and Row, 1966, p. 61.

7 J. Derrida, *L'écriture et la différence*, Paris, Seuil, 1967, p. 204; trans. A. Bass, *Writing and Difference*, London, Routledge and Kegan Paul, 1978, p. 139.

8 M. Heidegger, *Platons Lehre von der Wahrheit, mit einem Brief über den 'Humanismus'*, Bern, Francke, 1947, pp. 53–119, see pp. 53, 115; *Wegmarken*, Frankfurt, Klostermann, 1967, pp. 145–94, see pp. 145, 191, *Gesamtausgabe*, vol. 9, ed. F.-W. von Herrmann, Frankfurt am Main, Klostermann, 1976, pp. 313–64, see pp. 313, 361; 'Letter on Humanism', in D. F. Krell (ed.), *Martin Heidegger: Basic Writings*, London, Routledge and Kegan Paul, 1978, pp. 193, 239. But for an admission that the expression is not particularly illuminating,

see M. Heidegger, *Unterwegs zur Sprache*, Pfullingen, Neske, 1975, p. 90; trans. P. D. Hertz, *On the Way to Language*, New York, Harper and Row, 1971, p. 5.

9   See also the Introduction to M. Heidegger, *Prolegomena zur Geschichte des Zeitbegriffs*, *Gesamtausgabe*, vol. 20, ed. Petra Jaeger, Frankfurt am Main, Klostermann, 1979; trans. T. Kisiel, *History of the Concept of Time: Prolegomena*, Bloomington, Ind., Indiana University Press, 1985.

7 BEFORE AND BEYOND THE FACE

1   S. Alexander, *Space, Time, and Deity*, London, Macmillan, 1920, vol. I, pp. 12ff. and *passim*.

2   Levinas is reporting the paraphrase of B. Snell, *The Discovery of the Mind*, Oxford, Blackwell, 1953, pp. 200–1, given by K. Löwith, *Gesammelte Abhandlungen: zur Kritik der geschichtlichen Existenz*, Stuttgart, Kohlhammer, 1960, p. 222.

8 THE MANIFOLD OF ALTERITY

1   'My friends know that I have composed an entire book with *ça* (the sign of the Saussurian signifier, of Hegel's Absolute Knowing, in French: *savoir absolu*, of Freud's Id [the *Ça*], the feminine possessive pronoun [*sa*]).' J. Derrida, *Limited Inc, Glyph 2* Supplement, Baltimore, Johns Hopkins University Press, 1977, p. 81; trans. S. Weber, 'Limited Inc a b c . . .', pp. 162–254 in *Glyph 2: Johns Hopkins Textual Studies*, S. Weber and H. Sussman (eds), Baltimore, Johns Hopkins University Press, 1977, p. 254; and pp. 29–110 in J. Derrida, *Limited Inc*, ed. G. Graff, Evanston, Ill., Northwestern University Press, 1988, pp. 109–10. The 'entire book' (which is neither entire nor a book) is Derrida's *Glas*, Paris, Galilée, 1974; trans. J. P. Leavey and R. Rand, *Glas*, Lincoln, Nebr., University of Nebraska Press, 1986. See J. Llewelyn, 'Approaches to Semioethics', in H. J. Silverman (ed.), *Cultural Semiosis: Tracing the Signifier*, New York, Routledge, forthcoming.

2   E. Husserl, Archive MS D 17, 'Umsturz der kopernikanischen Lehre in der gewöhnlichen weltanschaulichen Interpretation. Die Urarche Erde bewegt sich nicht. . . .'; trans. F. Kersten, 'Foundational Investigations of the Phenomenological Origin of the Spatiality of Nature', in P. McCormick and F. A. Elliston (eds), *Husserl: Shorter Works*, Notre Dame, Ind., Notre Dame University Press, 1981, pp. 222–33.

3   M. Heidegger, 'Was ist Metaphysik?', in *Wegmarken*, Frankfurt am Main, Klostermann, 1967, pp. 1–19; *Gesamtausgabe* 9, ed. F.-W. von Herrmann, Frankfurt am Main, Klostermann, 1976, pp. 103–22, trans. R. F. C. Hull and A. Crick, 'What is Metaphysics?', in *Existence and Being*, London, Vision, 1949, pp. 355–80; trans. D.F. Krell, in *Martin Heidegger: Basic Writings*, ed. D.F. Krell, London, Routledge and Kegan Paul, 1978, pp. 95–112.

4   See, including references to Georges Bataille, J. Derrida, 'De l'économie restreinte à l'économie générale: un hégélianisme sans réserve', in *L'écriture et la différence*, Paris, Seuil, 1967, pp. 369–407; trans. A. Bass, 'From Restricted to General Economy: A Hegelianism without Reserve', in *Writing and Difference*, London, Routledge and Kegan Paul, 1978, pp. 251–77.

9 FROM SENSIBILITY TO SENSE

1 M. Merleau-Ponty, *La phénoménologie de la perception*, Paris, Gallimard, 1945; trans. Colin Smith, *Phenomenology of Perception*, London, Routledge and Kegan Paul, 1962.

2 Compare J. Hyppolite, *Genèse et structure de la Phénoménologie de l'esprit de Hegel*, Paris, Montaigne, 1946; trans. S. Cherniak and J. Heckman, *Genesis and Structure of Hegel's Phenomenology of Spirit*, Evanston, Ill., Northwestern University Press, 1974.

3 For a specimen of paragraph with paragraph comparison between Hegel, the *Phenomenology of Spirit* and *Otherwise than Being* see J. Llewelyn, *The Middle Voice of Ecological Conscience: A Chiasmic Reading of Responsibility in the Neighbourhood of Levinas, Heidegger and Others*, London, Macmillan, 1991, pp. 43–5.

4 As, on this definition of mysticism, it would be to interpret in this way anything that is said or shown in Wittgenstein's *Tractatus*. See L. Wittgenstein, *Tractatus Logico-Philosophicus*, trans. D. Pears and B. McGuinness, London, Routledge and Kegan Paul, 1961, 6.522: 'There are, indeed, things that cannot be put into words. They *make themselves manifest*. They are what is mystical.'

5 F. H. Bradley, *Ethical Studies*, Oxford, Clarendon Press, 1927, p. 172.

6 M. Heidegger, 'Der Spruch des Anaximander', *Holzwege*, Frankfurt am Main, Klostermann, 1972, p. 336; trans. D. F. Krell and F. A. Capuzzi, 'The Anaximander Fragment', in *Early Greek Thinking*, New York, Harper and Row, 1975, pp. 50–1. See also J. Derrida, '*Ousia et Grammè*: note sur une note de *Sein und Zeit*', in *Marges de la philosophie*, Paris, Minuit, 1972, pp. 76–8; trans. A. Bass, '*Ousia* and *Grammê*: Note on a Note from *Being and Time*', in *Margins of Philosophy*, Chicago, The University of Chicago Press, 1982, pp. 66–7.

10 GENERATIONS

1 R. A. F. Thurman, 'Wisdom and Compassion: The Heart of Tibetan Culture', in M. M. Rhie and R. A. F. Thurman (eds), *Wisdom and Compassion: The Sacred Art of Tibet*, New York, Harry N. Abrams Inc., 1991, pp. 17–19.

2 R. A. Cohen, *Face to Face with Levinas*, Albany, NY, State University of New York Press, 1986, p. 18.

3 I am grateful to Pascale-Anne Brault for ending my search for the source of the Rimbaud citation.

4 I. Kant, *Critique of Pure Reason*, Bvii.

5 F. Hölderlin, 'In lieblicher Bläue . . .', *Poems and Fragments*, trans. M. Hamburger, Cambridge, Cambridge University Press, 1980, p. 602.

6 See J. Llewelyn, *The Middle Voice of Ecological Conscience: A Chiasmic Reading of Responsibility in the Neighbourhood of Levinas, Heidegger and Others*, London, Macmillan, 1991, esp. chs 5, 9; 'L'intentionnalité inverse', in E. Escoubas (ed.), *Dossier: art et phénoménologie: La Part de l'Oeil*, Brussels, Presses de l'Académie des Beaux-Arts de Bruxelles, 1991, pp. 92–101; 'Regarding Regarding', in H. J. Silverman and W. S. Wurzer (eds), *Painting and Truth*, Atlantic Highlands, NJ, Humanities Press, forthcoming.

7   On the zig-zag reading of Husserl, see J.-L. Marion, *Réduction et donation: recherches sur Husserl, Heidegger et la phénoménologie*, Paris, Presses Universitaires de France, 1989, pp. 21–5.

8   J. Derrida, 'Violence et métaphysique', in *L'écriture et la différence*, Paris, Seuil, 1967, p. 125; trans. A. Bass, 'Violence and Metaphysics', in *Writing and Difference*, Chicago, University of Chicago Press, 1978, p. 84.

9   For a discussion of the hermeneutic theories of Friedrich Schleiermacher and Wilhelm Dilthey, and for bibliographical information concerning them, see. H.-G. Gadamer, *Truth and Method*, London, Sheen and Ward, 1979, second part. See also J. Llewelyn, *Beyond Metaphysics? The Hermeneutic Circle in Contemporary Continental Philosophy*, Atlantic Highlands, NJ, Humanities Press, 1985, ch. 6.

10   M. Heidegger, *Die Grundbegriffe der Metaphysik. Welt – Endlichkeit – Einsamkeit, Gesamtausgabe*, vol. 29–30, ed. F.-W. von Herrmann, Frankfurt am Main, Klostermann, 1983.

11   J. Derrida, *Spurs: Nietzsche's Styles*, trans. B. Harlow, Chicago, University of Chicago Press, 1978, p. 51.

12   M. Merleau-Ponty, *La phénoménologie de la perception*, Paris, Gallimard, 1945; trans. C. Smith, *Phenomenology of Perception*, London, Routledge and Kegan Paul, 1962, ch. 6.

13   Derrida, *Spurs*, pp. 46–7, citing section 60 of Nietzsche's *Die Fröhliche Wissenschaft* (1882). F. Nietzsche, *The Gay Science*, trans. W. Kaufmann, New York, Vintage, 1974, pp. 123–4.

14   E. Husserl, *Die Krisis der europäischen Wissenschaft und die transendentale Philosophie: Eine Einleitung in die Phänomenologie*, The Hague, Nijhoff, 1954; trans. D. Carr, *The Crisis of European Sciences and Transcendental Phenomenology: An Introduction to Phenomenological Philosophy*, Evanston, Ill., Northwestern University Press, 1970.

15   J. Derrida, 'Force de loi: le "fondement mystique de l'autorité"', trans. M. Quaintance, 'Force of Law: The "Mystical Foundation of Authority"', in P. Brusiloff, *Deconstruction and the Possibility of Justice, Cardozo Law Review*, vol. 11, 1990, pp. 920–1045; Derrida, 'Fors', preface to N. Abraham and M. Torak, *Cryptonymie: le verbier de l'homme aux loups*, Paris, Aubier–Flammarion, 1976, pp. 7–73; trans. N. Rand, *The Wolf Man's Magic Word: A Cryptonymy*, Minneapolis, University of Minnesota Press, 1986, pp. xi–xlviii.

16   M. Heidegger, 'Nachwort' to 'Was ist Metaphysik?', pp. 99–108 in *Wegmarken*, Frankfurt am Main, Klostermann, 1967, pp. 105–6, pp. 303–12 in *Gesamtausgabe*, vol. 9, ed. F.-W. von Herrmann, Frankfurt am Main, Klostermann, 1976, pp. 309–11; trans. R. F. C. Hull and A. Crick, Postscript to 'What is Metaphysics?', pp. 380–92 in *Existence and Being*, London, Vision, 1949, pp. 389ff.

17   Ibid. Compare J. Sallis, *Echoes After Heidegger*, Bloomington, Ind., Indiana University Press, 1990, especially pp. 151–3.

11   LIBERTY, EQUALITY, FRATERNITY

1   Duns Scotus, *Opera omnia*, ed. L. Wadding O. F. M., Lyons, 1638, vol. 11, *Reportata Parisiensia*, Bk 1, pt II, dist. 12, quaest. 6, nos 8, 13.

2 M. Foucault, *Naissance de la clinique. Une archéologie du regard médical*, Paris, Presses Universitaires de France, 1963, revised edn 1972; trans. A. M. Sheridan, *The Birth of the Clinic. An Archeology of Medical Perception*, London, Tavistock, 1973.

3 M. Scheler, *Wesen und Formen der Sympathie*, Bonn, Cohen, 1923; trans. P. Heath, *The Nature of Sympathy*, Hamden, Conn., Archon, 1970.

12 ATHEOLOGY

1 F. Rosenzweig, *Der Stern der Erlösung*, Frankfurt am Main, Kaufmann, 1921, 2nd edn 1930, p. 477; trans. W. W. Hallo, *The Star of Redemption*, Notre Dame, Ind., University of Notre Dame Press, 1985, p. 380. All the other words cited from *The Star* in chapter 12 can be found in the first book of its first part. This so-called book is in fact what would usually be called a chapter. And it is short, so short that with one exception I deem it unnecessary to interrupt my analysis of the argument in the first half of that book by giving references to specific pages.

2 F. Nietzsche, *Ecce Homo, Werke*, ed. K. Schlechta, Munich, Hanser, 1954–6, vol. 2, p. 1109; trans. W. Kaufmann, *On the Genealogy of Morals* and *Ecce Homo*, New York, Vintage, 1969, p. 272.

3 Rosenzweig, *Star*, pp. 26–7; *Stern*, p. 36.

4 R. Gibbs, *Correlations in Rosenzweig and Levinas*, Princeton, NJ, Princeton University Press, 1992, pp. 32–3.

5 F. de Saussure, *Cours de linguistique générale*, Paris, Payot, 1971, p. 37; trans. J. Culler, *Course in General Linguistics*, London, Fontana–Collins, 1974, pp. 18–19.

6 J. Derrida, 'En ce moment même dans cet ouvrage me voici', *Psyché*, Paris, Galilée, 1987, p. 187; trans. R. Berezdivin 'At This Very Moment in This Work Here I Am', in R. Bernasconi and S. Critchley (eds), *Re-Reading Levinas*, Bloomington, Ind., Indiana University Press, 1991, pp. 34–5.

7 F. W. J. Schelling, *Die Weltalter*, ed. M. Schröter, Munich, Biederstein, 1946; trans. F. de W. Bolman, *The Ages of the World*, New York, Columbia University Press, 1967.

8 J. Austin, *How to Do Things with Words*, Oxford, Clarendon Press, 1962, lecture XI.

9 *Aussprache mit Martin Heidegger an 06/XI/1951*, University of Zurich Committee for Guest Lecturers, Zurich, 1952. This is not, as far as I am aware, commercially available, but it is reproduced in part with acknowledgement to Jean Beaufret by J.-L. Marion, *Dieu sans l'être*, Paris, Communio/Fayard, 1982, p. 93, and translated into French by J. Greisch in R. Kearney and J. S. O'Leary (eds), *Heidegger et la question de Dieu*, Paris, Grasset, 1980, pp. 333–4, and by D. Saatdjian and F. Fédier in *Poésie* 1980, vol. 13, pp. 60–1. Here is my English translation putting into their context the remarks I have cited in the text: 'This question ['Can being and God be identified with each other?'] is put to me almost every other week, since for perfectly understandable reasons it worries theologians and because it is linked to the development of European history already from the Middle Ages due to the fact that Aristotle and Plato invaded respectively theology and the New Testament. What happens here is a

process the scope of which it is difficult to imagine. I asked a sympathetic Jesuit to indicate the places in Thomas Aquinas where it is said what "*esse*" means and what is signified by the affirmation "*Deus est suum esse*". So far I have received no reply. – God and being are not identical. (When Rickert deems the concept of being too loaded he takes being in a very narrow sense, the sense in which reality is distinguished from values.) Being and God are not identical, and I shall never attempt to think the essence of God by means of being. Some people are perhaps aware that I have a background in theology and that I retain a long-standing love for it and know a bit about it. If I were to write another theology, as I am occasionally tempted to do, the expression "being" would not be permitted to figure in it. Faith has no need of the thinking of being. If it needs that it is already no longer faith. Luther understood this. Yet even within his own Church this seems to be forgotten. I do not believe that pretentious claims can be made as to the suitability of being for thinking God theologically. There is no question of being here. I believe that being can never be thought as the ground and essence of God, but that on the contrary the experience of God and His revelation (so far as this comes man's way) takes place in the dimension of being, which in no case means that being could rank as a predicate of God. Here entirely new distinctions and delimitations are called for.'

Distinctions and delimitations not made, for example, by Hegel as characterized with assistance from Eckhart when Heidegger writes that when understood speculatively '"Being is God" means "Being 'ises' ['*istet*'] God", that is to say, Being lets God be God. "Is" is transitive and active. Only Being itself thus developed enables being-God. [*Erst das entfaltete Sein selbst ermöglicht das Gott-sein*]: It is only *being* developed up to itself (in the way it is in the *Logic*) that (by backlash) enables being-God (M. Heidegger, Le Thor seminar of 1968, in *Questions IV*, Paris, Gallimard, 1976, p. 258). Compare 'Being is the property of God', *Meister Eckhart*, trans. R. B. Blakney, New York, Harper and Row, 1941, Sermon 'Being is More than Life', p. 171.

10 Rudolf Otto, *The Idea of the Holy*, trans. J. W. Harvey, London, Penguin Books, 1959. The line in question is that spoken by Faust in Act 1 of the second part of Goethe's *Faust: Das Schaudern ist der Menschheit bester Teil* ('It is in shuddering that humanity shows itself at its best').

11 'I prefer the word *épreuve* to *expérience* because in the word *expérience* a knowing of which the self is master is always said. In the word *épreuve* there is at once the idea of life and of a critical "verification" which overflows the self of which it is only the "scene"' (interview in S. Malka, *Lire Levinas*, Paris, Cerf, 1984, p. 108).

12 'Yes', according to James Joyce, as well as being 'the most positive word in the human language', is also 'the female word.' See R. Ellmann, *James Joyce*, Oxford, Oxford University Press, 1983, pp. 501, 522.

13 M. Blanchot, *L'écriture du désastre*, Paris, Gallimard, 1980. M. Heidegger, *Aus der Erfahrung des Denkens*, Pfullingen, Neske, 1954, p. 7: 'Auf einen Stern zugehen, nur dieses.'

14 F. Nietzsche, *Also Sprach Zarathustra*, in *Werke*, ed. K. Schlechta, Munich, Hanser, 1954–6, vol. 2, p. 544; trans. W. Kaufmann, in *Thus Spoke Zarathustra*, in W. Kaufmann (ed.), *The Portable Nietzsche*, New York, Viking Press, 1954, p. 421.

13 ANTHOLOGY

1 Rabbi Hayyim de Volozhyn, *L'âme de la vie (Nefesh Hahayyim)*, trans. B. Gross, Paris, Verdier, 1986. See also J. Llewelyn, *The Middle Voice of Ecological Conscience: A Chiasmic Reading of Responsibility in the Neighbourhood of Heidegger, Levinas and Others*, London, Macmillan, 1991, p. 112 and n. 13, where are distinguished some of the places where Levinas omits and some of the places where he does not omit the phrase 'and for everything' that follows Markel's statement 'everyone is responsible to all men'. For example, they are included at *DVI* 119, at *EEI* 107 (*EI* 101), but omitted from 'The Paradox of Morality: An Interview with Emmanuel Levinas', trans. A. Benjamin and T. Wright, in R. Bernasconi and D. Wood (eds), *The Provocation of Levinas: Rethinking the Other*, London, Routledge, 1988, pp. 168–80. See F. Dostoevsky, *The Brothers Karamazov*, trans. E. Garnett, London, Dent, 1927, vol. 1, pp. 296–8.

2 J. Delhomme, *La pensée interrogative*, Paris, Presses Universitaires de France, 1954; *La pensée et le réel*, Paris, Presses Universitaires de France, 1966. E. Fink, *Spiel als Weltsymbol*, Stuttgart, Kohlhammer, 1960.

3 F. Nietzsche, 'Über Wahrheit und Lüge im aussermoralischen Sinn', pp. 309–22 in *Werke*, ed. K. Schlechta, Munich, Hanser, 1954–6, vol. 3, p. 314; trans. M. A. Mügge, 'On Truth and Falsity in their Ultramoral Sense', pp. 171–92 in F. Nietzsche, *The Complete Works of Friedrich Nietzsche*, ed. O. Levy, vol. 2, *Early Greek Philosophy*, Edinburgh, Foulis, 1911, pp. 180–1; pp. 42–7 in W. Kaufmann (ed.), *The Portable Nietzsche*, (ed.) W. Kaufmann, New York, Viking, 1954.

4 J. Derrida, 'Violence et métaphysique', *L'écriture et la différence*, Paris, Seuil, 1967, pp. 117–228, text reference to p. 226; trans. A. Bass, 'Violence and Metaphysics', *Writing and Difference*, London, Routledge and Kegan Paul, 1978, pp. 79–153, text reference to p. 152.

5 F. Hölderlin, 'Brot und Wein', in *Poems and Fragments*, trans. M. Hamburger, Cambridge, Cambridge University Press, 1980, p. 248. A. France, *Le jardin d'Epicure*, Paris, Calmann-Levy, n.d.

6 J. Derrida, *Marges de la philosophie*, Paris, Minuit, 1972, pp. 247–324; trans. A. Bass, *Margins of Philosophy*, Chicago, University of Chicago Press, 1982, pp. 207–71.

7 Derrida, *Marges*, p. 323; *Margins*, p. 271.

8 Derrida, *La dissémination*, Paris, Seuil, 1972, pp. 198–318; trans. B. Johnson, *Dissemination*, Chicago, University of Chicago Press, 1981, pp. 172–286.

9 S. Mallarmé, 'Magie', in *Oeuvres complètes* (Pléiade), Paris, Gallimard, 1945, pp. 399–400.

10 Derrida, *Psyché: Inventions de l'autre*, Paris, Gallimard, 1987, pp. 145–58, p. 158.

11 Derrida, *Glas*, Paris, Galilée, 1974, 106a; trans. J. P. Leavey and R. Rand, *Glas*, Lincoln, Nebr., University of Nebraska Press, 1984, 92a.

12 Ibid., 12a–13a; 6a–7a.

13 The Vedic analysis runs: '"The breath is seated on the shining one in the bushel of the part it takes in what is altogether loosed (or subtle)", whence we easily get as a next step: "He whose breath is a sign of life, man, that is, will find a place (no doubt after the breath has been exhaled) in the divine fire, source and

home of life, and this place will be meted out to him according to the virtue that has been given him (by the demons, I imagine) of sending abroad his warm breath, this little invisible soul, across the free expanse (the blue of the sky, most likely)".' A. France, *Le jardin d'Epicure*, Paris, Calmann-Levy, pp. 276–7.

14 Derrida, *Marges*, pp. 298–99; *Margins* p. 250.
15 Ibid., p. 300; p. 251.
16 Ibid., p. 308; p. 258, cp. p. 262, n. 73.
17 Ibid., p. 261; pp. 219–20.
18 Ibid., p. 251; p. 211.
19 P. Ricoeur, *La métaphore vive*, Paris, Seuil, 1975; trans. R. Czerny with K. McLaughlin and J. Costello SJ, *The Rule of Metaphor. Multidisciplinary Studies of the Creation of Meaning in Language*, Toronto, University of Toronto Press, 1977.
20 J. Derrida, 'Le retrait de la métaphore', pp. 63–93 of *Psyché: Inventions de l'autre*, Paris, Gallimard, 1987, pp. 73–4.
21 Derrida, 'Le retrait de la métaphore', p. 72; 'La Différance', pp. 1–29 in *Marges*, p. 25; 'Differance', pp. 1–27 in *Margins*, p. 24.
22 For an exposition of the problems and attempted solutions, and for bibliographical information, see W. Kneale and M. Kneale, *The Development of Logic*, Oxford, Clarendon Press, 1962, chs 11, 12.
23 M. Heidegger, *Der Satz vom Grund*, Pfullingen, Neske, 1957, p. 89.
24 M. Heidegger, 'Das Wesen der Sprache', *Unterwegs zur Sprache*, Pfullingen, Neske, 1959, 1975, p. 207; trans. P. D. Hertz, 'The Nature of Language', in *On the Way to Language*, New York, Harper and Row, 1971, p. 100.
25 J. Greisch, 'Les mots et les roses. La métaphore chez Martin Heidegger', *Revue des sciences philosophiques et théologiques*, vol. 57, 3, 1973, pp. 443–56.
26 Heidegger, *Der Satz vom Grund*, p. 89.
27 Levinas himself takes this risk when he says in paragraphs cited on the jacket of the French edition of *Otherwise than Being* that the expressions *désintéressement* and *pour-l'autre* must be understood in a rigorous manner. They are the metaphors of [and perhaps in, JL] the literal sense of the words: disengagement from being (and non-being), and responsibility for the other incumbent upon the hostage.
28 *AE* 138, 141, *OB* 109–10. Compare Levinas's 'mieux que les métaphores' with Derrida's 'meilleur que la métaphore' in the passage to which note 10 is appended.
29 At B29 of the *Critique of Pure Reason* Kant refers to 'a common, but to us unknown, root', of sensibility and understanding, and at B180 to schematism as 'an art concealed in the depths of the human soul'. This doctrine of 'some third thing' (B177) is emphasized by Heidegger throughout *Kant and the Problem of Metaphysics* and haunts his entire fundamental ontology (Heidegger, *Kant und das Problem der Metaphysik*, Frankfurt am Main, Klostermann, 1973; trans. R. Taft, *Kant and the Problem of Metaphysics*, Bloomington, Ind., Indiana University Press, 1990). For Derrida's remark see Derrida, *L'écriture et la différence*, p. 204; *Writing and Difference*, p. 139.
30 On page 139 of *Writing and Difference*, Derrida refers to Nietzsche's allusion to Heraclitus on 'warm breath'. See F. Nietzsche, 'Die Philosophie im tragischen Zeitalter der Griechen', pp. 349–413 in *Werke*, ed. K. Schlechta,

Munich, Hanser, vol. 1, p. 374; trans. M. A. Mügge, 'Philosophy in the Tragic Age of the Greeks', pp. 71–170 in *The Complete Works of Friedrich Nietzsche*, ed. O. Levy, vol. 2, *Early Greek Philosophy*, Edinburgh, Foulis, 1911, p. 105.

14 TROPES

1 M. Heidegger, 'Brief über den Humanismus', pp. 53–119 in *Platons Lehre von der Wahrheit, mit einem Brief über den 'Humanismus'*, Bern, Franke, 1947, pp. 115–16; pp. 145–94 in *Wegmarken*, Frankfurt am Main, Klostermann, 1967, pp. 191–2; pp. 313–64 in *Gesamtausgabe*, vol. 9, ed. F.-W. von Herrmann, Frankfurt am Main, Klostermann, pp. 361–2; trans. F. Capuzzi in cooperation with J. Glenn Gray, 'Letter on Humanism', pp. 193–242 in D. F. Krell (ed.), *Martin Heidegger: Basic Writings*, London, Routledge and Kegan Paul, 1978, p. 239. See also M. Heidegger, 'Aus einem Gespräch von der Sprache', pp. 83–155, in *Unterwegs zur Sprache*, Pfullingen, Neske, 1975, p. 111; trans. P. D. Hertz, 'A Dialogue on Language', pp. 1–54 in *On the Way to Language*, New York, Harper and Row, 1971, p. 26.

2 M. Heidegger, 'Der Spruch des Anaximander', *Holzwege*, Frankfurt, Klostermann, 1950, p. 318; trans. D. F. Krell and F. A. Capuzzi, 'The Anaximander Fragment', in *Early Greek Thinking*, New York, Harper and Row, 1975, p. 33.

3 P. Valéry, *Cahiers* (Pléiade), ed. J. Robinson, Paris, Gallimard, 1974, vol. 1, p. 1065. See also *Oeuvres complètes* (Pléiade), Paris, Gallimard, 1957, vol. 2, p. 637.

4 E. Husserl, *Die Krisis der europäischen Wissenschaft und die transzendentale Philosophie: Eine Einleitung in die phänomenologische Phänomenologie*, The Hague, Nijhoff, 1954; trans. D. Carr, *The Crisis of European Sciences and Transcendental Phenomenology: An Introduction to Phenomenological Philosophy*, Evanston, Ill., Northwestern University Press, 1970.

5 E. Husserl, *Erfahrung und Urteil: Untersuchungen zur Genealogie der Logik*, Hamburg, Claassen and Goverts, 1948; trans. J. S. Churchill and K. Ameriks, *Experience and Judgment: Investigations in a Genealogy of Logic*, London, Routledge and Kegan Paul, 1973.

6 M. Heidegger, *Der Satz vom Grund*, Pfullingen, Neske, 1957, p. 89: 'Wenn unser menschliches-sterbliches Hören und Blicken sein Eigentliches nicht im bloss sinnlichen Empfinden hat, dann ist es auch nicht völlig unerhört, dass Hörbares zugleich erblickt werden kann, wenn das Denken hörend blickt und blickend hört.'

7 R. G. Collingwood, *An Autobiography*, London, Pelican, 1944, pp. 24–33. See J. Llewelyn, 'Propositions as Answers', *American Philosophical Quarterly*, 1965, vol. 2, pp. 305–11.

8 B. Snell, *The Discovery of the Mind*, Oxford, Blackwell, 1953, pp. 200–1.

9 M. Buber, *Ich und Du*, in *Das Dialogische Prinzip*, Heidelberg, Schneider, 1979; trans. R. G. Smith, *I and Thou*, Edinburgh, Clark, 1937.

10 The nuances of Levinas's and Buber's exchange are delicately distinguished by Robert Bernasconi in '"Failure of Communication" as a Surplus: Dialogue and Lack of Dialogue between Buber and Levinas', in R. Bernasconi and D. Wood (eds), *The Provocation of Levinas: Rethinking the Other*, London, Routledge, 1988, pp. 100–35.

11 G. Marcel, *Etre et Avoir*, Paris, Aubier, 1968; trans. K. Farrer, *Being and Having*, London, Dacre, 1949.

12 *Phaedrus* 275. See J. Derrida, 'La pharmacie de Platon', in *La dissémination*, Paris, Seuil, 1972, pp. 69–197; trans. B. Johnson, 'Plato's Pharmacy', in *Dissemination*, Chicago, University of Chicago Press, 1981, pp. 61–171.

13 F. Nietzsche, *Menschliches, Allzumenschliches: Ein Buch für freie Geister*, pp. 434–1008 in *Werke*, ed. K. Schlechta, Munich, Hanser, 1954–5, vol. I, p. 526; trans. R. J. Hollingdale, *Human, All Too Human: A Book for Free Spirits*, Cambridge, Cambridge University Press, 1986, p. 66.

14 J. Derrida, '"Il faut bien manger" ou le calcul du sujet', in E. Weber (ed.), *Points de suspension. Entretiens*, Paris, Galilée, 1992, pp. 96–119; trans. P. Connor and A. Ronell, '"Eating Well", or the Calculation of the Subject: An Interview with Jacques Derrida', in E. Cadava, P. Connor and J.-L. Nancy (eds), *Who Comes After the Subject?*, New York, Routledge, 1991.

15 J. Derrida, 'En ce moment même dans cet ouvrage me voici', pp. 159–202 in *Psyché: Inventions de l'autre*, Paris, Galilée, 1987, pp. 192–202; 'At This Very Moment in This Work Here I Am', pp. 11–48 in R. Bernasconi and S. Critchley (eds), *Re-Reading Levinas*, Bloomington, Ind., Indiana University Press, 1991, pp. 39–48. See also J. Llewelyn, 'En ce moment même . . . une répétition qui n'en est pas une', in *Le passage des frontières: autour du travail de Jacques Derrida* (proceedings of the colloquium held at Cerisy in 1992), Paris, Galilée, 1994, pp. 245–8.

16 P. Ricoeur, *Soi-même comme un autre*, Paris, Seuil, 1990.

17 R. Descartes' Letter to Elizabeth, 28 June 1643, pp. 140–3 in *Descartes: Philosophical Letters*, ed. and trans. A. Kenny, Oxford, Blackwell, 1970, p. 141.

18 See M. Haar, 'L'obsession de l'autre. L'éthique comme traumatisme', in C. Chalier and M. Abensour (eds), *Emmanuel Levinas*, Paris, L'Herne, 1991, pp. 444–52.

19 'La réalité et son ombre', *Les Temps Modernes*, vol. 38, 1948, pp. 769–89.

20 'L'être, utopie et justice' (EN 253–62).

21 V. Grossman, *Life and Fate*, trans. R. Chandler, London, Fontana, 1986.

22 M. Heidegger, 'Der Ursprung des Kunstwerkes', pp. 7–68 in Heidegger, *Holzwege*, Frankfurt am Main, Klostermann, 1972, pp. 23–4; trans. A. Hofstadter, 'The Origin of the Work of Art', pp. 15–87 in *Poetry, Language, Thought*, New York, Harper and Row, 1971, pp. 31–2; (pp. 143–87 in *Martin Heidegger: Basic Writings*, ed. D. F. Krell, p. 163). See J. Derrida, 'Restitutions', pp. 291–436 in Derrida, *La vérité en peinture*, Paris, Flammarion, 1978; trans. G. Bennington and I. McLeod, 'Restitutions', pp. 255–382 in Derrida, *The Truth in Painting*, Chicago, University of Chicago Press, 1987. See also J. Llewelyn, 'Belongings', *Research in Phenomenology*, 1987, vol. 17, pp. 117–36.

23 For thoughts on an extension beyond see J. Llewelyn, 'L'intentionnalité inverse', in E. Escoubas (ed.), *Dossier: art et phénoménologie, La Part de L'Oeil*, Brussels, Presses de l'Académie des Beaux-Arts de Bruxelles, 1991, pp. 93–101; 'Regarding Regarding', in H. J. Silverman and W. S. Wurzer (eds), *Painting and Truth*, Atlantic Highlands, NJ, Humanities Press, forthcoming; and *The Middle Voice of Ecological Conscience: A Chiasmic Reading of Responsibility in the Neighbourhood of Levinas, Heidegger and Others*, London, Macmillan, New York, St Martin's Press, 1991, chs 5–7.

15   ETHICAL AGORAPHOBIA

1   M. Heidegger, 'Brief über den Humanismus', pp. 53–119 in *Platons Lehre von der Wahrheit mit einem Brief über den 'Humanismus'*, Bern, Francke, 1954, p. 54; pp. 145–94 in *Wegmarken*, Frankfurt am Main, Klostermann, 1967, p. 145; pp. 313–64 in *Gesamtausgabe*, vol. 9, ed. F.-W. von Herrmann, 1976, Frankfurt am Main, Klostermann, pp. 313–14; trans. F. Capuzzi in cooperation with J. Glenn Gray 'Letter on Humanism', pp. 193–242 in D. F. Krell (ed.), *Martin Heidegger: Basic Writings*, London, Routledge and Kegan Paul, 1978, p. 194.

2   *EN* 107ff. E. Levinas, 'Useless Suffering', trans. R. Cohen, in R. Bernasconi and D. Wood (eds), *The Provocation of Levinas: Rethinking the Other*, London, Routledge, 1988, pp. 156–67.

3   *EN* 116; Levinas, 'Useless Suffering', p. 163.

4   See especially J. Lacan, 'L'instance de la lettre dans l'inconscient ou la raison depuis Freud', in *Ecrits*, Paris, Seuil, 1966, pp. 493–528; trans. A. Sheridan, 'The Agency of the Letter in the Unconscious or Reason since Freud', in *Ecrits: A Selection*, New York, Norton, pp. 146–78.

5   I do not imagine for one moment that diversion of this kind will take place in M.-A. Lescourret, *Emmanuel Levinas*, Paris, Flammarion, 1994. I thank Catherine Chalier for drawing my attention to the announcement of this biography.

6   This epigraph and the one about to be cited are, respectively, *Pensées* 295 and 451 as numbered in *Oeuvres de Blaise Pascal*, ed. L. Brunschvicg, Paris, Hachette, 1925, vol. 13, *Pensées*, vol. 2.

7   *AE* 158n., *OB* 198n. P. Nemo, *Job et l'excès du mal*, Paris, Grasset, 1978, pp. 63–111.

8   In *Die Philosophen* Friedrich Schiller has the Kantian proclaim: 'Gladly, I serve my friends, but alas I do it with pleasure. / Hence I am plagued with the doubt that I am not a virtuous person.' To which the reply goes: 'Sure, your only resource is to try to despise them entirely, / And then with aversion to do what your duty enjoins you' (*Schillers Sämtliche Werke*, vol. 1, *Gedichte*, Stuttgart, Cotta, 1904; the translation is taken from H. Rashdall, *The Theory of Good and Evil*, Oxford, Oxford University Press, 1924, vol. 1, p. 120).

9   Ezekiel 6:2, 13:17, 20:46, 21:2, 25:2, 28:21, 29:2, 35:2, 38:2. See K. W. Carley, *Ezekiel among the Prophets*, London, SCM, 1975, pp. 40–2, 93.

10   E. Jabès, *Le livre des ressemblances*, Paris, Gallimard, 1976, p. 116.

11   E. Jabès, *Le petit livre de la subversion hors de soupçon*, Paris, Gallimard, 1982, p. 47.

12   Cited by E. de Fontenay, introducing the symposium entitled 'Le scandale du mal. Catastrophes naturelles et crimes de l'homme', pp. 2–17 in *Les Nouveaux Cahiers*, vol. 22, 1986, p. 5.

13   Jabès, *Le livre des ressemblances*, p. 67.

14   Nietzsche, *Werke: Kritische Gesamtausgabe*, ed. G. Colli and M. Montinari, Berlin, W. de Gruyter, from 1973. G. Deleuze, *Nietzsche et la philosophie*, Paris, Presses Universitaires de France, 1970. M. Heidegger, *Nietzsche*, vols 1, 2, Pfullingen, Neske, 1961; trans. P. Klossowski, Paris, Gallimard, 1971. Mention should also be made of P. Klossowski, *Nietzsche et le cercle vicieux*, Paris, Mercure de France, 1969.

15   Illelleity is treated in J. Llewelyn, 'En ce moment même . . . une répétition qui

n'en est pas une', in *Le passage des frontières: Autour du travail de Jacques Derrida*, Colloque de Cerisy, Paris, Galilée, 1994. It should be said that while *illéité* is Levinas's coinage, I must answer for 'illelleity', 'elleity' and 'ilyaity'.

16   Levinas, 'Modèle de l'occident', *ADV* 29–50, *BTV* 13–33.

17   F. Nietzsche, *Thus Spoke Zarathustra* (1883–5) pt III, 'On Apostates'.

18   S. Malka, *Lire Levinas*, Paris, Cerf, 1984, p. 105.

19   Levinas, 'Useless Suffering', trans. R. Cohen, in R. Bernasconi and D. Wood (eds) *The Provocation of Levinas*, pp. 161–4.

20   'Was there latent in Sylvia Plath's sensibility, as in that of many of us who remember only by fiat of imagination, a fearful envy, a dim resentment at not having been there, of having missed the rendezvous with hell?' G. Steiner, 'Dying as an Art', in *Language and Silence: Essays 1958–1966*, London, Faber and Faber, 1967, p. 330, cited in Lawrence L. Langer, *The Holocaust and the Literary Imagination*, New Haven, Conn., Yale University Press, 1975, p. 19.

21   E. L. Fackenheim, 'Transcendence in Contemporary Culture: Philosophical Reflections and Jewish Theology', in H. W. Richardson and D. R. Cutler (eds), *Transcendence*, Boston, Beacon Press, 1969, p. 150. See also Fackenheim, *God's Presence in History: Jewish Affirmations and Philosophical Reflections*, New York, Harper and Row, 1972, and *To Mend the World: Foundations of Jewish Thought*, New York, Schocken, 1982.

22   *EN* 116; Levinas, 'Useless Suffering', p. 163.

Bibliography

The most detailed bibliography is R. Burggraeve, *Emmanuel Levinas: une biblio-graphie primaire et secondaire (1929–89)*, Leuven, Centre for Metaphysics and Philosophy of God, Peeters,1990, and to be brought up to date. In the following lists I have marked with the letter B some of the publications that include bibliographies of secondary literature on Levinas.

BOOK-LENGTH STUDIES OF LEVINAS'S WORKS

Chalier, C., *Figures du féminin: lectures d'Emmanuel Levinas*, Paris, La nuit survéillée, 1982.
—— *La Persévérance du mal*, Paris, La nuit survéillée–Cerf, 1987.
Ciaramelli, F., *Transcendance et éthique: essai sur Levinas*, Brussels, Ousia, 1989.
Davies, P., *Experience and Distance: Heidegger, Blanchot, Levinas*, Albany, NY, State University of New York Press, forthcoming.
Feron, E., *De l'idée de transcendance à la question du langage: l'itinéraire philo-sophique d'Emmanuel Levinas*, Grenoble, Millon, 1992. (B)
Finkielkraut, A., *La sagesse de l'amour*, Paris, Gallimard, 1984.
Forthomme, B., *Une philosophie de la transcendance: la métaphysique d'Emmanuel Levinas*, Paris, Vrin, 1979. (B)
Gibbs, R., *Correlations in Rosenzweig and Levinas*, Princeton, NJ, Princeton University Press, 1992.
Guibal, F., *. . . et combien de dieux nouveaux, approches contemporaines*, vol. 2, *Levinas*, Paris, Aubier–Montaigne, 1980.
Libertson, J., *Proximity. Levinas, Blanchot, Bataille and Communication*, The Hague, Nijhoff, 1982.
Llewelyn, J., *The Middle Voice of Ecological Conscience: A Chiasmic Reading of Responsibility in the Neighbourhood of Levinas, Heidegger and Others*, London, Macmillan, 1991.
Malka, S., *Lire Levinas*, Paris, Cerf, 1984.
Ouaknin, M.-A., *Méditations érotiques: essai sur Emmanuel Levinas*, Paris, Balland, 1992.
Peperzak, A., *To the Other: An Introduction to the Philosophy of Emmanuel Levinas*, West Lafayette, Ind., Purdue University Press, 1993. (B)

Petrosino, S., and Rolland, J., *La vérité nomade: introduction à Emmanuel Levinas*, Paris, La Découverte, 1984.

Poirié, R., *Emmanuel Levinas. Qui êtes-vous?*, Lyon, La Manufacture, 1987.

Smith, S. G., *The Argument to the Other: Reason Beyond Reason in the Thought of Karl Barth and E. Levinas*, Chico, Calif.: Scholars Press, 1983.

Strasser, S., *Jenseits von Sein und Zeit: eine Einführung in Emmanuel Levinas' Philosophie*, The Hague, Nijhoff, 1978.

Vries, H. de, *Theologie im Pianissimo & Zwischen Rationalität und Dekonstruktion*, Kampen, Kok, 1989. (B)

Wyschogrod, E., *Emmanuel Levinas: The Problem of Ethical Metaphysics*, The Hague, Nijhoff, 1974.

COLLECTIONS, ARTICLES AND CHAPTERS

Aeschlimann, J.-Chr. (ed.) *Répondre d'autrui: Emmanuel Levinas*, Neuchâtel, La Baconnière, 1989.

Aubay, F., 'Conscience, immanence et non-présence: E. Levinas, lecteur de Husserl (1)', *Alter*, 1993, vol. 1, pp. 297–318.

Benso, S., 'Levinas – Another Ascetic Priest?', *Journal of the British Society for Phenomenology*, forthcoming.

Bernasconi, R., 'Levinas Face to Face – with Hegel', *Journal of the British Society for Phenomenology*, 1982, vol. 13, pp. 267–76.

—— 'The Trace of Levinas in Derrida', in D. Wood and R. Bernasconi (eds), *Derrida and Difference*, Coventry, Parousia Press, 1985, pp. 17–44.

—— 'Hegel and Levinas: The Possibility of Forgiveness and Reconciliation', *Archivio di Filosofia*, 1986, vol. 54, pp. 325–46.

—— 'Deconstruction and the Possibility of Ethics', in J. Sallis (ed.), *Deconstruction and Philosophy: The Texts of Jacques Derrida*, Chicago, Chicago University Press, 1987, pp. 122–39.

—— 'Fundamental Ontology, Metontology and the Ethics of Ethics', *Irish Philosophical Journal*, 1987, vol. 4, pp. 76–93.

—— 'The Silent Anarchic World of the Evil Genius', in G. Moneta, J. Sallis and J. Taminiaux (eds), *The Collegium Phaenomenologicum: The First Ten Years*, Dordrecht, Kluwer, 1988, pp. 257–72.

—— 'Rereading *Totality and Infinity*', in A. B. Dallery and C. E. Scott (eds), *The Question of the Other*, Albany, NY, State University of New York Press, 1989, pp. 23–34.

Bernasconi, R. and Critchley, S. (eds), *Re-Reading Levinas*, Bloomington, Ind. Indiana University Press, 1991.

Bernasconi, R. and Wood, D. (eds), *The Provocation of Levinas: Rethinking the Other*, Warwick Studies in Philosophy and Literature, London, Routledge, 1988. (B)

Boer, Theo de, 'Judaism and Hellenism in the Philosophy of Levinas and Heidegger', *Archivio di Filosofia*, 1985, vol. 53, pp. 192–215.

Blum, R. P., 'Emmanuel Levinas' Theory of Commitment', *Philosophy and Phenomenological Research*, 1983–4, vol. 44, pp. 145–68.

Casey, E., 'Levinas on Memory and the Trace', in G. Moneta, J. Sallis and J. Taminiaux (eds), *The Collegium Phaenomenologicum: The First Ten Years*, Dordrecht, Kluwer, 1988, pp. 241–55.

Chalier, C., and Abensour, M. (eds), *Emmanuel Levinas*, Paris, L'Herne, 1991. (B)

Chanter, T., 'The Question of Death: The Time of the I and the Time of the Other', *Irish Philosophical Journal*, 1987, vol. 4, pp. 94–119.

—— 'The Alterity and Immodesty of Time: Death as Future and Eros as Feminine in Levinas', in D. Wood (ed.), *Writing the Future*, London, Routledge, 1990, pp. 137–54.

Ciaramelli, F., 'Le rôle du judaïsme dans l'oeuvre de Levinas', *Revue Philosophique de Louvain*, 1983, vol. 52, pp. 580–99.

Cohen, R. A. (ed.), *Face to Face with Levinas*, Albany, NY, State University of New York Press, 1986.

—— 'Absolute Positivity and Ultrapositivity: Husserl and Levinas', in A. B. Dallery and C. E. Scott (eds), *The Question of the Other*, Albany, NY, State University of New York Press, 1989, pp. 35–43.

Davies, P., 'Difficult Friendship', *Research in Phenomenology*, 1988, vol. 18, pp. 149–72.

Derrida, J., 'Violence et métaphysique', in *L'écriture et la différence*, Paris, Seuil, 1967, pp. 117–228; trans. A. Bass, 'Violence and Metaphysics', in *Writing and Difference*, Chicago, Chicago University Press, 1978, pp. 79–153.

—— 'En ce moment même dans cet ouvrage me voici', in *Psyché: Inventions de l'autre*, Paris, Gallimard, 1987, pp. 159–202; trans. R. Berezdivin, 'At This Moment In This Very Work Here I Am', in R. Bernasconi and S. Critchley (eds), *Re-Reading Levinas*, Bloomington, Ind., Indiana University Press, pp. 11–48.

Etudes Phénoménologiques, 1990, vol. 6, no. 12, *Emmanuel Levinas*.

Exercices de la patience: Cahiers de philosophie, no. 1, *Levinas*, Paris, Obsidiane, 1980.

Greisch, J., 'L'être, l'autre, l'étranger', *Cahiers de l'Ecole des Sciences Philosophiques et Religieuses*, 1987, no. 1, pp. 127–51.

Greisch, J. and Rolland, J. (eds), *Emmanuel Levinas: l'éthique comme philosophie première* (proceedings of the colloquium held at Cerisy, 1992), Paris, La nuit survéillée–Cerf, 1993.

Lingis, A., 'Phenomenology of the Face and Carnal Intimacy', in *Libido: The French Existential Theories*, Bloomington, Ind., Indiana University Press, 1985, pp. 58–73.

—— 'The Elemental Imperative', *Research in Phenomenology*, 1988, vol. 18, pp. 3–21.

—— 'Face to Face', in *Deathbound Subjectivity*, Bloomington, Ind., Indiana University Press, 1989, pp. 135–55.

Llewelyn, J., 'Levinas, Derrida and Others Vis-à-Vis', in *Beyond Metaphysics? The Hermeneutic Circle in Contemporary Continental Philosophy*, Atlantic Highlands, NJ, Humanities Press, 1985, pp. 185–206.

—— 'Jewgreek or Greekjew', in G. Moneta, J. Sallis and J. Taminiaux (eds), *The Collegium Phaenomenologicum: The First Ten Years*, Dordrecht, Kluwer, 1988, pp. 273–87.

—— 'En ce moment même . . . une répétition qui n'en est pas une', in *Le passage des frontières: Autour du travail de Jacques Derrida* (proceedings of the colloquium held at Cerisy, 1994, Paris, Galilée, 1994, pp. 245–8.

Olivetti, M. M., 'Intersoggettività, Alterità, Etica. Domande filosofiche a E. Levinas', *Archivio di Filosofia*, 1985, vol. 53, pp. 265–88.

Peperzak, A., 'Beyond Being', *Research in Phenomenology*, 1978, vol. 8, pp. 239–61.

—— 'Emmanuel Levinas: Jewish Experience and Philosophy', *Philosophy Today*, 1983, vol. 27, pp. 281–3.

—— 'Phenomenology – Ontology – Metaphysics: Levinas' Perspective on Husserl and Heidegger', *Man and World*, 1983, vol. 16, pp. 113–27.

—— 'From Intentionality to Responsibility: On Levinas' Philosophy of Language', in A. B. Dallery and C. E. Scott (eds), *The Question of the Other*, Albany, NY, State University of New York Press, 1989, pp. 3–22.

—— (ed.), *Ethics as First Philosophy: The Significance of Emmanuel Levinas for Philosophy, Literature and Religion* (Proceedings of the conference held at Loyola University of Chicago and the University of Chicago in 1993), forthcoming.

Rolland, J. (ed.), *Les cahiers de la nuit survéillée, Emmanuel Levinas*, Lagrasse, Verdier, 1984.

Sebbah, F.-D., 'Eveil et naissance. Quelques remarques à partir d'Emmanuel Levinas et Michel Henri', *Alter*, 1993, vol. 1, pp. 213–39.

Soysal, A., 'Deux études sur la non-donation', *Alter*, 1993, vol. 1, pp. 241–64.

Strasser, S., 'Emmanuel Levinas (born 1906): Phenomenological Philosophy', in H. Spiegelberg, *The Phenomenological Movement: A Historical Introduction*, The Hague, Nijhoff, 1982, pp. 612-49.

Taylor, M., 'Infinity', in *Altarity*, Chicago, University of Chicago Press, 1987, pp. 185–216.

Watson, S., 'Reason and the Face of the Other', *Journal of the American Academy of Religion*, 1986, vol. 54, pp. 33–57.

—— 'The Face of Hibakushi: Levinas and the Trace of Apocalypse', in D. Wood (ed.), *Writing the Future*, London, Routledge, 1990, pp. 155–73.

Wyschogrod, E., 'The Moral Self: Emmanuel Levinas and Hermann Cohen', *DAAT*, 1980, no. 4, 35–58.

Ziarek, K., 'The Language of Praise: Levinas and Marion', *Religion & Literature*, 1990, vol. 22, pp. 93–107.

Many of the works listed above contain interviews with Levinas. The one reproduced in R.A. Cohen (ed.), *Face to Face with Levinas* appeared originally in R. Kearney (ed.), *Dialogues with Contemporary Continental Thinkers: The Phenomenological Heritage*, Manchester, Manchester University Press, 1984. See also R. Mortley (ed.), *French Philosophers in Conversation*, London, Routledge, 1991.

Index